Better Homes and Gardens®

THE COMPLETE GUIDE TO·

BREAD
MACHINE
BAKING

Better Homes and Gardens® Books
An imprint of Meredith® Books

**THE COMPLETE GUIDE TO
BREAD MACHINE BAKING**
Editor: Kristi M. Fuller
Associate Design Director: Mick Schnepf
Illustrator: Tom Nikosey Design
Photographer: Krantz Studio
Contributing Writers: Margaret Agnew, Karen Brown, Jane Horn, Marcia K. Stanley
Recipe Development: Better Homes and Gardens Test Kitchen, Linda Henry
Copy Chief: Catherine Hamrick
Copy and Production Editor: Terri Fredrickson
Contributing Editor: Kim Catanzarite
Contributing Proofreaders: Susie Kling, Sheila Mauck, Beth Popplewell
Electronic Production Coordinator: Paula Forest
Editorial and Design Assistants: Judy Bailey, Karen Schirm
Test Kitchen Director: Sharon Stilwell
Test Kitchen Product Supervisor: Marilyn Cornelius
Production Director: Douglas M. Johnston
Production Manager: Pam Kvitne
Assistant Prepress Manager: Marjorie J. Schenkelberg

Meredith® Books
Editor in Chief: James D. Blume
Design Director: Matt Strelecki
Managing Editor: Gregory H. Kayko

Director, Sales & Marketing, Retail: Michael A. Peterson
Director, Sales & Marketing, Special Markets: Rita McMullen
Director, Sales & Marketing, Home & Garden Center Channel: Ray Wolf
Director, Operations: George A. Susral

Vice President, General Manager: Jamie L. Martin

Better Homes and Gardens® Magazine
Editor in Chief: Jean LemMon
Executive Food Editor: Nancy Byal

Meredith Publishing Group
President, Publishing Group: Christopher M. Little
Vice President, Consumer Marketing & Development: Hal Oringer

Meredith Corporation
Chairman and Chief Executive Officer: William T. Kerr

Chairman of the Executive Committee: E. T. Meredith III

All of us at Better Homes and Gardens® Books are dedicated to providing you with the information and ideas you need to create delicious foods. We welcome your comments and suggestions. Write to us at: Better Homes and Gardens® Books, Cookbook Editorial Department, 1716 Locust St., Des Moines, IA 50309-3023.

If you would like to purchase any of our books, please check wherever books are sold.

Our seal assures you that every recipe in *The Complete Guide to Bread Machine Baking* has been tested in the Better Homes and Gardens® Test Kitchen. This means that each recipe is practical and reliable, and meets our high standards of taste appeal. We guarantee your satisfaction with this book for as long as you own it.

BREAD MACHINE BAKING

BASICS

Making bread just got a whole lot easier—and more enjoyable. The bread machine has created a new way to make homemade bread, one of life's little pleasures. Not only has the machine simplified the process of bread baking, it also has made this lost art accessible to those cooks who don't have a lot of spare time.

This collection of recipes helps you make the most of your bread machine—and allows you to have fun doing it. With **180 tempting recipes** to choose from, you'll enjoy limitless possibilities—classic, sourdough, shaped, sweet, holiday, and savory breads. The tips and a thorough primer (see pages 6 to 11) guarantee success, while the **beautiful full-color photography** promises inspiration.

The recipes in this book can be made in a 1½- or 2-pound bread machine. Many recipes use the machine's kneading feature, which allows for **versatility** in the types of breads you can create, such as pizza, calzones, braids, rings, and more. Read through the helpful tips, choose your recipe, and get ready for some **unforgettable homemade breads.**

Recipe Success

All recipes were tested by our experienced home economists in the Better Homes and Gardens® Test Kitchen. Recipes are judged on ease of preparation, texture, appeal, and flavor. No recipe can receive the Test Kitchen Seal of Approval until it meets the Test Kitchen's high standards. To ensure success, the recipes were tested in machines from a variety of manufacturers including Black & Decker, Breadman, Hitachi, Mr. Coffee, Mr. Loaf, Oster, Panasonic, Regal, Sanyo, Singer, Trillium, Toastmaster, West Bend, Welbilt, and Zojirushi. All recipes were tested in 1½- and 2-pound machines.

Bread machines have their own unique differences. Because of these differences, it's important to learn the features of your own particular model by reading the owner's manual that comes with your machine. In the information that follows, we've gone a step further to give you everything you need to know about baking with a bread machine.

Know Your Machine

Brands of bread machines vary when it comes to cycles, baking times, and temperatures. Here is a listing of several common cycles and settings to compare with the ones listed in your owner's manual.

Basic White: An all-purpose setting used for most breads.

Whole Grain: This cycle provides the longer rising times necessary for heavier breads that contain whole wheat, rye flour, or other varieties of whole grains.

Dough: This cycle mixes and kneads the bread dough and usually allows it to rise once before the cycle is complete. After this point, remove the dough for shaping, rising, and baking in your conventional oven.

Raisin: Some machines have an optional cycle that signals about 5 minutes prior to the end of the second kneading cycle. This signal indicates that raisins, dried fruits, nuts, or other similar ingredients can be added. If your machine doesn't have this option, try adding these ingredients about 15 minutes into the kneading cycle.

Sweet: The amount of sugar in a bread recipe affects its rising time and baking temperature. Some machines include this cycle for breads that have a high proportion of sugar. Follow the manufacturer's directions for when to use this cycle. If you find that bread baked on this cycle has gummy areas, try baking the bread on the basic white cycle.

Rapid: Some machines offer a cycle that reduces the total time needed for the machine to mix, rise, and bake a loaf of bread. Follow the manufacturer's directions to determine when to use this cycle.

Time Baked: This feature allows ingredients to be added to the machine at one time and the processing to begin at a later time. Do not use the time-bake cycle with recipes that include fresh milk, eggs, cheese, and other perishable foods. Allowing these ingredients to stand at room temperature for long periods will cause them to spoil. (See the chart on page 7 to substitute dry milk powder for fresh milk.)

Crust Color Setting: This useful feature lets you alter the baking time to control the brownness of the crust. For most breads, the best choice is the medium setting. If you find that your machine browns breads excessively, try a light-crust setting. Recipes that are high in sugar also may benefit from a lighter setting. Keep in mind, however, that with a lighter setting the bread may be slightly gummy.

Ingredient Tips and Substitutions

All the recipes for loaves in this book call for between 1 and 1½ teaspoons of active dry yeast or bread machine yeast. You may notice that this is less yeast than is used in many recipes supplied by bread machine manufacturers. In our testing, we found this amount of yeast makes a nicely risen loaf with an attractive shape. Adding more yeast typically produces a loaf with a very coarse and/or uneven texture. Also, it may cause the dough to rise too high then fall or stick to the lid of your machine or run over the edges of the pan.

Use the following equivalents to substitute dry milk powder for fresh milk:

Fresh Milk	=	Dry Milk Powder	Water
½ cup		2 tablespoons	½ cup
⅔ cup		2 tablespoons	⅔ cup
¾ cup		3 tablespoons	¾ cup
1 cup		¼ cup	1 cup
1¼ cups		⅓ cup	1¼ cups
1⅓ cups		⅓ cup + 1 tablespoon	1¼ cups
1½ cups		½ cup	1⅓ cups

☞ Sour milk is a good substitute for buttermilk. To make 1 cup sour milk, add 1 tablespoon vinegar or lemon juice to a 1-cup liquid measuring cup. Add enough low-fat milk to measure 1 cup liquid. Dry buttermilk powder also is available.

☞ Refrigerated or thawed frozen egg product can be used in place of whole eggs (1 egg equals ¼ cup egg product). Egg whites also can be used instead of whole eggs (2 egg whites equal 1 whole egg).

☞ For best results when using margarine, choose a margarine or a stick spread that contains at least 80 percent vegetable oil. Do not use an "extra light" spread, which contains only about 40 percent vegetable oil. It will result in an inferior finished product. In some cases, when necessary, butter is recommended by our test kitchen for quality assurance and is listed first.

☞ When you are using more than 2 tablespoons of either margarine or butter, cut it into small pieces to ensure that it will blend properly with the other ingredients.

Choosing a Recipe

The easiest way to ensure great results is to read a recipe completely through before you start. This helps familiarize you with the recipe steps and ensures that you have all the ingredients on hand. The recipes in this book list ingredients for both 1½- and 2-pound loaves so you can select the appropriate size to fit your needs and your machine. For the most part, recipe directions apply to both sizes. Occasionally, however, there are special directions for the 2-pound recipe.

You'll find that some recipes include this note: "For the 1½-pound loaf, the bread machine pan must have a capacity of 10 cups or more. For the 2-pound loaf, the bread machine pan must have a capacity of 12 cups or more." Check your owner's manual to see if it lists your machine's pan capacity. If it doesn't, you'll need to measure the capacity of your pan. Here's how: Remove the pan from the bread machine. Keeping track of the total amount of water added to the pan, use a liquid measuring cup to fill the pan with water until it is filled to the brim. For future reference, note the pan capacity in your owner's manual.

Measuring Up

Measuring accurately is crucial when baking. Incorrect proportions of liquid to dry ingredients may cause the recipe to fail. To avoid problems, follow these suggestions:

Flour. Stir the flour to lighten it before measuring and use metal or plastic measuring cups designed for dry ingredients. Gently spoon the flour into the cup and level off the top with the straight edge of a knife or metal spatula. Never dip your measuring cup into the flour or shake it after filling it with flour. This results in an excess of flour, possibly causing your dough to be too dry.

7

Bread flour vs. All-purpose flour

Many recipes in this book call for bread flour rather than all-purpose flour. In making yeast breads, kneading causes gluten, a type of protein in flour, to form an elasticlike consistency. Gluten traps bubbles of carbon dioxide that form when the yeast "feeds" on sugars in the dough. Gluten holds the gas bubbles, causing the dough to rise. The more gluten, the higher a baked product rises. Bread flour is specially formulated for bread baking because it contains more gluten than all-purpose, pastry, or cake flour. This allows products made from bread flour to rise higher and form better structurally than other flours. Use bread flour for the recipes in this book unless directed otherwise.

Liquid Ingredients. Use a glass or clear plastic measuring cup for liquids. Place the cup on a level surface and bend down so your eye is level with the marking you wish to read. Fill the cup to the marking. Don't lift the cup off the counter to your eye—it's impossible to hold the cup steady enough for an accurate reading. When using a measuring spoon to measure a liquid, pour the liquid just to the top of the spoon without letting it spill over. Don't hold the spoon over the machine pan while adding the liquid because the liquid could overflow from the spoon into the pan.

Margarine or Butter. For premeasured sticks, use a sharp knife to cut off the amount needed, following the guidelines on the wrapper. (Use one ¼-pound stick for ½ cup or half of a stick for ¼ cup.) For butter that's not in premeasured sticks, soften it and measure as directed for shortening.

Shortening. Using a rubber spatula, press the shortening firmly into a measuring cup designed for dry ingredients or into a measuring spoon. Level it off with the straight edge of a knife or metal spatula.

Sugar. Press brown sugar firmly into a measuring cup designed for dry ingredients. The sugar should hold the shape of the cup when turned out. To measure granulated sugar, spoon the sugar into the measuring cup or spoon, then level it off with the straight edge of a knife or metal spatula.

Perfect Dough Consistency

Occasionally, no matter how carefully you measure, a dough may become either too wet or too dry. This often is due to the fact that some types (and brands)

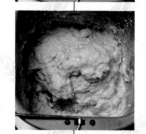

of flour absorb slightly more or less liquid than others. By checking the dough's consistency during the first 3 to 5 minutes of kneading, however, you can make sure the ratio of liquid to dry ingredients is perfect.

If the dough looks too dry and crumbly (see photo, top left) or forms two or more balls, add additional liquid, 1 teaspoon at a time, until one smooth ball forms. If the dough has too much moisture and does not form a ball (see photo, center left), add additional bread flour, 1 tablespoon at a time, until a ball forms. Bread dough with the correct amount of flour and liquid will form a smooth ball (see photo, bottom left).

Adding Ingredients To Your Machine

It's important to add ingredients to your machine according to the directions given in the owner's manual. Generally, manufacturers recommend adding the *liquids first, followed by the dry ingredients.* The *yeast goes in last.* The reason for this order is to keep the yeast separated from the liquid ingredients until the kneading cycle begins. This is the order our Test Kitchen recommends; however, it may not be the order the manufacturer recommends for your specific machine. Check your owner's manual and use the order recommended by the manufacturer of your machine.

Also in this book, any ingredients listed after the yeast, such as dried fruits or nuts, should be added at the raisin bread cycle, if your machine has one. If not, add them according to the manufacturer's directions, or 15 minutes into the kneading cycle.

Storing Breads or Doughs

Baked. Knowing how to store bread properly will keep it fresh for an extended period of time. Follow these tips:

☞ Remove hot bread from the machine as soon as it is done and turn it out on a wire rack to cool completely. (If the bread cools in the machine, it may become damp and soggy.)

☞ To store at room temperature, wrap the cooled bread in foil or plastic wrap, or place it in a plastic bag. Store it in a cool, dry place for up to 3 days.

☞ To freeze, place cooled bread in a freezer bag or container. Freeze loaf for up to 3 months. To serve the frozen bread, thaw it in the packaging for 1 hour. Or, remove from packaging, wrap frozen bread in foil, and thaw it in a 300° oven about 20 minutes.

Unbaked. Tailor bread machine recipes to fit your schedule. Make the dough as directed, refrigerate or freeze it, shape, and bake it later. Here's how:

☞ To refrigerate bread dough, place it in an airtight container and refrigerate for up to 24 hours. (Make sure the container is at least twice the size of the dough. The dough could rise enough to burst out of a small container.) Bring the dough to room temperature before shaping.

☞ To freeze bread dough, place it in an airtight container. Seal, label, and freeze for up to 3 months. To use the dough, let it stand at room temperature for 3 hours or until thawed. Or, thaw it overnight in the refrigerator. Shape and bake the bread as directed in the recipe.

Pointers From Our Test Kitchen

Here are some helpful suggestions from our Test Kitchen to help make your bread machine reliable and easy to use.

☞ Use bread flour for each of the recipes in this book unless directed otherwise. This high-protein flour is especially formulated for bread baking. (See tip box, page 8, "Bread flour vs. All-purpose flour.")

☞ If you store flour or specialty grains in the freezer, warm the measured amount to room temperature before using.

☞ Adding gluten flour to a bread that contains whole grain flour, especially rye flour, improves the texture of the loaf. (See gluten flour in glossary, page 11.)

☞ Salt is necessary when making yeast bread because it controls the growth of yeast, which aids the rising of dough. If you're on a sodium-restricted diet you'll be happy to find most of the recipes in this book are lower in sodium than purchased breads. If you want to reduce the sodium further, experiment by reducing the salt a little at a time. Because bread needs some salt or the bread may collapse, don't eliminate it altogether.

☞ Yeast is important in bread baking. When baking bread at high altitudes, it may be necessary to reduce the amount of yeast in the recipe. (See "High Altitude Tips," page 10.)

☞ Store packages of dry yeast in a cool, dry place. Once a jar of yeast has been opened, store it tightly covered in the refrigerator. Use yeast before the expiration date stamped on the package or jar.

☞ Spray the bread pan with nonstick coating before adding the ingredients. This makes for easy removal.

☞ Make cleanup easy by spraying the kneading paddle of your machine with nonstick coating before using.

☞ If the kneading paddle stays in the bread when you remove the hot loaf from the machine, use the handle of a wooden spoon to help remove it.

☞ Fill the machine's pan with hot soapy water immediately after removing baked bread. (Do not immerse pan in water.) Soak the kneading paddle separately if it comes out with the loaf of bread.

9

What Went Wrong?

Small and Heavy Loaf

The dough may not have risen enough.

- check measurements (ratio of flour to liquid must be exact)
- make sure yeast is fresh (use before expiration date)
- check dough consistency as dough kneads. (You may need to add more liquid or flour, see page 8)

Gummy Texture

Usually means bread is underbaked.

- if recipe is too large for pan, heat will not penetrate to center of loaf
- make sure you're using the right setting on your machine (The light color setting may be too short in duration to completely bake some rich breads)
- experiment with a darker setting if you have this option

Collapsed Loaf

- recipe is too large for pan
- ratio of liquid to dry ingredients unbalanced (recheck measurements/check consistency as dough kneads)
- too much yeast
- salt has been omitted
- warm, humid weather causes dough to rise too fast, then collapses before baking begins—bake during coolest part of day, use refrigerated liquids, try rapid cycle if your machine has this feature

Mushroom-shaped Loaf

- recipe is too large for pan
- ratio of liquid to dry ingredients unbalanced (recheck measurements/check consistency as dough kneads)

- warm weather—bake during coolest part of day, use refrigerated liquids, try rapid cycle if your machine has this feature

Open, Holey Texture

- ratio of liquid to dry ingredients unbalanced (recheck measurements/check consistency as dough kneads)
- too much yeast
- salt has been omitted
- warm weather/high humidity

Bumpy, Uneven Top/Very Dense Texture

- flour no longer fresh—it may be dried out
- too much flour (check dough consistency while kneading—may need to add more liquid)
- if you live at high altitude, see "High Altitude Tips" below

High-Altitude Tips

If you live in an area that is more than 1,000 feet above sea level, you'll need to make some adjustments to your bread machine recipes because of the lower atmospheric pressure. First check your owner's manual for specific high-altitude directions. If no directions are given, start by reducing the yeast by ¼ teaspoon. At higher altitudes, breads will rise higher than at sea level, so they need less yeast. If your bread still rises too high, reduce the yeast by another ¼ teaspoon the next time you make the recipe.

Also, keep in mind that flour tends to be drier at high altitudes and sometimes will absorb more liquid. Watch the dough carefully as it mixes in the machine. If the dough seems too dry, add additional liquid, 1 teaspoon at a time. Keep a record of the total amount of liquid you use as a reference for the next time you make the bread.

Rise up

When using the dough cycle, you often need to let the shaped dough rise before baking. For the best results, our Test Kitchen suggests using a warm, draft-free area where the temperature is between 80° and 85°. An unheated oven is an ideal place for raising dough. Place the oven's lower rack in the lowest position. Set a large pan of hot water on the rack. Cover the shaped dough loosely with a clean cloth; place it on the top rack of the oven. Close the door; let the dough rise until nearly doubled. Remove the dough and water from the oven; preheat the oven.

Ingredients Glossary

All-purpose Flour, a white flour, is generally a combination of soft and hard wheats, or medium-protein wheats. It works well for all types of baked products, including yeast breads, cakes, cookies, and quick breads. All-purpose flour usually is sold presifted. It is available bleached and unbleached. Either is suitable for home baking and can be used interchangeably.

Barley, a cereal grain, has a mild, starchy flavor and a slightly chewy texture. Pearl barley, the most popular form used for cooking, has the outer hull removed and has been polished or "pearled." It is sold in regular and quick-cooking forms. Store barley in an airtight container in a cool, dry place for up to 1 year.

Bread Flour, the type recommended for recipes in this book, is made from hard wheat. It has a higher gluten content than all-purpose flour. Gluten, a protein, provides structure and height to breads, making bread flour well suited for the task. Store bread flour in an airtight container in a cool, dry place for up to 5 months, or freeze it for up to 1 year.

Bulgur, a parched, cracked wheat product, is made by soaking, cooking, and drying whole wheat kernels. Part of the bran is removed and what remains of the hard kernels is cracked into small pieces. Bulgur has a delicate, nutty flavor. Store it in an airtight container in a cool, dry place for up to 6 months, or freeze it for up to 1 year.

Cornmeal, a finely ground corn product, is made from dried yellow, white, or blue corn kernels. Cornmeal labeled "stone ground" is slightly coarser than regular cornmeal. Store cornmeal in an airtight container in a cool, dry place for up to 6 months, or freeze it for up to 1 year.

Gluten Flour, sometimes called wheat gluten, is made by removing most of the starch from high-protein, hard-wheat flour. If you can't find gluten flour at your supermarket, look for it at a health-food store. Store it in an airtight container in a cool, dry place for up to 5 months, or freeze it for up to 1 year.

Millet, a cereal grain with tiny, round, yellow kernels, tastes slightly nutty and has a chewy texture. Store millet in an airtight container in a cool, dry place for up to 2 years.

Oats are the cereal grain produced by the cereal grass of the same name. Whole oats minus the hulls are called groats. Oats have a nutty flavor and a chewy texture. Store oats in an airtight container in a cool, dry place for up to 6 months, or freeze for up to 1 year. Two popular forms include old-fashioned and quick-cooking oats.

Old-fashioned Rolled Oats are oat groats that have been steamed then flattened by steel rollers.

Quick-cooking Rolled Oats are oat groats that have been cut into small pieces—to shorten the cooking time—then flattened.

Rye Flour is made from finely ground rye, a cereal grain that has dark brown kernels and a distinctive robust flavor. Light rye flour is sifted and contains less bran than dark rye flour. Store rye flour in an airtight container in a cool, dry place, for up to 5 months, or freeze for up to 1 year.

Wheat Germ, the embryo or sprouting portion of the wheat kernel, is sold both raw and toasted. It is extremely perishable. Once opened, store in the refrigerator no more than 3 months.

Whole Wheat Flour, unlike all-purpose and bread flour, is ground from the complete wheat berry, and contains the wheat germ as well as the wheat bran. It is coarser in texture and does not rise as well as all-purpose or bread flour. Store whole wheat flour in an airtight container in a cool, dry place for up to 5 months, or freeze for up to 1 year.

Wild Rice is the long, dark brown or black, nutty-flavored seed of an annual marsh grass. Wild rice is not actually a rice but a cereal grain. Store uncooked wild rice indefinitely in a cool, dry place or in the refrigerator.

BREAD MACHINE BAKING

CLASSIC

{ PUMPKIN PECAN BREAD }

see recipe, page 35

WHITE BREAD

This tender classic with its golden crust and delicate flavor is the bread supermarket loaves aspire to be. One taste, and your family will accept no substitutes. With a bread machine, you can easily oblige.

DIRECTIONS

☞ Select the loaf size. Add the ingredients to the machine according to the manufacturer's directions. Select the basic white bread cycle.
☞ ***NOTE:** Our Test Kitchen recommends ¼ cup water for either size recipe.

Prep time: 10 minutes
Nutrition facts per slice: 114 calories, 2 g total fat (0 g saturated fat), 1 mg cholesterol, 119 mg sodium, 21 g carbohydrate, 1 g fiber, 4 g protein.

1½-POUND (16 slices)	INGREDIENTS	2-POUND (22 slices)
1 cup	milk	1¼ cups
¼ cup	water*	¼ cup
4 teaspoons	margarine, butter, or olive oil	2 tablespoons
3 cups	bread flour	4 cups
4 teaspoons	sugar	2 tablespoons
¾ teaspoon	salt	1 teaspoon
1 teaspoon	active dry yeast or bread machine yeast	1¼ teaspoons

14

The aroma of toasted whole wheat bread is one of the best things around. Have this bread on hand for everyday eating—for turkey sandwiches, toasted cheese sandwiches, or just toast.

DIRECTIONS

☞ Select the loaf size. Add the ingredients to the machine according to the manufacturer's directions. If available, select the whole grain cycle, or select the basic white bread cycle.

May We Suggest?

If you prefer the flavor of whole wheat bread over regular white, substitute this basic whole wheat dough. Recipes that use a regular white bread dough, such as Pizza Rustica (page 219), Calzones (page 230), and Bread Soup Bowls (page 222), adapt well to this whole wheat dough.

WHOLE WHEAT BREAD

Prep time: 10 minutes

Nutrition facts per slice: 105 calories, 1 g total fat (0 g saturated fat), 1 mg cholesterol, 117 mg sodium, 20 g carbohydrate, 2 g fiber, 4 g protein.

1½-POUND (16 slices)	INGREDIENTS	2-POUND (22 slices)
1 cup	milk	1⅓ cups
3 tablespoons	water	¼ cup
4 teaspoons	honey or sugar	2 tablespoons
1 tablespoon	margarine or butter	4 teaspoons
1½ cups	whole wheat flour	2 cups
1½ cups	bread flour	2 cups
¾ teaspoon	salt	1 teaspoon
1 teaspoon	active dry yeast or bread machine yeast	1¼ teaspoons

15

ZUCCHINI WHEAT BREAD

Shredded zucchini highlights the unique flavor of whole wheat. A little brown sugar and lemon peel add additional flavor notes. Try it toasted with Lemon Butter (see recipe, page 116).

Prep time: 15 minutes

Nutrition facts per slice: 112 calories, 2 g total fat (1 g saturated fat), 1 mg cholesterol, 109 mg sodium, 19 g carbohydrate, 2 g fiber, 4 g protein.

1½-POUND (16 slices)	INGREDIENTS	2-POUND (22 slices)
1 cup	milk*	1 cup
1 cup	coarsely shredded zucchini (lightly packed)	1½ cups
2 tablespoons	shortening*	2 tablespoons
2 cups	whole wheat flour	2⅔ cups
1 cup	bread flour	1⅓ cups
2 tablespoons	gluten flour*	2 tablespoons
1 tablespoon	brown sugar	4 teaspoons
1½ teaspoons	finely shredded lemon peel	2 teaspoons
¾ teaspoon	salt	1 teaspoon
1 teaspoon	active dry yeast or bread machine yeast	2 teaspoons

DIRECTIONS

☞ Select the loaf size. Add the ingredients to the machine according to the manufacturer's directions, adding the zucchini with the milk. If available, select the whole grain cycle, or select the basic white bread cycle.

☞ ***NOTE:** Our Test Kitchen recommends 1 cup milk, 2 tablespoons shortening, and 2 tablespoons gluten flour for either size recipe.

HOT TIP

When purchasing lemons for zesting or juicing, choose those that are smooth with evenly yellow skin. Avoid any dry, wrinkled lemons, which most likely are old. A medium-size lemon will yield 3 tablespoons of juice and 2 teaspoons of shredded peel.

16

CHEESY POTATO BREAD

This fragrant cheese bread has just a hint of caraway. It's excellent for sandwiches—or try it toasted, spread with Parmesan-Garlic Butter (see recipe, page 117).

DIRECTIONS

☞ Select loaf size. In a small saucepan combine the water and potato. Bring to boiling; reduce heat. Cover and simmer about 10 minutes or until potato is very tender. Do not drain. Mash potato in the water. Measure potato-water mixture. If necessary, add water to equal ¾ cup mixture for the 1½-pound loaf or 1 cup mixture for the 2-pound loaf; discard any excess mixture. Cool slightly.

☞ Add the potato mixture and remaining ingredients to the machine according to the manufacturer's directions. Select the basic white bread cycle.

Prep time: 25 minutes

Nutrition facts per slice: 118 calories, 2 g total fat (1 g saturated fat), 3 mg cholesterol, 101 mg sodium, 21 g carbohydrate, 1 g fiber, 4 g protein.

1½-POUND (16 slices)	INGREDIENTS	2-POUND (22 slices)
¾ cup	water	1 cup
½ cup	chopped, peeled potato	⅔ cup
⅓ cup	milk	½ cup
⅓ cup	shredded cheddar cheese	½ cup
2 teaspoons	margarine or butter	1 tablespoon
3 cups	bread flour	4 cups
1 tablespoon	sugar	4 teaspoons
¾ teaspoon	onion salt	1 teaspoon
¼ teaspoon	caraway seed, crushed (optional)	½ teaspoon
1 teaspoon	active dry yeast or bread machine yeast	1¼ teaspoons

17

GARDEN PATCH BREAD

This cream-of-the crop loaf is chockful of garden flavors—basil, tomato, green pepper, carrot, and onion. Update your next BLT sandwich with this colorful bread.

Prep time: 15 minutes

Nutrition facts per slice: 83 calories, 1 g total fat (0 g saturated fat), 0 mg cholesterol, 102 mg sodium, 16 g carbohydrate, 1 g fiber, 3 g protein.

DIRECTIONS

☞ Select the loaf size. Add the ingredients to the machine according to the manufacturer's directions. Select the basic white bread cycle.
☞ *NOTE: Our Test Kitchen recommends 1 teaspoon yeast for either size recipe.

1½-POUND (20 slices)	INGREDIENTS	2-POUND (27 slices)
½ cup	water	⅔ cup
½ cup	coarsely shredded carrots	⅔ cup
⅓ cup	tomato juice	½ cup
2 tablespoons	coarsely chopped green pepper	3 tablespoons
2 tablespoons	sliced green onion	3 tablespoons
1 tablespoon	margarine, butter, or cooking oil	4 teaspoons
3 cups	bread flour	4 cups
1 teaspoon	sugar	1½ teaspoons
¾ teaspoon	salt	1 teaspoon
¼ teaspoon	dried basil, crushed	½ teaspoon
1 teaspoon	active dry yeast or bread machine yeast*	1 teaspoon

18

RUSSIAN RYE BREAD

A flavor trinity of coffee, molasses, and cocoa powder creates an exotic taste blend. For a real taste treat, wrap this bread around grilled links of sausage.

DIRECTIONS

☞ Select the loaf size. Add the ingredients to the machine according to the manufacturer's directions. If available, select the whole grain cycle, or select the basic white bread cycle.

Prep time: 10 minutes

Nutrition facts per slice: 102 calories, 1 g total fat (0 g saturated fat), 0 mg cholesterol, 110 mg sodium, 20 g carbohydrate, 1 g fiber, 3 g protein.

1½-POUND (16 slices)	INGREDIENTS	2-POUND (22 slices)
¾ cup	water	1 cup
¼ cup	strong coffee	⅓ cup
2 tablespoons	mild-flavored molasses	3 tablespoons
1 tablespoon	margarine or butter	2 tablespoons
2 cups	bread flour	2⅔ cups
1 cup	rye flour	1⅓ cups
2 tablespoons	unsweetened cocoa powder	3 tablespoons
1 teaspoon	gluten flour	1½ teaspoons
¾ teaspoon	salt	1 teaspoon
¾ teaspoon	caraway seed	1 teaspoon
¼ teaspoon	fennel seed, crushed	½ teaspoon
1¼ teaspoons	active dry yeast or bread machine yeast	1½ teaspoons

20

PUMPERNICKEL BREAD

Bring the best to your table with this perennial favorite. With just a hint of molasses, it's good served warm with hearty meals—or sliced later for sandwiches. Let it become your specialty.

DIRECTIONS

☞ Select the loaf size. Add the ingredients to the machine according to the manufacturer's directions. If available, select the whole grain cycle, or select the basic white bread cycle.

☞ **★NOTE:** For the 1½-pound loaf, the bread machine pan must have a capacity of 10 cups or more. For the 2-pound loaf, the bread machine pan must have a capacity of 12 cups or more.

May We Suggest?

Measuring and pouring molasses (or honey or corn syrup) can prove a sticky problem. Smooth the way by first spraying the measuring cup or measuring spoon with vegetable spray or brushing it with an unflavored oil. The molasses will slide right out.

Prep time: 10 minutes

Nutrition facts per slice: 109 calories, 2 g total fat (0 g saturated fat), 0 mg cholesterol, 102 mg sodium, 21 g carbohydrate, 1 g fiber, 3 g protein.

1½-POUND★ (16 slices)	INGREDIENTS	2-POUND★ (22 slices)
¾ cup	water	1 cup
¼ cup	mild-flavored molasses	⅓ cup
4 teaspoons	cooking oil	2 tablespoons
2 cups	bread flour	2⅔ cups
1 cup	rye flour	1⅓ cups
2 teaspoons	caraway seed	1 tablespoon
¾ teaspoon	salt	1 teaspoon
1¼ teaspoons	active dry yeast or bread machine yeast	1½ teaspoons

21

WILD RICE BREAD

Take a walk on the wild side of bread with a loaf that gets its nutty zip and chewy texture from wild rice. Pair it with smoked turkey or cheese for a sophisticated, satisfying sandwich.

Prep time: 10 minutes

Nutrition facts per slice: 108 calories, 1 g total fat (0 g saturated fat), 0 mg cholesterol, 180 mg sodium, 20 g carbohydrate, 2 g fiber, 4 g protein.

1½-POUND (16 slices)	INGREDIENTS	2-POUND (22 slices)
1 cup	water	1¼ cups
¾ cup	cooked wild rice, well drained and cooled*	1 cup
4 teaspoons	margarine or butter	2 tablespoons
2 cups	bread flour	2⅔ cups
1 cup	whole wheat flour	1⅓ cups
1 tablespoon	sugar	2 tablespoons
1¼ teaspoons	instant chicken bouillon granules	1½ teaspoons
¾ teaspoon	salt	1 teaspoon
½ teaspoon	dried thyme, crushed	1 teaspoon
1 teaspoon	active dry yeast or bread machine yeast	1¼ teaspoons

DIRECTIONS

☞ Select the loaf size. Add the ingredients to the machine according to the manufacturer's directions. If available, select the whole grain cycle, or select the basic white bread cycle.

☞ *NOTE: For ¾ cup cooked wild rice, start with ¾ cup water and ¼ cup uncooked wild rice. For 1 cup cooked wild rice, start with 1 cup water and ⅓ cup uncooked wild rice. In a small saucepan bring water to boiling; add wild rice. Reduce heat to low. Simmer, covered, about 40 minutes or until rice is just tender. Drain well; cool completely.

HOT TIP

The dehydrated form of broth—instant bouillon granules or cubes—supplies rich, homey chicken flavor. Either is convenient because you can make as little or as much broth as you like. Both keep for months if stored in airtight containers.

22

This bread brings to mind the rough country breads found in France and Italy. It often is shaped into long loaves, called baguettes, which have a wonderful golden brown crust.

FRENCH BREAD

Prep time: 20 minutes **Rise time:** 35 minutes **Bake time:** 32 minutes
Nutrition facts per slice: 103 calories, 0 g total fat (0 g saturated fat), 0 mg cholesterol, 111 mg sodium, 20 g carbohydrate, 1 g fiber, 4 g protein.

DIRECTIONS

☞ Select loaf size. Add first 4 ingredients to machine according to the manufacturer's directions. Select the dough cycle.

☞ When cycle is complete, remove dough. Punch down. Cover and let rest 10 minutes. Divide 1½-pound dough in half. On a lightly floured surface, roll each half into a 10×8-inch rectangle. (Divide 2-pound dough in half; roll each half into a 15×10-inch rectangle.) Starting from a long side, roll up into a spiral; seal edge. Pinch and pull ends to taper.

☞ Place, seams down, on a greased baking sheet sprinkled with cornmeal. Combine egg white and 1 tablespoon water; brush some over top of loaves. Cover and let rise in a warm place for 35 to 45 minutes or until nearly double. With a very sharp knife, make 3 or 4 diagonal cuts about ¼ inch deep across the top of each loaf.

☞ Bake in a 375° oven for 20 minutes. Brush with remaining egg white mixture. Bake for 12 to 15 minutes more or until bread sounds hollow when lightly tapped. Remove from baking sheet; cool on wire rack.

1½-POUND (15 slices)	INGREDIENTS	2-POUND (20 slices)
1 cup	water	1⅓ cups
3 cups	bread flour	4 cups
¾ teaspoon	salt	1 teaspoon
1 teaspoon	active dry yeast or bread machine yeast	1½ teaspoons
	Yellow cornmeal	
1	slightly beaten egg white	1
1 tablespoon	water	1 tablespoon

23

Bagels originated from an Eastern European-Jewish baking tradition. Do you want to know the secret to their chewy texture and sheen? Boiling them in water before baking them.

BAGELS

Prep time: 25 minutes **Rise time:** 20 minutes **Broil time:** 3 minutes
Cook time: 7 minutes per batch **Bake time:** 25 minutes
Nutrition facts per bagel: 183 calories, 2 g total fat (0 g saturated fat), 0 mg cholesterol, 186 mg sodium, 35 g carbohydrate, 1 g fiber, 6 g protein.

DIRECTIONS

☞ Select recipe size. Add first 6 ingredients to machine according to the manufacturer's directions. Select the dough cycle. When cycle is complete, remove dough from machine. Punch down. Cover and let rest 10 minutes.

☞ Divide 1½-pound dough into 9 portions (divide 2-pound dough into 12 portions). Working quickly, shape each into a smooth ball. Punch a hole in center; pull gently to make a 2-inch hole. Place on a greased large baking sheet. Cover; let rise for 20 minutes (start timing after first bagel is shaped). Broil, 5 inches from heat, 3 to 4 minutes, turning once (tops should not brown).

☞ Meanwhile, in large pot bring 6 cups water and 1 tablespoon sugar to boiling. Reduce heat. Add bagels, 4 or 5 at a time, and simmer for 7 minutes, turning once. Drain on paper towels. (If some bagels fall slightly, they may rise when baked.) Place on a well-greased large baking sheet. Mix the egg white and the 1 tablespoon water; brush over bagels. If desired, sprinkle with poppy or sesame seeds. Bake in a 375° oven for 25 to 30 minutes or until tops are golden. Remove from baking sheets; cool on racks.

1½-POUND (9 bagels)	INGREDIENTS	2-POUND (12 bagels)
1 cup	water	1⅓ cups
2 teaspoons	cooking oil	1 tablespoon
3 cups	bread flour	4 cups
1 tablespoon	sugar	4 teaspoons
¾ teaspoon	salt	1 teaspoon
1 teaspoon	active dry yeast or bread machine yeast	1¼ teaspoons
1	slightly beaten egg white	1
1 tablespoon	water	1 tablespoon
	Poppy seeds or sesame seeds (optional)	

25

OATMEAL BREAD

Layer shaved smoked turkey, provolone cheese, lettuce leaves, and thinly sliced tomato between two slices of this hearty, oaty bread for an out-of-the ordinary lunchtime meal.

Prep time: 25 minutes

Nutrition facts per slice: 117 calories, 2 g total fat (0 g saturated fat), 1 mg cholesterol, 115 mg sodium, 22 g carbohydrate, 1 g fiber, 4 g protein.

1½-POUND (16 slices)	INGREDIENTS	2-POUND (22 slices)
1 cup	quick-cooking rolled oats	1⅓ cups
⅔ cup	milk	¾ cup
⅓ cup	water	½ cup
1 tablespoon	margarine, butter, or shortening	2 tablespoons
2½ cups	bread flour	3⅓ cups
3 tablespoons	packed brown sugar	¼ cup
¾ teaspoon	salt	1 teaspoon
1 teaspoon	active dry yeast or bread machine yeast	1¼ teaspoons

DIRECTIONS

☞ Select the loaf size. Spread the oats in a shallow baking pan. Bake in a 350° oven for 15 to 20 minutes or until light brown, stirring occasionally. Cool.

☞ Add the ingredients to the machine according to the manufacturer's directions, adding the oats with the flour. If available, select the whole grain cycle, or select the basic white bread cycle.

Good Advice!

Not all rolled oats—the husked oat grain sliced, steamed, flattened, and dried—are created equal (although you can use them equally for baking). Old-fashioned rolled oats are thicker, adding rustic texture to breads and other baked goods. Quick-cooking rolled oats are thinner, smaller flakes that create smoother doughs.

26

Turn your hum-drum spaghetti dinner into a feast with this homemade Italian bread alongside. Serve with our Parmesan-Garlic Butter (page 117) and get ready for rave reviews.

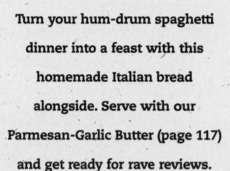

DIRECTIONS

☞ Select the loaf size. Add the ingredients to the machine according to the manufacturer's directions. Select the basic white bread cycle.

☞ **NOTE:** For the 1½-pound loaf, the bread machine pan must have a capacity of 10 cups or more. For the 2-pound loaf, the bread machine pan must have a capacity of 12 cups or more.

☞ **NOTE:** Our Test Kitchen recommends 1 egg for either size recipe.

ITALIAN BREAD

Prep time: 10 minutes

Nutrition facts per slice: 110 calories, 2 g total fat (0 g saturated fat), 14 mg cholesterol, 85 mg sodium, 19 g carbohydrate, 1 g fiber, 4 g protein.

1½-POUND★ (16 slices)	INGREDIENTS	2-POUND★ (22 slices)
¾ cup	milk	1 cup
1	egg★★	1
3 tablespoons	water	¼ cup
1 tablespoon	margarine or butter	4 teaspoons
3 cups	bread flour	4 cups
½ teaspoon	salt	¾ teaspoon
1 teaspoon	active dry yeast or bread machine yeast	1¼ teaspoons

27

RYE BREAD

An earthy European-style rye is easy to love, but hard to make because the dough can be difficult to handle—in other words, the perfect recipe for a bread machine.

DIRECTIONS

☞ Select the loaf size. Add the ingredients to the machine according to the manufacturer's directions. If available, select the whole grain cycle, or select the basic white bread cycle.

Prep time: 10 minutes

Nutrition facts per slice: 108 calories, 2 g total fat (0 g saturated fat), 0 mg cholesterol, 118 mg sodium, 20 g carbohydrate, 2 g fiber, 3 g protein.

1½-POUND (16 slices)	INGREDIENTS	2-POUND (22 slices)
1 cup	water	1⅓ cups
2 tablespoons	margarine or butter, cut up; shortening; or cooking oil	3 tablespoons
2 cups	bread flour	2⅔ cups
1 cup	rye flour	1⅓ cups
2 tablespoons	gluten flour	3 tablespoons
2 tablespoons	brown sugar	3 tablespoons
1½ teaspoons	caraway seed (optional)	2 teaspoons
¾ teaspoon	salt	1 teaspoon
1 teaspoon	active dry yeast or bread machine yeast	1¼ teaspoons

28

Buckwheat is actually an herb—not a grain or cereal. Therefore, it does not contain gluten—necessary in making breads rise—which means it must be used along with other flours in baking.

BUCKWHEAT BREAD

DIRECTIONS

☞ Select the loaf size. Add the ingredients to the machine according to the manufacturer's directions. If available, select the whole grain cycle, or select the basic white bread cycle.

☞ *NOTE: Our Test Kitchen recommends 2 tablespoons gluten flour and 2 tablespoons brown sugar for either size recipe.

May We Suggest?

Despite its name, buckwheat is not kin to wheat, although it is ground and used as a flour like wheat. Fans love its earthy, nutty flavor. Keep this specialty flour in the refrigerator or freezer for up to three months. Bring to room temperature before using, or it will retard yeast activity.

Prep time: 10 minutes

Nutrition facts per slice: 104 calories, 1 g total fat (0 g saturated fat), 0 mg cholesterol, 101 mg sodium, 20 g carbohydrate, 2 g fiber, 4 g protein.

1½-POUND (16 slices)	INGREDIENTS	2-POUND (22 slices)
1 cup	water	1¼ cups
1 tablespoon	shortening	2 tablespoons
2 cups	bread flour	2⅔ cups
1 cup	buckwheat flour	1½ cups
2 tablespoons	gluten flour*	2 tablespoons
2 tablespoons	brown sugar*	2 tablespoons
¾ teaspoon	salt	1 teaspoon
1¼ teaspoons	active dry yeast or bread machine yeast	1½ teaspoons

29

PRETZELS

DIRECTIONS

☞ Select the recipe size. Add the first 7 ingredients to the machine according to the manufacturer's directions. Select the dough cycle. When cycle is complete, remove dough from machine. Punch down. Cover and let rest for 10 minutes.

☞ On a lightly floured surface, roll the 1½-pound dough into a 12×8-inch rectangle. Cut into sixteen 12×½-inch strips. (Roll the 2-pound dough into a 12×11-inch rectangle; cut into twenty-two 12×½-inch strips.) Gently pull the strips into 16-inch-long ropes. Shape each pretzel by crossing one end over the other to form a circle, overlapping about 4 inches from each end. Take one end of dough in each hand and twist once at the point where the dough overlaps. Carefully lift each end across to the edge of the circle opposite it. Tuck ends under edges to make a pretzel shape; moisten ends and press to seal. Place on 2 greased large baking sheets.

☞ Bake in a 475° oven for 4 minutes.★ Remove from the oven. Reduce the oven temperature to 350°. Meanwhile, in a large pot bring 8 cups water and 2 tablespoons salt to boiling. Add pretzels, 3 or 4 at a time, and boil gently for 2 minutes, turning once. Using a slotted spoon, remove pretzels from water and drain on paper towels. Let stand a few seconds. Place pretzels about ½ inch apart on 2 well-greased large baking sheets.

☞ In a small bowl combine egg white and 1 tablespoon water; brush over pretzels. Sprinkle with sesame seeds or coarse salt. Bake in the 350° oven for 20 to 25 minutes or until golden brown. Remove from baking sheets; cool on wire racks.

☞ ★**NOTE:** For crisper pretzels, bake in upper half of oven 4 to 5 inches from the top.

Prep time: 40 minutes **Bake time:** 24 minutes **Cook time:** 2 minutes per batch
Nutrition facts per pretzel: 119 calories, 2 g total fat (0 g saturated fat), 1 mg cholesterol, 245 mg sodium, 21 g carbohydrate, 1 g fiber, 4 g protein.

1½-POUND (16 pretzels)	INGREDIENTS	2-POUND (22 pretzels)
1 cup	milk	1⅓ cups
2 tablespoons	water	3 tablespoons
1 tablespoon	cooking oil	4 teaspoons
3 cups	bread flour	4 cups
2 tablespoons	sugar	3 tablespoons
¾ teaspoon	salt	1 teaspoon
1¼ teaspoons	active dry yeast or bread machine yeast	1½ teaspoons
1	slightly beaten egg white	1
1 tablespoon	water	1 tablespoon
	Sesame seeds or coarse salt	

31

CRESCENT ROLLS

Arbiters of good taste at dinner tables everywhere agree: Classic crescent rolls reign supreme. And these are especially irresistible— light, flaky, and oh-so-buttery. What's not to like?

Prep time: 25 minutes   **Rise time:** 30 minutes   **Bake time:** 8 minutes
Nutrition facts per roll: 153 calories, 5 g total fat (3 g saturated fat), 39 mg cholesterol, 156 mg sodium, 22 g carbohydrate, 1 g fiber, 4 g protein.

1½-POUND (16 rolls)	INGREDIENTS	2-POUND (24 rolls)
½ cup	milk	⅔ cup
2	eggs*	2
¼ cup	butter or margarine, cut up	⅓ cup
3 cups	bread flour	3¾ cups
3 tablespoons	sugar	¼ cup
¾ teaspoon	salt	1 teaspoon
1¼ teaspoons	active dry yeast or bread machine yeast	1½ teaspoons
2 tablespoons	butter or margarine, melted	3 tablespoons

32

DIRECTIONS

☞ Select the recipe size. Add the first 7 ingredients to the machine according to the manufacturer's directions. Select the dough cycle. When the cycle is complete, remove dough from machine. Punch down. Cover and let rest for 10 minutes.

☞ *For the 1½-pound recipe:* Divide the dough in half. On a lightly floured surface, roll each half into a 12-inch circle. Brush each circle with half of the melted butter or margarine. Cut each circle into 8 wedges. Starting at the wide end of each wedge, loosely roll toward the point. Place rolls, points down, 2 to 3 inches apart on greased baking sheets. Cover; let rise in a warm place for 30 to 40 minutes or until nearly double.

☞ Bake in a 375° oven for 8 to 10 minutes or until golden. Remove from baking sheets; cool on wire racks.

☞ *For the 2-pound recipe:* Prepare as above, except divide the dough into thirds. After rolling, brush each circle with one-third of the melted butter or margarine.

☞ ***NOTE:** Our Test Kitchen recommends 2 eggs for either size recipe.

More than a little bit nutty, this delectable bread is one of the best things to ever happen to a walnut. Try it in your favorite bread pudding recipe for some extra razzle-dazzle.

DIRECTIONS

☞ Select the loaf size. Add the ingredients to the machine according to the manufacturer's directions. Select the basic white bread cycle.

HOT TIP

When a jar of honey gets as thick as sludge and won't pour, don't throw it out—microwave it. Using 100 percent power (high), microwave the honey (metal cap off, if it's a jar) until it softens, from 5 to 20 seconds, depending on the amount.

HONEYED WALNUT BREAD

Prep time: 15 minutes

Nutrition facts per slice: 132 calories, 5 g total fat (0 g saturated fat), 0 mg cholesterol, 86 mg sodium, 20 g carbohydrate, 1 g fiber, 3 g protein.

1½-POUND (20 slices)	INGREDIENTS	2-POUND (27 slices)
1 cup	water	1⅓ cups
¼ cup	honey	5 tablespoons
2 tablespoons	walnut oil or cooking oil	3 tablespoons
3 cups	bread flour	4 cups
¼ cup	nonfat dry milk powder	⅓ cup
¾ teaspoon	salt	1 teaspoon
1 teaspoon	active dry yeast or bread machine yeast	1¼ teaspoons
¾ cup	coarsely chopped walnuts, toasted	1 cup

33

PINEAPPLE CARROT BREAD

The enticing aroma of this delicious loaf will lure hungry appetites to your kitchen. When lunch rolls around, it makes a terrific peanut butter and jelly sandwich.

Prep time: 15 minutes

Nutrition facts per slice: 107 calories, 1 g total fat (0 g saturated fat), 0 mg cholesterol, 116 mg sodium, 21 g carbohydrate, 2 g fiber, 4 g protein.

1½-POUND (16 slices)	INGREDIENTS	2-POUND (22 slices)
¾ cup	buttermilk	1 cup
one 8-ounce can	crushed pineapple (juice packed), well drained	one 15¼-ounce can
½ cup	coarsely shredded carrot	⅔ cup
1 tablespoon	shortening or cooking oil	4 teaspoons
2 cups	whole wheat flour	2⅔ cups
1 cup	bread flour	1⅓ cups
1 tablespoon	brown sugar	4 teaspoons
¾ teaspoon	salt	1 teaspoon
1 teaspoon	active dry yeast or bread machine yeast	1¼ teaspoons

DIRECTIONS

☞ Select the loaf size. Add the ingredients to the machine according to the manufacturer's directions, adding the pineapple and carrot with the buttermilk. If available, select the whole grain cycle, or select the basic white bread cycle.

Good Advice!

If you use buttermilk infrequently, but you appreciate its virtues for baking, use buttermilk powder instead of liquid buttermilk. It tenderizes in exactly the same way and has a long shelf life. Always reconstitute with water before using as directed on the label.

34

Win warm accolades for all the favorite flavors of pumpkin pie baked into bread. Great served on its own or tasty with a quick spread of Cream Cheese Butter (see recipe, page 116).

PUMPKIN PECAN BREAD

(Pictured on page 13.)

Prep time: 15 minutes

Nutrition facts per slice: 159 calories, 6 g total fat (1 g saturated fat), 14 mg cholesterol, 126 mg sodium, 23 g carbohydrate, 1 g fiber, 4 g protein.

DIRECTIONS

☞ Select the loaf size. Add the ingredients to the machine according to the manufacturer's directions. Select the basic white bread cycle.

☞ *NOTE: For the 1½-pound loaf, the bread machine pan must have a capacity of 10 cups or more. For the 2-pound loaf, the bread machine pan must have a capacity of 12 cups or more.

☞ **NOTE: Our Test Kitchen recommends 1 egg and ¼ teaspoon ground ginger for either size recipe.

1½-POUND* (16 slices)	INGREDIENTS	2-POUND)* (22 slices)
½ cup	milk	⅔ cup
½ cup	canned pumpkin	⅔ cup
1	egg**	1
2 tablespoons	margarine or butter, cut up	3 tablespoons
3 cups	bread flour	4 cups
3 tablespoons	packed brown sugar	¼ cup
¾ teaspoon	salt	1 teaspoon
¼ teaspoon	ground nutmeg	½ teaspoon
¼ teaspoon	ground ginger**	¼ teaspoon
⅛ teaspoon	ground cloves	¼ teaspoon
1 teaspoon	active dry yeast or bread machine yeast	1¼ teaspoons
¾ cup	coarsely chopped pecans	1 cup

35

CINNAMON SWIRL BREAD

The aroma of cinnamon bread is enough to wake even the sleepiest of sleepyheads. Discover the delights of this comfort food for breakfast, or anytime you're in need of some T.L.C.

Prep time: 25 minutes **Rise time:** 30 minutes **Bake time:** 30 minutes
Nutrition facts per slice: 171 calories, 5 g total fat (1 g saturated fat), 14 mg cholesterol, 145 mg sodium, 26 g carbohydrate, 1 g fiber, 4 g protein.

1½-POUND (16 slices)	INGREDIENTS	2-POUND (24 slices)
¾ cup	milk	1 cup
1	egg(s)	2
3 tablespoons	margarine or butter	¼ cup
3 cups	bread flour	4 cups
3 tablespoons	granulated sugar	¼ cup
¾ teaspoon	salt	1 teaspoon
1¼ teaspoons	active dry yeast or bread machine yeast	1½ teaspoons
⅓ cup	chopped walnuts or pecans, toasted	½ cup
⅓ cup	packed brown sugar	½ cup
1½ teaspoons	ground cinnamon	2 teaspoons
1 tablespoon	margarine or butter	2 tablespoons
	Sifted powdered sugar	

DIRECTIONS

☞ Select loaf size. Add the first 7 ingredients to machine according to the manufacturer's directions. Select the dough cycle. When cycle is complete, remove dough. Punch down. Cover and let rest for 10 minutes.

☞ Meanwhile, for filling, in a medium bowl stir together the walnuts or pecans, brown sugar, and cinnamon. Set aside.

☞ *For the 1½-pound recipe:* On a lightly floured surface, roll dough into a 14×9-inch rectangle. Spread with 1 tablespoon margarine or butter and sprinkle with filling. Starting from both short sides, roll up each side into a spiral toward the center. Place, rolled side up, in a greased 9×5×3-inch loaf pan. Cover; let rise about 30 minutes or until nearly double.

☞ Bake in a 350° oven about 30 minutes or until bread sounds hollow when lightly tapped. If necessary, loosely cover with foil the last 10 minutes to prevent overbrowning. Remove from pan; cool on wire rack. Before serving, sprinkle with powdered sugar.

☞ *For the 2-pound recipe:* Prepare as above, except divide the dough and margarine or butter in half. Form 2 loaves; place in 2 greased 9×5×3- or 8×4×2-inch loaf pans.

BANANA WALNUT BREAD

Make this yeast bread when your bananas look their sorriest—very dark, brown-speckled skin. That's when they are at their ripe-and-ready best.

Prep time: 15 minutes

Nutrition facts per slice: 167 calories, 6 g total fat (1 g saturated fat), 14 mg cholesterol, 124 mg sodium, 25 g carbohydrate, 1 g fiber, 5 g protein.

1½-POUND★ (16 slices)	INGREDIENTS	2-POUND★ (22 slices)
⅓ cup	milk	½ cup
½ cup	mashed ripe banana	⅔ cup
1	egg★★	1
2 tablespoons	margarine or butter★★	2 tablespoons
3 cups	bread flour	4 cups
3 tablespoons	sugar	¼ cup
¾ teaspoon	salt	1 teaspoon
¼ teaspoon	ground cinnamon★★ (optional)	¼ teaspoon
1 teaspoon	active dry yeast or bread machine yeast	1¼ teaspoons
¾ cup	chopped walnuts or pecans, toasted	1 cup

DIRECTIONS

☞ Select the loaf size. Add the ingredients to the machine according to the manufacturer's directions, adding the banana with the milk. Select the basic white bread cycle.

☞ ★**NOTE:** For the 1½-pound loaf, the bread machine pan must have a capacity of 10 cups or more. For the 2-pound loaf, the bread machine pan must have a capacity of 12 cups or more.

☞ ★★**NOTE:** Our Test Kitchen recommends 1 egg, 2 tablespoons margarine or butter, and ¼ teaspoon cinnamon for either size recipe.

38

APPLE BREAD

This apple bread tastes great without any adornments. But if you want to turn it into a kid's favorite, serve it toasted and spread with Nut 'n' Honey Butter (see recipe, page 117).

DIRECTIONS

☞ Select the loaf size. Add the ingredients to the machine according to the manufacturer's directions. If available, select the whole grain cycle, or select the basic white bread cycle.

☞ ★**NOTE:** Our Test Kitchen recommends using 1 tablespoon margarine or butter for either size recipe.

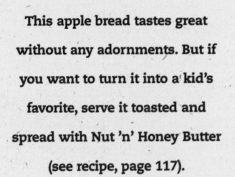

May We Suggest?

Extra-moist, fruit breads are great keepers. In the event that a portion of this wonderfully autumnal bread makes it to Day Two, wrap it tightly with plastic wrap and store at room temperature.

Prep time: 10 minutes

Nutrition facts per slice: 109 calories, 1 g total fat (0 g saturated fat), 0 mg cholesterol, 110 mg sodium, 21 g carbohydrate, 1 g fiber, 3 g protein.

1½-POUND (16 slices)	INGREDIENTS	2-POUND (22 slices)
¾ cup	apple juice	1 cup
⅓ cup	applesauce	½ cup
1 tablespoon	margarine or butter★	1 tablespoon
1 tablespoon	honey	4 teaspoons
2 cups	bread flour	2½ cups
1 cup	whole wheat flour	1½ cups
1½ teaspoons	ground cinnamon	2 teaspoons
¾ teaspoon	salt	1 teaspoon
1 teaspoon	active dry yeast or bread machine yeast	2 teaspoons

RAISIN RUM LOAF

So delicious, so easy, and so good describes this spirited bread. Subtle overtones of rum complement the plump, moist raisins in the loaf.

Prep time: 10 minutes

Nutrition facts per slice: 147 calories, 3 g total fat (1 g saturated fat), 17 mg cholesterol, 114 mg sodium, 25 g carbohydrate, 1 g fiber, 4 g protein.

1½-POUND★ (16 slices)	INGREDIENTS	2-POUND★ (22 slices)
½ cup	dairy sour cream	⅔ cup
⅓ cup	water	½ cup
1	egg★★	1
3 tablespoons	dark or light rum	¼ cup
2 teaspoons	margarine or butter	1 tablespoon
1 teaspoon	vanilla	1½ teaspoons
3 cups	bread flour	4 cups
3 tablespoons	sugar	¼ cup
¾ teaspoon	salt	1 teaspoon
1 teaspoon	active dry yeast or bread machine yeast	1¼ teaspoons
½ cup	dark raisins	⅔ cup

DIRECTIONS

☞ Select the loaf size. Add the ingredients to the machine according to the manufacturer's directions. Select the basic white bread cycle.

☞ ★**NOTE:** For the 1½-pound loaf, the bread machine pan must have a capacity of 10 cups or more. For the 2-pound loaf, the bread machine pan must have a capacity of 12 cups or more.

☞ ★★**NOTE:** Our Test Kitchen recommends 1 egg for either size recipe.

Good Advice!

When raisins are called for in bread machine-baked recipes, our Test Kitchen recommends using dark raisins rather than light raisins. Light raisins are generally treated with a sulphur substance, which reacts with the yeast in the bread dough. This reaction results in breads that will not rise properly.

40

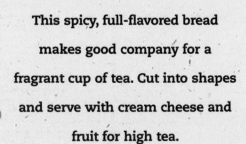

This spicy, full-flavored bread makes good company for a fragrant cup of tea. Cut into shapes and serve with cream cheese and fruit for high tea.

GINGERBREAD LOAF

Prep time: 15 minutes

Nutrition facts per slice: 138 calories, 3 g total fat (1 g saturated fat), 14 mg cholesterol, 136 mg sodium, 23 g carbohydrate, 1 g fiber, 4 g protein.

DIRECTIONS

☞ Select the loaf size. Add the ingredients, except the Lemon Icing, to the machine according to the manufacturer's directions. Select the basic white bread cycle. If desired, drizzle the cooled loaf with Lemon Icing.

☞ *Lemon Icing:* In a small mixing bowl stir together ½ cup sifted powdered sugar, 1 teaspoon lemon juice, and ¼ teaspoon vanilla. Stir in enough milk (1 to 3 teaspoons) to make an icing of drizzling consistency.

☞ **★NOTE:** For the 1½-pound loaf, the bread machine pan must have a capacity of 10 cups or more. For the 2-pound loaf, the bread machine pan must have a capacity of 12 cups or more.

1½-POUND★ (16 slices)	INGREDIENTS	2-POUND★ (22 slices)
⅔ cup	milk	¾ cup
1	egg(s)	2
¼ cup	mild-flavored molasses	⅓ cup
3 tablespoons	margarine or butter, cut up	¼ cup
3 cups	bread flour	4 cups
1 tablespoon	brown sugar	4 teaspoons
¾ teaspoon	salt	1 teaspoon
¾ teaspoon	ground cinnamon	1 teaspoon
¾ teaspoon	ground ginger	1 teaspoon
1 teaspoon	active dry yeast or bread machine yeast	1½ teaspoons
	Lemon Icing (optional)	

BREAD MACHINE BAKING

SAVORY

{ GREEK BREAD }

see recipe, page 47

BURRITO BREAD

Cilantro and refried beans fill this loaf with authentic Southwestern flavor. The result is a savory, protein-rich bread that pairs nicely with Mexican-style entrées.

Prep time: 15 minutes

Nutrition facts per slice: 123 calories, 2 g total fat (1 g saturated fat), 2 mg cholesterol, 108 mg sodium, 21 g carbohydrate, 1 g fiber, 4 g protein.

DIRECTIONS

☞ Select the loaf size. In a small saucepan cook the onion in hot oil for 3 to 4 minutes or until tender. Cool slightly.

☞ Add the onion mixture and the remaining ingredients to the machine according to the manufacturer's directions. Select the basic white bread cycle.

1½-POUND (16 slices)	INGREDIENTS	2-POUND (22 slices)
⅓ cup	chopped onion	½ cup
1 tablespoon	cooking oil	4 teaspoons
½ cup	milk	⅔ cup
⅓ cup	water	½ cup
⅓ cup	refried beans	½ cup
¼ cup	shredded cheddar cheese	⅓ cup
2 tablespoons	snipped fresh cilantro	3 tablespoons
3 cups	bread flour	4 cups
1 tablespoon	sugar	4 teaspoons
2 teaspoons	chili powder	1 tablespoon
½ teaspoon	salt	¾ teaspoon
1 teaspoon	active dry yeast or bread machine yeast	1¼ teaspoons

44

Chilies lend a provocative and spicy flavor that embraces the sharp cheddar cheese—a perfect combination for tomato soup. For extra zing, choose well-aged cheddar cheese.

DIRECTIONS

☞ Select the loaf size. Add the ingredients to the machine according to the manufacturer's directions, adding the cheese and chili peppers with the milk. Select the basic white bread cycle.

May We Suggest?

The blend of ground dried red chilies and other spices sold as chili powder came to be, some say, to shortcut preparation of the famous Texas bowl of red. These blends vary in flavor (and heat) from label to label, so experiment with different brands.

CHILI CHEESE BREAD

Prep time: 15 minutes

Nutrition facts per slice: 133 calories, 3 g total fat (2 g saturated fat), 8 mg cholesterol, 132 mg sodium, 20 g carbohydrate, 1 g fiber, 5 g protein.

1½-POUND (16 slices)	INGREDIENTS	2-POUND (22 slices)
½ cup	milk	⅔ cup
1 cup	shredded sharp cheddar cheese	1⅓ cups
½ of a 4-ounce can	diced green chile peppers, drained	one 4-ounce can
¼ cup	water	⅓ cup
2 teaspoons	margarine or butter	1 tablespoon
3 cups	bread flour	4 cups
1½ teaspoons	sugar	2 teaspoons
¾ teaspoon	chili powder	1 teaspoon
½ teaspoon	salt	¾ teaspoon
1 teaspoon	active dry yeast or bread machine yeast	1¼ teaspoons

45

FETA DILL BREAD

The combination of feta cheese and dill provides a melding of flavors so rich, this bread is a meal in itself. Team with wine, assorted cheeses, and your favorite dining companion.

Prep time: 15 minutes

Nutrition facts per slice: 127 calories, 2 g total fat (1 g saturated fat), 17 mg cholesterol, 170 mg sodium, 21 g carbohydrate, 1 g fiber, 5 g protein.

1½-POUND★ (16 slices)	INGREDIENTS	2-POUND★ (22 slices)
1 cup	water	1¼ cups
⅔ cup	crumbled feta cheese	¾ cup
1	egg★★	1
1 tablespoon	margarine or butter	4 teaspoons
3 cups	bread flour	4 cups
⅓ cup	packaged instant mashed potato flakes or buds	½ cup
¼ cup	nonfat dry milk powder	⅓ cup
1 tablespoon	sugar	4 teaspoons
1 teaspoon	dried dill or	1¼ teaspoons
1 tablespoon	snipped fresh dill	4 teaspoons
¾ teaspoon	salt	1 teaspoon
1 teaspoon	active dry yeast or bread machine yeast	1¼ teaspoons

DIRECTIONS

☞ Select the loaf size. Add the ingredients to the machine according to the manufacturer's directions. Select the basic white bread cycle.

☞ ★**NOTE:** For the 1½-pound loaf, the bread machine pan must have a capacity of 10 cups or more. For the 2-pound loaf, the bread machine pan must have a capacity of 12 cups or more.

☞ ★★**NOTE:** Our Test Kitchen recommends 1 egg for either size recipe.

HOT TIP

If you've bought more feta—a soft, white, brine-cured, crumbly goat or sheep-milk cheese—than you can use right away, freeze it. You'll have it conveniently at hand for another loaf, or a great Greek salad. Thaw in the refrigerator before using.

46

GREEK BREAD

(Pictured on page 43.)

Fans of Greek salad will find much to like here. The key flavors—piquant kalamata olives, tangy feta cheese, and a touch of rosemary—reinvent moist, high-rising country loaf.

DIRECTIONS

☞ Select the loaf size. Add the ingredients to the machine according to the manufacturer's directions. Select the basic white bread cycle.

☞ **NOTE:** For the 1½-pound loaf, the bread machine pan must have a capacity of 10 cups or more. For the 2-pound loaf, the bread machine pan must have a capacity of 12 cups or more.

Prep time: 15 minutes

Nutrition facts per slice: 110 calories, 2 g total fat (1 g saturated fat), 4 mg cholesterol, 118 mg sodium, 18 g carbohydrate, 1 g fiber, 4 g protein.

1½-POUND★ (18 slices)	INGREDIENTS	2-POUND★ (24 slices)
1 cup	milk	1¼ cups
½ cup	crumbled feta cheese	¾ cup
⅓ cup	chopped pitted kalamata olives	½ cup
2 tablespoons	water	3 tablespoons
2 teaspoons	shortening or cooking oil	1 tablespoon
3 cups	bread flour	4 cups
1 tablespoon	sugar	4 teaspoons
1 teaspoon	dried rosemary, crushed, or	1¼ teaspoons
1 tablespoon	snipped fresh rosemary	4 teaspoons
½ teaspoon	salt	¾ teaspoon
1 teaspoon	active dry yeast or bread machine yeast	1¼ teaspoons

47

PARMESAN PINE NUT BREAD

Italian seasoning infuses this bread with mild herb flavor, while pine nuts contribute delightful crunchy texture. It's the perfect partner for lasagna or ravioli.

Prep time: 10 minutes

Nutrition facts per slice: 125 calories, 4 g total fat (1 g saturated fat), 14 mg cholesterol, 104 mg sodium, 18 g carbohydrate, 1 g fiber, 5 g protein.

1½-POUND★ (18 slices)	INGREDIENTS	2-POUND★ (24 slices)
1 cup	milk	1⅓ cups
1	egg★★	1
1 tablespoon	olive oil or cooking oil	4 teaspoons
3 cups	bread flour	4 cups
⅓ cup	grated Parmesan or Asiago cheese	½ cup
1 teaspoon	dried Italian seasoning, crushed	1½ teaspoons
½ teaspoon	salt	¾ teaspoon
¼ teaspoon	sugar	½ teaspoon
1 teaspoon	active dry yeast or bread machine yeast	1¼ teaspoons
⅓ cup	pine nuts	½ cup

DIRECTIONS

☞ Select the loaf size. Add the ingredients to the machine according to the manufacturer's directions. Select the basic white bread cycle.

☞ ★**NOTE:** For the 1½-pound loaf, the bread machine pan must have a capacity of 10 cups or more. For the 2-pound loaf, the bread machine pan must have a capacity of 12 cups or more.

☞ ★★**NOTE:** Our Test Kitchen recommends 1 egg for either size recipe.

Good Advice!

Italians call the rich and buttery pine nut—which does come from pine trees—pignoli. They enjoy these tiny treasures in everything from pesto sauce to cookies to stuffings. Flavors like cheeses, herbs, and spices marry well with their nutty, creamy personality. Keep pine nuts fresh by refrigerating them up to two weeks, or freezing up to three months.

DRIED TOMATO BREAD

If you like the taste of pizza, you'll love this variation on the theme. Subtly spiced with oregano, onion, and dried tomatoes, it's a perfect accompaniment to minestrone.

DIRECTIONS

☞ Select the loaf size. In a small saucepan cook onion in hot oil until tender. Cool mixture slightly.

☞ Add the ingredients to the machine according to the manufacturer's directions, adding the onion mixture and the dried tomatoes with the water. Select the basic white bread cycle.

Prep time: 15 minutes

Nutrition facts per slice: 109 calories, 2 g total fat (0 g saturated fat), 0 mg cholesterol, 110 mg sodium, 20 g carbohydrate, 1 g fiber, 3 g protein.

1½-POUND (16 slices)	INGREDIENTS	2-POUND (22 slices)
½ cup	finely chopped onion	⅔ cup
4 teaspoons	olive oil or cooking oil	2 tablespoons
¾ cup + 2 tablespoons	water	1¼ cups
2 tablespoons	snipped dried tomatoes (not oil-packed)	3 tablespoons
3 cups	bread flour	4 cups
1 tablespoon	sugar	4 teaspoons
1 teaspoon	dried oregano, crushed, or	1¼ teaspoons
1 tablespoon	snipped fresh oregano	4 teaspoons
¾ teaspoon	salt	1 teaspoon
1 teaspoon	active dry yeast or bread machine yeast	1¼ teaspoons

49

PEPPERONI PIZZA LOAF

Three simple ingredients— Parmesan cheese, pepperoni, and fennel seed—turn ordinary bread into pizza! For a zippy lunch with pizzazz, try it in your next grilled cheese sandwich.

DIRECTIONS

☞ Select the loaf size. Add the ingredients to the machine according to the manufacturer's directions. Select the basic white bread cycle. Store in the refrigerator.

☞ **NOTE:** For the 1½-pound loaf, the bread machine pan must have a capacity of 10 cups or more. For the 2-pound loaf, the bread machine pan must have a capacity of 12 cups or more.

May We Suggest?

Stuck time after time with leftover canned tomato paste that goes to waste? Tomato paste in a screw-cap tube lets you squirt out a tablespoon or two—perfect for many recipes—and safely store the rest for next time. A tube of tomato paste keeps in the refrigerator for a couple of months.

Prep time: 15 minutes
Nutrition facts per slice: 142 calories, 5 g total fat (1 g saturated fat), 7 mg cholesterol, 188 mg sodium, 20 g carbohydrate, 1 g fiber, 5 g protein.

1½-POUND★ (16 slices)	INGREDIENTS	2-POUND★ (22 slices)
¾ cup	water	1 cup
½ cup	finely chopped pepperoni	¾ cup
¼ cup	chopped green pepper	⅓ cup
2 tablespoons	olive oil or cooking oil	3 tablespoons
1 tablespoon	tomato paste	2 tablespoons
3 cups	bread flour	4 cups
¼ cup	grated Parmesan cheese	⅓ cup
2 teaspoons	sugar	1 tablespoon
1 teaspoon	fennel seed, crushed	1½ teaspoons
½ teaspoon	salt	¾ teaspoon
1 teaspoon	active dry yeast or bread machine yeast	1¼ teaspoons

51

SODA BREAD

Think cozy corner booth and a waitress that calls you "Hon." In the best sandwich shop tradition, this homestyle bread gets its tender crumb and rich brown crust from a big pinch of baking soda.

Prep time: 10 minutes

Nutrition facts per slice: 112 calories, 2 g total fat (0 g saturated fat), 1 mg cholesterol, 139 mg sodium, 20 g carbohydrate, 1 g fiber, 4 g protein.

1½-POUND (16 slices)	INGREDIENTS	2-POUND (22 slices)
¾ cup	milk	1 cup
¼ cup	water	⅓ cup
4 teaspoons	margarine or butter	2 tablespoons
3 cups	bread flour	4 cups
4 teaspoons	sugar	2 tablespoons
¾ teaspoon	salt	1 teaspoon
¼ teaspoon	baking soda	½ teaspoon
1 teaspoon	active dry yeast or bread machine yeast	1¼ teaspoons

DIRECTIONS

☞ Select the loaf size. Add the ingredients to the machine according to the manufacturer's directions. Select the basic white bread cycle.

Good Advice!

Is there a way to tell if a dried herb is still fresh? Yes. If you've had an herb on the shelf awhile, you can check it by crushing a small amount of the herb in the palm of your hand. It should still be aromatic. If the aroma is weak, it's time to buy a new jar. Faded or straw-colored herbs should also be discarded.

52

Louisiana-style seasonings supply the spice for this rich and hearty bread—made even better—with whole wheat flour. It's sure to jazz up your everyday meals or Cajun-inspired dinners.

DIRECTIONS

☞ Select the loaf size. In a small saucepan cook the onion and green pepper in hot oil until onion is tender. Stir in the Cajun seasoning; cook for 30 seconds more. Cool mixture slightly.

☞ Add the ingredients to the machine according to the manufacturer's directions, adding the onion mixture with the milk. If available, select the whole grain cycle, or select the basic white bread cycle.

CAJUN WHOLE WHEAT BREAD

Prep time: 15 minutes

Nutrition facts per slice: 113 calories, 2 g total fat (0 g saturated fat), 1 mg cholesterol, 26 mg sodium, 21 g carbohydrate, 2 g fiber, 4 g protein.

1½-POUND (16 slices)	INGREDIENTS	2-POUND (22 slices)
⅓ cup	chopped onion	½ cup
⅓ cup	chopped green pepper	½ cup
4 teaspoons	chili oil or cooking oil	2 tablespoons
1½ teaspoons	Cajun seasoning	2 teaspoons
1 cup	milk	1⅓ cups
2 tablespoons	honey or mild-flavored molasses	3 tablespoons
2 cups	whole wheat flour	2⅔ cups
1 cup	bread flour	1⅓ cups
1 tablespoon	gluten flour	2 tablespoons
1 teaspoon	active dry yeast or bread machine yeast	1¼ teaspoons

53

WHOLE WHEAT HERB BREAD

As a bonus, this hearty rosemary- and thyme-scented wheat bread offers the option of blending in shelled sunflower seeds. The seeds give the whole grain bread a slightly crunchy texture.

Prep time: 10 minutes

Nutrition facts per slice: 105 calories, 2 g total fat (0 g saturated fat), 1 mg cholesterol, 109 mg sodium, 19 g carbohydrate, 3 g fiber, 5 g protein.

DIRECTIONS

☞ Select the loaf size. Add the ingredients to the machine according to the manufacturer's directions. If available, select the whole grain cycle, or select the basic white bread cycle.

1½-POUND (16 slices)	INGREDIENTS	2-POUND (22 slices)
1 cup	milk	1⅓ cups
3 tablespoons	water	¼ cup
1 tablespoon	cooking oil	4 teaspoons
3 cups	whole wheat flour	4 cups
¼ cup	gluten flour	⅓ cup
4 teaspoons	sugar	2 tablespoons
1 teaspoon	dried thyme, crushed, or	1¼ teaspoons
1 tablespoon	snipped fresh thyme	4 teaspoons
¾ teaspoon	salt	1 teaspoon
¼ teaspoon	dried rosemary, crushed, or	½ teaspoon
1 teaspoon	snipped fresh rosemary	1½ teaspoons
1 teaspoon	active dry yeast or bread machine yeast	1¼ teaspoons
¼ cup	shelled sunflower seeds (optional)	⅓ cup

54

ANISE WHEAT BREAD

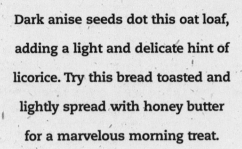

Dark anise seeds dot this oat loaf, adding a light and delicate hint of licorice. Try this bread toasted and lightly spread with honey butter for a marvelous morning treat.

DIRECTIONS

☞ Select the loaf size. Spread the oats in a shallow baking pan. Bake in a 350° oven about 15 minutes or until light brown, stirring occasionally. Cool. Transfer to a blender container or food processor bowl; cover and blend or process until finely ground.

☞ Add the ingredients to the machine according to the manufacturer's directions, adding the ground oats with the flours. If available, select the whole grain cycle, or select the basic white bread cycle.

☞ **NOTE:** Our Test Kitchen recommends ¼ cup water for either size recipe.

Prep time: 25 minutes

Nutrition facts per slice: 104 calories, 2 g total fat (0 g saturated fat), 1 mg cholesterol, 118 mg sodium, 19 g carbohydrate, 1 g fiber, 3 g protein.

1½-POUND (16 slices)	INGREDIENTS	2-POUND (22 slices)
½ cup	regular or quick-cooking rolled oats	¾ cup
¾ cup	milk	1 cup
¼ cup	water*	¼ cup
4 teaspoons	margarine, butter, or cooking oil	2 tablespoons
1¾ cups	bread flour	2 cups
¾ cup	whole wheat flour	1 cup
2 tablespoons	sugar	3 tablespoons
¾ teaspoon	salt	1 teaspoon
½ teaspoon	anise seed	¾ teaspoon
1¼ teaspoons	active dry yeast or bread machine yeast	1½ teaspoons

55

CURRIED WHEAT LOAF

Satisfy culinary wanderlust without leaving home. A blend of Indian spices, known as curry, is added to this whole grain bread. Peanuts, a traditional ingredient of curries, also are added.

Prep time: 10 minutes

Nutrition facts per slice: 130 calories, 3 g total fat (1 g saturated fat), 14 mg cholesterol, 138 mg sodium, 22 g carbohydrate, 1 g fiber, 5 g protein.

DIRECTIONS

☞ Select the loaf size. Add the ingredients to the machine according to the manufacturer's directions. If available, select the whole grain cycle, or select the basic white bread cycle.

☞ ***NOTE:** For the 1½-pound loaf, the bread machine pan must have a capacity of 10 cups or more. For the 2-pound loaf, the bread machine pan must have a capacity of 12 cups or more.

1½-POUND★ (16 slices)	INGREDIENTS	2-POUND★ (22 slices)
¾ cup	milk	1 cup
1	egg(s)	2
3 tablespoons	water	¼ cup
1 tablespoon	margarine or butter	2 tablespoons
2½ cups	bread flour	3⅓ cups
¾ cup	whole wheat flour	1 cup
1 tablespoon	brown sugar	2 tablespoons
1 teaspoon	curry powder	1¼ teaspoons
¾ teaspoon	salt	1 teaspoon
1¼ teaspoons	active dry yeast or bread machine yeast	1½ teaspoons
¼ cup	chopped peanuts	⅓ cup

HOT TIP

Salty peanuts or salt-free? On this contentious culinary issue, fans line up on both sides of the salt shaker. In most recipes, including those for baking, it's a taste toss-up that makes no difference to success. Unless a market form is specified, choose the one you prefer.

56

SWISS ONION BREAD

Your mouth will water when you slice into this freshly baked loaf and detect the aromatic blend of onion, Swiss cheese, and caraway seed. Spread with a little butter and enjoy!

Prep time: 15 minutes

Nutrition facts per slice: 132 calories, 4 g total fat (2 g saturated fat), 20 mg cholesterol, 102 mg sodium, 19 g carbohydrate, 1 g fiber, 6 g protein.

1½-POUND★ (16 slices)	INGREDIENTS	2-POUND★ (22 slices)
¼ cup	chopped onion	⅓ cup
1 tablespoon	margarine or butter	4 teaspoons
½ cup	milk	⅔ cup
1 cup	shredded Swiss cheese	1⅓ cups
¼ cup	water	⅓ cup
1	egg★★	1
2¼ cups	bread flour	2¾ cups
¾ cup	whole wheat flour	1¼ cups
¾ teaspoon	caraway seed	1 teaspoon
½ teaspoon	salt	¾ teaspoon
1 teaspoon	active dry yeast or bread machine yeast	1¼ teaspoons

DIRECTIONS

☞ Select the loaf size. In a small saucepan cook the onion in hot margarine or butter until tender. Cool slightly.

☞ Add the ingredients to the machine according to the manufacturer's directions, adding the onion mixture and the cheese with the milk. If available, select the whole grain cycle, or select the basic white bread cycle.

☞ ★**NOTE:** For the 1½-pound loaf, the bread machine pan must have a capacity of 10 cups or more. For the 2-pound loaf, the bread machine pan must have a capacity of 12 cups or more.

☞ ★★**NOTE:** Our Test Kitchen recommends 1 egg for either size recipe.

The light- and even-grained texture, the golden-hued crust, and a heavenly scent of garlic make this bread a winner. So versatile, serve it with soups in the winter or salads in the summer.

DIRECTIONS

☞ Select the loaf size. Add the ingredients to the machine according to the manufacturer's directions. If available, select the whole grain cycle, or select the basic white bread cycle.

May We Suggest?

Bottled minced or chopped roasted garlic is a new convenience product found in the produce section of the supermarket. One teaspoonful is the equivalent of two to three cloves of fresh roasted garlic. You get great garlic flavor with none of the fuss. Store opened jars in the refrigerator.

ROASTED GARLIC WHEAT BREAD

Prep time: 10 minutes
Nutrition facts per slice: 99 calories, 1 g total fat (1 g saturated fat), 2 mg cholesterol, 104 mg sodium, 18 g carbohydrate, 2 g fiber, 4 g protein.

1½-POUND (16 slices)	INGREDIENTS	2-POUND (22 slices)
¾ cup	water	1 cup
⅓ cup	dairy sour cream	½ cup
1½ teaspoons	bottled minced roasted garlic	2 teaspoons
1½ cups	bread flour	2 cups
1½ cups	whole wheat flour	2 cups
2 teaspoons	gluten flour	1 tablespoon
1 teaspoon	sugar	1½ teaspoons
¾ teaspoon	salt	1 teaspoon
1 teaspoon	active dry yeast or bread machine yeast	1¼ teaspoons

59

BLACK WALNUT BREAD

The Cadillac of walnut varieties, black walnuts are native to America and are particularly tasty in baked goods. This tender loaf, abundant with nutty nuggets, showcases them perfectly.

DIRECTIONS

☞ Select the loaf size. Add the ingredients to the machine according to the manufacturer's directions. Select the basic white bread cycle.

☞ *NOTE: For the 1½-pound loaf, the bread machine pan must have a capacity of 10 cups or more. For the 2-pound loaf, the bread machine pan must have a capacity of 12 cups or more.

☞ **NOTE: Our Test Kitchen recommends 1 egg for either size recipe.

Prep time: 15 minutes

Nutrition facts per slice: 156 calories, 6 g total fat (1 g saturated fat), 14 mg cholesterol, 110 mg sodium, 21 g carbohydrate, 1 g fiber, 5 g protein.

1½-POUND★ (16 slices)	INGREDIENTS	2-POUND★ (22 slices)
⅔ cup	milk	¾ cup
1	egg**	1
3 tablespoons	water	¼ cup
2 tablespoons	walnut oil or cooking oil	3 tablespoons
3 cups	bread flour	4 cups
2 tablespoons	sugar	3 tablespoons
¾ teaspoon	salt	1 teaspoon
1 teaspoon	active dry yeast or bread machine yeast	1¼ teaspoons
⅔ cup	chopped black walnuts or English walnuts	¾ cup

60

Good Advice!

In French villages, fresh walnuts are cold-pressed following time-honored methods to extract their aromatic oils—a traditional culinary specialty. Just a splash of this nutty elixir elevates a simple salad dressing into something special, or intensifies the flavor of a nut bread. Store this delicate oil away from light and heat.

MUSTARD RYE BREAD

Stone-ground mustard gives zip to this flavorful rye. Its dense, even texture makes it sandwich-worthy. Wrap a slice around a grilled hotdog or brat for a super summertime meal.

Prep time: 10 minutes

Nutrition facts per slice: 114 calories, 2 g total fat (0 g saturated fat), 0 mg cholesterol, 152 mg sodium, 21 g carbohydrate, 2 g fiber, 4 g protein.

DIRECTIONS

☞ Select the loaf size. Add the ingredients to the machine according to the manufacturer's directions. If available, select the whole grain cycle, or select the basic white bread cycle.

☞ ***NOTE:** Our Test Kitchen recommends 1 teaspoon caraway seed for either size recipe.

1½-POUND (16 slices)	INGREDIENTS	2-POUND (22 slices)
1¼ cups	water	1½ cups
¼ cup	stone-ground mustard	⅓ cup
1 tablespoon	shortening	2 tablespoons
2 cups	bread flour	2⅔ cups
1½ cups	rye flour	2 cups
2 tablespoons	gluten flour	3 tablespoons
1 tablespoon	brown sugar	4 teaspoons
1 teaspoon	caraway seed*	1 teaspoon
¾ teaspoon	salt	1 teaspoon
1 teaspoon	active dry yeast or bread machine yeast	1¼ teaspoons

62

STOUT RYE BREAD

"Brew-in-a-bread" describes this finely textured rye. The flavors of beer and caraway upgrade a simple roast pork or beef sandwich to new heights.

DIRECTIONS

☞ Select the loaf size. Add the ingredients to the machine according to the manufacturer's directions. If available, select the whole grain cycle, or select the basic white bread cycle.

☞ *NOTE: Our Test Kitchen recommends 1 tablespoon shortening, 2 tablespoons gluten flour, and 1 teaspoon caraway seed for either size recipe.

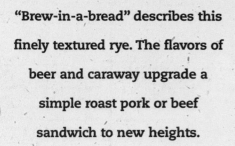

May We Suggest?

There is no doubt that beer and bread have a special affinity—pass the pretzels, please. A foamy brew with a pub-goer's lunch of crusty bread and cheese is a famous menu marriage. Another is rye bread, smoked meats, and dark, full-bodied stout, an ale with lots of malt. A good rule of thumb: Light beers pair well with lighter foods; robust brews require heartier dishes.

Prep time: 10 minutes

Nutrition facts per slice: 105 calories, 1 g total fat (0 g saturated fat), 0 mg cholesterol, 102 mg sodium, 19 g carbohydrate, 1 g fiber, 3 g protein.

1½-POUND (16 slices)	INGREDIENTS	2-POUND (22 slices)
1 cup	stout or other dark beer	1¼ cups
1 tablespoon	shortening*	1 tablespoon
2 cups	bread flour	2⅔ cups
1 cup	rye flour	1⅓ cups
2 tablespoons	gluten flour*	2 tablespoons
1 tablespoon	brown sugar	4 teaspoons
1 teaspoon	caraway seed*	1 teaspoon
¾ teaspoon	salt	1 teaspoon
1 teaspoon	active dry yeast or bread machine yeast	1½ teaspoons

63

Don't be surprised by the surprise ingredient in this bread. A jar of baby food lends convenience and flavor to this sweet potato loaf. Try deli turkey tucked between a couple of slices.

DIRECTIONS

☞ Select the loaf size. Add the ingredients to the machine according to the manufacturer's directions. Select the basic white bread cycle.

☞ *NOTE: Our Test Kitchen recommends one 6-ounce jar sweet potato baby food for either size recipe.

SWEET POTATO ONION BREAD

Prep time: 15 minutes

Nutrition facts per slice: 107 calories, 1 g total fat (0 g saturated fat), 0 mg cholesterol, 111 mg sodium, 20 g carbohydrate, 1 g fiber, 3 g protein.

1½-POUND (16 slices)	INGREDIENTS	2-POUND (22 slices)
one 6-ounce jar	sweet potato baby food*	one 6-ounce jar
⅓ cup	water	½ cup
⅓ cup	sliced green onions	½ cup
1 tablespoon	margarine or butter	4 teaspoons
3 cups	bread flour	4 cups
1 teaspoon	sugar	1¼ teaspoons
1 teaspoon	dried thyme, crushed, or	1¼ teaspoons
1 tablespoon	snipped fresh thyme	4 teaspoons
¾ teaspoon	salt	1 teaspoon
1 teaspoon	active dry yeast or bread machine yeast	1¼ teaspoons

65

CUCUMBER DILL BREAD

The traditional flavors of a Scandinavian smorgasbord—cucumber, dill, and sour cream—reprise in a bread that requires only silken slices of smoked salmon or gravlax.

DIRECTIONS

☞ Select the loaf size. Drain the cucumber, pressing out excess liquid. Add the ingredients to the machine according to manufacturer's directions. Select the basic white bread cycle.

☞ ***NOTE:** Our Test Kitchen recommends 1 teaspoon yeast for either size recipe.

Prep time: 15 minutes

Nutrition facts per slice: 95 calories, 1 g total fat (1 g saturated fat), 2 mg cholesterol, 92 mg sodium, 17 g carbohydrate, 1 g fiber, 3 g protein.

1½-POUND (18 slices)	INGREDIENTS	2-POUND (24 slices)
¾ cup	coarsely shredded, seeded cucumber	1 cup
½ cup	water	⅔ cup
⅓ cup	dairy sour cream	½ cup
3 cups	bread flour	4 cups
2 teaspoons	sugar	1 tablespoon
¾ teaspoon	salt	1 teaspoon
½ teaspoon	dried dill	¾ teaspoon
	or	
1½ teaspoons	snipped fresh dill	2 teaspoons
1 teaspoon	active dry yeast or bread machine yeast*	1 teaspoon

66

Like flecks of colorful jewels, vegetables add nutrition and visual impact to this healthful bread. Thyme is the suggested herb, but add your favorite, such as basil or oregano, if you prefer.

DIRECTIONS

☞ Select the loaf size. Add the ingredients to the machine according to the manufacturer's directions. Select the basic white bread cycle.

☞ **★NOTE:** Dough may appear stiff until the vegetables have released some of their liquid during the kneading cycle. Watch closely; it may be necessary to add 1 to 3 tablespoons additional bread flour.

CONFETTI BREAD

Prep time: 20 minutes

Nutrition facts per slice: 103 calories, 1 g total fat (0 g saturated fat), 0 mg cholesterol, 111 mg sodium, 20 g carbohydrate, 1 g fiber, 3 g protein.

1½-POUND (16 slices)	INGREDIENTS	2-POUND (22 slices)
¾ cup	water	1 cup
½ cup	shredded carrot	⅔ cup
⅓ cup	shredded zucchini	½ cup
¼ cup	sliced green onions	⅓ cup
¼ cup	finely chopped red sweet pepper	⅓ cup
1 tablespoon	margarine or butter	4 teaspoons
3 cups	bread flour★	4 cups
1 teaspoon	sugar	1½ teaspoons
¾ teaspoon	salt	1 teaspoon
½ teaspoon	dried thyme, crushed, or	¾ teaspoon
1½ teaspoons	snipped fresh thyme	2 teaspoons
1 teaspoon	active dry yeast or bread machine yeast	1¼ teaspoons

67

CELERY SEED BREAD

Just a couple of basic ingredients transforms an ordinary loaf of bread into something noteworthy. Here, onion powder and celery seed are the notable flavor stars.

Prep time: 10 minutes

Nutrition facts per slice: 109 calories, 1 g total fat (0 g saturated fat), 1 mg cholesterol, 108 mg sodium, 20 g carbohydrate, 1 g fiber, 4 g protein.

1½-POUND★ (16 slices)	INGREDIENTS	2-POUND★ (22 slices)
1 cup	milk	1¼ cups
¼ cup	water★★	¼ cup
2 teaspoons	shortening or cooking oil	1 tablespoon
3 cups	bread flour	4 cups
1 tablespoon	sugar	4 teaspoons
¾ teaspoon	salt	1 teaspoon
¾ teaspoon	onion powder	1 teaspoon
½ teaspoon	celery seed	¾ teaspoon
1 teaspoon	active dry yeast or bread machine yeast	1¼ teaspoons

DIRECTIONS

☞ Select the loaf size. Add the ingredients to the machine according to the manufacturer's directions. Select the basic white bread cycle.

☞ ★**NOTE:** For the 1½-pound loaf, the bread machine pan must have a capacity of 10 cups or more. For the 2-pound loaf, the bread machine pan must have a capacity of 12 cups or more.

☞ ★★**NOTE:** Our Test Kitchen recommends ¼ cup water for either size recipe.

SAGE & ONION BREAD

Serve the flavors of Thanksgiving in a sandwich. Top this bread with sliced roasted turkey and a spoonful of cranberry-orange relish for a taste of the holiday without all the fuss.

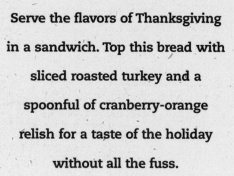

DIRECTIONS

☞ Select the loaf size. In a small saucepan cook the onion in hot margarine or butter until tender. Cool slightly.

☞ Add the onion mixture and the remaining ingredients to the machine according to the manufacturer's directions. Select the basic white bread cycle.

☞ **NOTE:** Our Test Kitchen recommends 3 tablespoons water for either size recipe.

HOT TIP

Dried herbs have rightly earned their place as a convenient staple. When using them, keep these tips in mind: Always crush dried herbs before using to release their aromatic oils. The easiest way to do this is to rub the leaves between your fingers. Replace unused dried herbs every six months as their flavor fades with time.

Prep time: 15 minutes
Nutrition facts per slice: 113 calories, 2 g total fat (0 g saturated fat),1 mg cholesterol, 119 mg sodium, 20 g carbohydrate, 1 g fiber, 4 g protein.

1½-POUND (16 slices)	INGREDIENTS	2-POUND (22 slices)
⅓ cup	finely chopped onion	½ cup
4 teaspoons	margarine or butter	2 tablespoons
1 cup	milk	1¼ cups
3 tablespoons	water*	3 tablespoons
3 cups	bread flour	4 cups
2 teaspoons	sugar	1 tablespoon
2 teaspoons	dried sage, crushed, or	1 tablespoon
2 tablespoons	snipped fresh sage	3 tablespoons
¾ teaspoon	salt	1 teaspoon
1 teaspoon	active dry yeast or bread machine yeast	1¼ teaspoons

69

FRUIT & BEER BREAD

The art of fermentation finds its ultimate expression in this savory whole grain yeast bread boosted with cherry stout beer and brightened with morsels of dried tart cherries.

Prep time: 15 minutes

Nutrition facts per slice: 117 calories, 1 g total fat (0 g saturated fat), 0 mg cholesterol, 110 mg sodium, 23 g carbohydrate, 2 g fiber, 3 g protein.

DIRECTIONS

☞ Select the loaf size. Add the ingredients to the machine according to the manufacturer's directions. If available, select the whole grain cycle, or select the basic white bread cycle.

1½-POUND (16 slices)	INGREDIENTS	2-POUND (22 slices)
1 cup	cherry stout beer	1¼ cups
2 tablespoons	water	3 tablespoons
1 tablespoon	margarine or butter	4 teaspoons
2 cups	bread flour	2½ cups
1 cup	whole wheat flour	1½ cups
4 teaspoons	sugar	2 tablespoons
1 teaspoon	dried savory, crushed, or	1¼ teaspoons
1 tablespoon	snipped fresh savory	4 teaspoons
¾ teaspoon	salt	1 teaspoon
1 teaspoon	active dry yeast or bread machine yeast	1¼ teaspoons
½ cup	snipped dried tart cherries	⅔ cup

PARMESAN CORN BREAD

Boldly-flavored Parmesan cheese and full-flavored herbs provide an easy update to this all-American classic. Served alongside piping-hot chili, it will really warm up your cold winter nights.

DIRECTIONS

☞ Select the loaf size. Add the ingredients to the machine according to the manufacturer's directions. Select the basic white bread cycle.

Good Advice!

Here's the grind on cooking with cornmeal: For baking, use finely ground cornmeal, the familiar meal sold next to flour in every supermarket. The cornmeal used for polenta—the Italian cornmeal pudding—is a more coarsely ground cornmeal. Look for it at specialty and Italian markets.

Prep time: 10 minutes
Nutrition facts per slice: 114 calories, 2 g total fat (0 g saturated fat), 1 mg cholesterol, 131 mg sodium, 21 g carbohydrate, 1 g fiber, 4 g protein.

1½-POUND (16 slices)	INGREDIENTS	2-POUND (22 slices)
1 cup	water	1⅓ cups
2 teaspoons	olive oil or cooking oil	1 tablespoon
2¾ cups	bread flour	3⅔ cups
½ cup	yellow cornmeal	⅔ cup
¼ cup	grated Parmesan cheese	⅓ cup
2 teaspoons	sugar	1 tablespoon
¾ teaspoon	salt	1 teaspoon
¾ teaspoon	dried basil, crushed, or	1 teaspoon
2 teaspoons	snipped fresh basil	1 tablespoon
1 teaspoon	active dry yeast or bread machine yeast	1¼ teaspoons

71

SMOKED CHEDDAR LOAF

Choose smoked cheddar cheese at the supermarket to impart the best flavor in this rich, moist bread. Also, use light-colored rather than dark beer.

DIRECTIONS

☞ Select the loaf size. Add the ingredients to the machine according to the manufacturer's directions, adding the cheese with the beer. Select the basic white bread cycle.

☞ *NOTE: For the 1½-pound loaf, the bread machine pan must have a capacity of 10 cups or more. For the 2-pound loaf, the bread machine pan must have a capacity of 12 cups or more.

☞ **NOTE: Our Test Kitchen recommends 1 egg for either size recipe.

May We Suggest?

Although flat beer is dismal to drink, it's better for cooking because it's easier to measure free of fizz. Let the beer lose its carbonation, then pour just what you need. No more waiting for the foamy head to subside to check the real volume.

Prep time: 15 minutes
Nutrition facts per slice: 141 calories, 4 g total fat (2 g saturated fat), 23 mg cholesterol, 160 mg sodium, 20 g carbohydrate, 1 g fiber, 6 g protein.

1½-POUND* (16 slices)	INGREDIENTS	2-POUND* (22 slices)
¾ cup	mild-flavored beer	1 cup
1¼ cups	shredded smoked cheddar cheese	1⅔ cups
1	egg**	1
3 cups	bread flour	4 cups
1 tablespoon	sugar	4 teaspoons
¾ teaspoon	salt	1 teaspoon
1 teaspoon	active dry yeast or bread machine yeast	1¼ teaspoons

73

SAGE CORNMEAL LOAF

Stuffing comes to mind with the flavor of this bread. Of course it's great in sandwiches, but try cutting the cooled bread into cubes, drying it, and using it as bread stuffing for poultry or meat.

Prep time: 15 minutes

Nutrition facts per slice: 111 calories, 2 g total fat (0 g saturated fat), 1 mg cholesterol, 118 mg sodium, 20 g carbohydrate, 1 g fiber, 3 g protein.

1½-POUND (16 slices)	INGREDIENTS	2-POUND (22 slices)
⅓ cup	chopped onion	½ cup
4 teaspoons	margarine or butter	2 tablespoons
¾ cup	milk	1 cup
¼ cup	water	⅓ cup
2½ cups	bread flour	3½ cups
½ cup	yellow cornmeal	⅔ cup
1 tablespoon	ground sage or poultry seasoning	4 teaspoons
¾ teaspoon	salt	1 teaspoon
½ teaspoon	sugar	¾ teaspoon
1 teaspoon	active dry yeast or bread machine yeast	1¼ teaspoons

DIRECTIONS

☞ Select the loaf size. In a small saucepan cook the onion in hot margarine or butter until tender. Cool slightly.

☞ Add the onion mixture and remaining ingredients to the machine according to the manufacturer's directions. Select the basic white bread setting.

74

Cornmeal gives this whole wheat bread a crunchy, pleasantly dense texture and a golden crust—well suited for a bacon, lettuce, and tomato sandwich.

DIRECTIONS

☞ Select the loaf size. Add the ingredients to the machine according to the manufacturer's directions. If available, select the whole grain cycle, or select the basic white bread cycle.

HOT TIP

Cornmeal—ground from dried corn kernels—is as regional as an accent. Southern cooks prefer white cornmeal for their famous breads and batters, while in Southwest kitchens blue cornmeal ground from New Mexico's blue corn is favored. Most elsewhere, yellow cornmeal is favored, but all colors are interchangeable. Store cornmeal tightly covered up to one year in a cool, dry place.

WHOLE WHEAT CORNMEAL BREAD

Prep time: 10 minutes

Nutrition facts per slice: 118 calories, 2 g total fat (0 g saturated fat), 1 mg cholesterol, 109 mg sodium, 22 g carbohydrate, 1 g fiber, 4 g protein.

1½-POUND (16 slices)	INGREDIENTS	2-POUND (22 slices)
1 cup	milk	1¼ cups
¼ cup	water	⅓ cup
1 tablespoon	shortening or cooking oil	2 tablespoons
2 cups	bread flour	2⅔ cups
¾ cup	whole wheat flour	1 cup
½ cup	yellow cornmeal	⅔ cup
1 tablespoon	gluten flour	4 teaspoons
1 tablespoon	sugar	4 teaspoons
1½ teaspoons	dried basil or thyme, crushed, or	2 teaspoons
1 tablespoon	snipped fresh basil or thyme	4 teaspoons
¾ teaspoon	salt	1 teaspoon
1¼ teaspoons	active dry yeast or bread machine yeast	1½ teaspoons

75

TOMATO HERB LOAF

Every soup supper needs bread to complete the meal—and this is it. Whole wheat flour makes it hearty, while tomato and oregano deliver goodness from the garden.

Prep time: 15 minutes

Nutrition facts per slice: 101 calories, 1 g total fat (0 g saturated fat), 0 mg cholesterol, 136 mg sodium, 20 g carbohydrate, 2 g fiber, 3 g protein.

1½-POUND (16 slices)	INGREDIENTS	2-POUND (22 slices)
⅔ cup	water	¾ cup
3 tablespoons	snipped dried tomatoes (not oil-packed)	¼ cup
½ cup	tomato sauce	¾ cup
1 tablespoon	margarine or butter	4 teaspoons
2 cups	bread flour	2⅔ cups
1 cup	whole wheat flour	1⅓ cups
1 tablespoon	brown sugar	2 tablespoons
1 teaspoon	dried oregano, crushed, or	1½ teaspoons
1 tablespoon	snipped fresh oregano	4 teaspoons
½ teaspoon	salt	¾ teaspoon
1 teaspoon	active dry yeast or bread machine yeast	1¼ teaspoons

DIRECTIONS

☞ Select the loaf size. Add the ingredients to the machine according to the manufacturer's directions, adding the dried tomatoes with the water. If available, select the whole grain cycle, or select the basic white bread cycle.

Good Advice!

Dried tomatoes have gone mainstream. Once stocked only by upscale markets that imported them from Italy, these intensely flavored nuggets are now staples at every corner grocery, and are produced stateside. Common market forms include oil-packed and dry, in jars or bags, bulk and prepackaged. To chop them, as most recipes suggest, snip with scissors.

76

FENNEL CHEESE BREAD

Enhance the flavor of a loaf of bread with fennel and hazelnuts. Ricotta cheese produces the light, airy texture in this much-loved loaf. It's so good, you may want to eat it straight from the oven.

DIRECTIONS

☞ Select the loaf size. Add the ingredients to the machine according to the manufacturer's directions. Select the basic white bread cycle.

☞ **★NOTE:** For the 1½-pound loaf, the bread machine pan must have a capacity of 10 cups or more. For the 2-pound loaf, the bread machine pan must have a capacity of 12 cups or more.

Prep time: 15 minutes
Nutrition facts per slice: 153 calories, 5 g total fat (1 g saturated fat), 18 mg cholesterol, 141 mg sodium, 22 g carbohydrate, 1 g fiber, 6 g protein.

1½-POUND★ (16 slices)	INGREDIENTS	2-POUND★ (22 slices)
¾ cup	part-skim ricotta cheese	1 cup
⅔ cup	milk	¾ cup
1	egg(s)	2
2 tablespoons	margarine or butter, cut up	3 tablespoons
3 cups	bread flour	4 cups
2 tablespoons	brown sugar	3 tablespoons
1½ teaspoons	fennel seed, crushed	2 teaspoons
¾ teaspoon	salt	1 teaspoon
1 teaspoon	active dry yeast or bread machine yeast	1¼ teaspoons
⅓ cup	finely chopped hazelnuts, toasted	½ cup

77

BREAD MACHINE BAKING
SOURDOUGH

{ **MAPLE WALNUT SOURDOUGH BREAD** }

see recipe, page 88

SOURDOUGH STARTER

This pleasantly pungent mixture of flour, liquid, yeast, and sugar ferments; then a portion is used to leaven bread, lending a "sour" flavor. Starters are replenished and used again and again.

Prep time: 10 minutes   **Stand time:** 5 days

AMOUNT
(4 cups)

AMOUNT (4 cups)	INGREDIENTS
1½ teaspoons	active dry yeast or bread machine yeast
¾ cup	warm water (105° to 115°)
3 cups	warm water (105° to 115°)
3 cups	all-purpose flour
4 teaspoons	granulated sugar or brown sugar

80

DIRECTIONS

☞ *To make starter:* Dissolve the yeast in the ¾ cup warm water. Add the 3 cups warm water; stir in flour and sugar. Beat with an electric mixer on medium speed just until smooth. Cover with 100-percent-cotton cheesecloth. Let stand at room temperature (75° to 85°) for 5 to 10 days or until mixture has a sour, fermented aroma, stirring 2 or 3 times every day. (A warmer room speeds the process.) When the starter has fermented, transfer to a 2-quart or larger plastic container with a tight-fitting lid; refrigerate.

☞ *To use starter:* Stir starter thoroughly after removing it from refrigerator. Measure amount needed; bring to room temperature. (The cold starter should be the consistency of buttermilk or thin pancake batter. If necessary, add water to thin the starter after it is stirred and before measuring.)

☞ For each cup of starter used, replenish remaining starter by stirring in ¾ cup all-purpose flour, ¾ cup water, and 1 teaspoon granulated or brown sugar. Cover; let mixture stand at room temperature for at least 1 day or until bubbly. Refrigerate. If not used within 10 days, stir in 1 teaspoon granulated or brown sugar. Repeat every 10 days unless starter is replenished.

RYE SOURDOUGH STARTER

Sourdough starter, like a seed, needs time to grow. This version uses rye flour, giving it a different flavor than the starter on page 80. Use it in Pumpernickel Sourdough Bread, page 104.

Prep time: 10 minutes **Stand time:** 5 days

AMOUNT (2½ cups)	INGREDIENTS
1 package	active dry yeast or bread machine yeast
½ cup	warm water (105° to 115°)
2 cups	warm water (105° to 115°)
2 cups	rye flour
1 tablespoon	sugar or honey

DIRECTIONS

☞ *To make starter:* Dissolve the yeast in the ½ cup warm water. Add the 2 cups warm water; stir in rye flour and sugar or honey. Beat with an electric mixer on medium speed just until smooth. Cover with 100-percent-cotton cheesecloth. Let stand at room temperature (75° to 85°) for 5 to 10 days or until mixture has a sour, fermented aroma, stirring 2 or 3 times every day. (A warmer room speeds the process.) When the starter has fermented, transfer to a jar and cover with 100-percent-cotton cheesecloth (do not cover tightly or use a metal lid); refrigerate.

☞ *To use starter:* Stir the starter thoroughly after removing it from refrigerator. Measure amount needed; bring to room temperature. (The cold starter should be the consistency of thin pancake batter. If necessary, add enough water to thin the starter after it is stirred and before measuring.)

☞ For each cup of starter used, replenish remaining starter by stirring in 1 cup water, ¾ cup rye flour, and 1 teaspoon sugar or honey. Cover; let mixture stand at room temperature for at least 1 day or until bubbly. Refrigerate. If not used within 10 days, stir in 1 teaspoon sugar or honey. Repeat every 10 days unless starter is replenished.

81

SOURDOUGH CINNAMON ROLLS

DIRECTIONS

☞ Select the recipe size. Add the first 8 ingredients to the machine according to the manufacturer's directions. Select the dough cycle. When cycle is complete, remove dough from machine. Punch down. Cover and let rest for 10 minutes.

☞ Meanwhile, for filling, in a small mixing bowl stir together the pecans, granulated sugar, brown sugar, and cinnamon.

☞ *For the 1½-pound recipe:* On a lightly floured surface, roll dough into a 12-inch square. Brush with the melted margarine or butter and sprinkle with filling. Roll up into a spiral; seal edge. Cut into 12 slices. Place, cut sides down, in a greased 13×9×2-inch baking pan. Cover and let rise in a warm place about 30 minutes or until nearly double. Drizzle whipping cream over rolls. Bake rolls in a 375° oven for 20 to 25 minutes or until golden brown. Cool in pan about 5 minutes; invert onto a wire rack. If desired, drizzle with Powdered Sugar Glaze.

☞ *For the 2-pound recipe:* Prepare as above, except roll dough into an 18×12-inch rectangle. Fill and roll up, starting from a long side. Cut into 18 slices; place in 2 greased 8×8×2-inch baking pans or 9×1½-inch round baking pans. Continue as above.

☞ *Powdered Sugar Glaze:* In a small mixing bowl stir together 1 cup sifted powdered sugar and ½ teaspoon vanilla. Stir in enough milk (1 to 2 tablespoons) to make a glaze of drizzling consistency.

☞ ***NOTE:** Our Test Kitchen recommends ⅓ cup water and 1 egg for either size recipe.

Prep time: 25 minutes   **Rise time:** 30 minutes   **Bake time:** 20 minutes
Nutrition facts per roll: 281 calories, 9 g total fat (2 g saturated fat), 25 mg cholesterol, 177 mg sodium, 44 g carbohydrate, 1 g fiber, 7 g protein.

1½-POUND (12 rolls)	INGREDIENTS	2-POUND (18 rolls)
1 cup	Sourdough Starter (see recipe, page 80)	1⅓ cups
⅓ cup	water*	⅓ cup
1	egg*	1
3 tablespoons	honey	¼ cup
1 tablespoon	margarine or butter	2 tablespoons
3 cups	bread flour	4 cups
¾ teaspoon	salt	1 teaspoon
1¼ teaspoons	active dry yeast or bread machine yeast	1¾ teaspoons
½ cup	chopped pecans	⅔ cup
⅓ cup	granulated sugar	½ cup
2 tablespoons	brown sugar	3 tablespoons
1½ teaspoons	ground cinnamon	2 teaspoons
2 tablespoons	margarine or butter, melted	3 tablespoons
¼ cup	whipping cream	⅓ cup
	Powdered Sugar Glaze (optional)	

83

HAZELNUT ESPRESSO SOURDOUGH BREAD

Wake up and smell the coffee, cinnamon, and toasted hazelnuts. Serve this full-flavored bread for breakfast or save it for a richly deserved afternoon treat.

Prep time: 15 minutes
Nutrition facts per slice: 149 calories, 3 g total fat (0 g saturated fat), 11 mg cholesterol, 93 mg sodium, 26 g carbohydrate, 1 g fiber, 4 g protein.

1½-POUND★ (20 slices)	INGREDIENTS	2-POUND★ (27 slices)
1 cup	Sourdough Starter★★ (see recipe, page 80)	1 cup
⅓ cup	milk	½ cup
1	egg★★	1
2 tablespoons	honey	3 tablespoons
1 tablespoon	margarine or butter	2 tablespoons
3 cups	bread flour	4 cups
1 tablespoon	instant espresso coffee powder or instant coffee crystals	4 teaspoons
¾ teaspoon	salt	1 teaspoon
¼ teaspoon	ground cinnamon	½ teaspoon
1 teaspoon	active dry yeast or bread machine yeast★★	1 teaspoon
½ cup	chopped hazelnuts or almonds, toasted	⅔ cup
	Coffee Glaze	

DIRECTIONS

☞ Select loaf size. Add ingredients, except the glaze, to machine according to manufacturer's directions. Select basic white bread cycle. Drizzle cooled loaf with Coffee Glaze.

☞ *Coffee Glaze:* In a small mixing bowl dissolve ½ teaspoon instant espresso powder or instant coffee crystals in 2 teaspoons milk. Stir in 1 cup sifted powdered sugar and enough additional milk (1 to 2 teaspoons) to make a glaze of drizzling consistency.

☞ **★NOTE:** For the 1½-pound loaf, the bread machine pan must have a capacity of 10 cups or more. For the 2-pound loaf, the bread machine pan must have a capacity of 12 cups or more.

☞ **★★NOTE:** Our Test Kitchen recommends 1 cup Sourdough Starter, 1 egg, and 1 teaspoon yeast for either size recipe.

84

Classic French bread is rediscovered using tangy sourdough flavor. Brush the unbaked loaf with a mixture of egg white and water for a beautiful shiny gold finish.

SOURDOUGH FRENCH BREAD

Prep time: 20 minutes **Rise time:** 35 minutes **Bake time:** 35 minutes
Nutrition facts per slice: 125 calories, 1 g total fat (0 g saturated fat), 0 mg cholesterol, 105 mg sodium, 25 g carbohydrate, 1 g fiber, 4 g protein.

DIRECTIONS

☞ Select the loaf size. Add first 5 ingredients to the machine according to manufacturer's directions. Select the dough cycle. When the cycle is complete, remove dough from machine. Cover and let rest for 10 minutes.

☞ On a lightly floured surface, roll the 1½-pound dough into a 12×8-inch rectangle (roll the 2-pound dough into a 15×10-inch rectangle). Starting from a long side, roll up into a spiral; seal edge. Pinch and pull ends to taper. Place, seam down, on a greased baking sheet sprinkled with cornmeal. Combine egg white and 1 tablespoon water; brush some over top of loaf.

☞ Cover and let rise in a warm place for 35 to 45 minutes or until nearly double. With a very sharp knife, make 3 to 5 diagonal cuts about ¼ inch deep across the top of loaf. Bake in a 375° oven for 20 minutes. Brush with remaining egg white mixture. Bake for 15 to 20 minutes more or until bread sounds hollow when lightly tapped. Remove from baking sheet; cool on a wire rack.

1½-POUND (16 slices)	INGREDIENTS	2-POUND (22 slices)
1¼ cups	Sourdough Starter (see recipe, page 80)	1¾ cups
2 tablespoons	water	¼ cup
3 cups	bread flour	4 cups
¾ teaspoon	salt	1 teaspoon
1 teaspoon	active dry yeast or bread machine yeast	1¼ teaspoons
	Yellow cornmeal	
1	slightly beaten egg white	1
1 tablespoon	water	1 tablespoon

85

OLIVE SOURDOUGH BREAD

The blend of olive oil, pimiento-stuffed green olives, and oregano produce a memorable bread. Even a bologna sandwich will take on a fresh personality with this bread.

Prep time: 15 minutes

Nutrition facts per slice: 138 calories, 2 g total fat (0 g saturated fat), 0 mg cholesterol, 212 mg sodium, 26 g carbohydrate, 1 g fiber, 4 g protein.

1½-POUND★ (16 slices)	INGREDIENTS	2-POUND★ (22 slices)
1¼ cups	Sourdough Starter (see recipe, page 80)	1¾ cups
¼ cup	water	⅓ cup
1 tablespoon	olive oil	2 tablespoons
3 cups	bread flour	4 cups
1 tablespoon	sugar	4 teaspoons
¾ teaspoon	salt	1 teaspoon
¾ teaspoon	dried oregano, crushed, or	1 teaspoon
2 teaspoons	snipped fresh oregano	1 tablespoon
1 teaspoon	active dry yeast or bread machine yeast	1¼ teaspoons
½ cup	chopped, pimiento-stuffed green olives	⅔ cup

DIRECTIONS

☞ Select the loaf size. Add the ingredients to the machine according to the manufacturer's directions. Select the basic white bread cycle.

☞ **★NOTE:** For the 1½-pound loaf, the bread machine pan must have a capacity of 10 cups or more. For the 2-pound loaf, the bread machine pan must have a capacity of 12 cups or more.

Did you know?

Tangy sourdough and salty olives have unquestioned California credentials. San Francisco's sourdough bread, famous since Gold Rush days, is unlike any other—thanks to the natural yeasts that thrive in the Bay Area's fog-filtered air. The first olive groves in this country were planted in the Golden State by early Spanish missionaries. California is now a major olive producer.

86

A chewy pretzel hot from a street cart is the ultimate comfort food in Philadelphia, where pretzels are prized. This version is extra-tangy, extra-easy, and extra-good.

SOURDOUGH BAKED PRETZELS

Prep time: 40 minutes   **Bake time:** 18 minutes
Nutrition facts per pretzel: 120 calories, 1 g total fat (0 g saturated fat), 13 mg cholesterol, 106 mg sodium, 24 g carbohydrate, 2 g fiber, 5 g protein.

DIRECTIONS

☞ Select recipe size. Add first 8 ingredients to the machine according to manufacturer's directions. Select the dough cycle. When cycle is complete, remove dough from machine. Punch down. Cover and let rest 10 minutes.

☞ On a lightly floured surface, roll the 1½-pound dough into a 14×8-inch rectangle. Cut into sixteen 14×½-inch strips. (Roll the 2-pound dough into a 14×10-inch rectangle; cut into twenty 14×½-inch strips.) Gently pull the strips into 16-inch-long ropes.

☞ Shape each pretzel by crossing one end over the other to form a circle, overlapping about 4 inches from each end. Take one end of dough in each hand and twist once at the point where dough overlaps. Carefully lift each end across to edge of circle opposite it. Tuck ends under edges to make a pretzel shape; moisten ends and press to seal. Place on 2 greased large baking sheets. *Do not let rise.* Mix egg and water; brush over pretzels. If desired, sprinkle with coarse salt or sesame seed. Bake in a 350° oven for 18 to 20 minutes or until golden. (Bake one baking sheet at a time, refrigerating other sheet to prevent rising.) Remove; cool.

1½-POUND (16 pretzels)	INGREDIENTS	2-POUND (20 pretzels)
1¼ cups	Sourdough Starter (see recipe, page 80)	1¾ cups
2 tablespoons	milk	¼ cup
1½ cups	bread flour	2 cups
1⅓ cups	whole wheat flour	1¾ cups
1 tablespoon	gluten flour	2 tablespoons
1 tablespoon	sugar	4 teaspoons
¾ teaspoon	salt	1 teaspoon
1 teaspoon	active dry yeast or bread machine yeast	1¼ teaspoons
1	beaten egg	1
1 tablespoon	water	1 tablespoon
	Coarse salt or sesame seed (optional)	

87

MAPLE WALNUT SOURDOUGH BREAD

(Pictured on page 79.)

The pairing of maple syrup and toasted walnuts provides a perfect balance to the sourdough base of this prize-winning recipe. Good enough to eat au naturel or for a very classy French toast.

Prep time: 15 minutes

Nutrition facts per slice: 172 calories, 4 g total fat (1 g saturated fat), 13 mg cholesterol, 114 mg sodium, 30 g carbohydrate, 1 g fiber, 5 g protein.

1½-POUND★ (16 slices)	INGREDIENTS	2-POUND★ (22 slices)
1 cup	Sourdough Starter (see recipe, page 80)	1⅓ cups
1	egg★★	1
3 tablespoons	water	¼ cup
2 tablespoons	maple-flavored syrup	3 tablespoons
1 tablespoon	margarine or butter	2 tablespoons
¼ teaspoon	maple extract	½ teaspoon
3 cups	bread flour	4 cups
¾ teaspoon	salt	1 teaspoon
¾ teaspoon	ground cinnamon	1 teaspoon
1 teaspoon	active dry yeast or bread machine yeast	1¼ teaspoon
½ cup	chopped walnuts, toasted	⅔ cup
½ cup	dark raisins	⅔ cup

DIRECTIONS

☞ Select the loaf size. Add the ingredients to the machine according to the manufacturer's directions. Select the basic white bread cycle.

☞ ★**NOTE:** For the 1½-pound loaf, the bread machine pan must have a capacity of 10 cups or more. For the 2-pound loaf, the bread machine pan must have a capacity of 12 cups or more.

☞ ★★**NOTE:** Our Test Kitchen recommends 1 egg for either size recipe.

That's a fact!

Maple syrup is tapped from maple trees late in winter when their sap begins to flow, then boiled until thick. One gallon of syrup requires over 30 gallons of sap. Lighter in taste and less expensive is maple-flavored syrup, which is a syrup such as corn syrup that has a small amount of maple syrup added. Syrups made from corn syrup plus maple extract are called pancake syrups.

TOFFEE SOURDOUGH BREAD

This bread begs to be saved for an afternoon coffee break. The combination of coffee and almond brickle is perfect for a midafternoon pick-me-up.

DIRECTIONS

☞ Select the loaf size. Dissolve the coffee crystals in the milk or water. Add the coffee mixture and the remaining ingredients to the machine according to the manufacturer's directions. Select the basic white bread cycle.

☞ *NOTE: For the 1½-pound loaf, the bread machine pan must have a capacity of 10 cups or more. For the 2-pound loaf, the bread machine pan must have a capacity of 12 cups or more.

☞ **NOTE: Our Test Kitchen recommends 2 tablespoons margarine or butter for either size recipe.

Prep time: 10 minutes
Nutrition facts per slice: 149 calories, 3 g total fat (0 g saturated fat), 2 mg cholesterol, 132 mg sodium, 26 g carbohydrate, 1 g fiber, 4 g protein.

1½-POUND* (18 slices)	INGREDIENTS	2-POUND* (24 slices)
2 teaspoons	instant coffee crystals	1 tablespoon
2 tablespoons	milk or water	⅓ cup
1¼ cups	Sourdough Starter (see recipe, page 80)	1½ cups
2 tablespoons	margarine or butter**	2 tablespoons
3 cups	bread flour	4 cups
4 teaspoons	sugar	2 tablespoons
¾ teaspoon	salt	1 teaspoon
1 teaspoon	active dry yeast or bread machine yeast	1¼ teaspoons
½ cup	almond brickle pieces	⅔ cup

89

PESTO SOURDOUGH LOAF

Pesto and Parmesan provide the perfect pairing of flavors to enhance this sourdough bread. Serve it with a full-bodied Merlot to experience a taste of life's simple pleasures.

DIRECTIONS

☞ Select the loaf size. Add the ingredients to the machine according to the manufacturer's directions. Select the basic white bread cycle. **★NOTE:** For the 1½-pound loaf, the bread machine pan must have a capacity of 10 cups or more. For the 2-pound loaf, the bread machine pan must have a capacity of 12 cups or more.

Prep time: 10 minutes
Nutrition facts per slice: 144 calories, 3 g total fat (0 g saturated fat), 2 mg cholesterol, 152 mg sodium, 24 g carbohydrate, 1 g fiber, 5 g protein.

1½-POUND★ (16 slices)	INGREDIENTS	2-POUND★ (22 slices)
1 cup	Sourdough Starter (see recipe, page 80)	1⅓ cups
¼ cup	water	⅓ cup
3 tablespoons	purchased pesto	¼ cup
3 cups	bread flour	4 cups
¼ cup	grated Parmesan cheese	⅓ cup
¾ teaspoon	salt	1 teaspoon
⅛ teaspoon	cracked black pepper	¼ teaspoon
1 teaspoon	active dry yeast or bread machine yeast	1¼ teaspoons

91

BROCCOLI CORN SOURDOUGH BREAD

Colorful yellow corn and green broccoli brighten this savory sourdough loaf. Serve slices spread with Herbed Feta Spread (see recipe, page 117) along with fresh garden salads.

Prep time: 15 minutes

Nutrition facts per slice: 123 calories, 2 g total fat (0 g saturated fat), 0 mg cholesterol, 91 mg sodium, 22 g carbohydrate, 1 g fiber, 4 g protein.

1½-POUND★ (18 slices)	INGREDIENTS	2-POUND★ (24 slices)
½ cup	finely chopped broccoli★★	½ cup
⅓ cup	frozen whole-kernel corn★★	⅓ cup
2 tablespoons	finely chopped onion★★	2 tablespoons
2 tablespoons	cooking oil★★	2 tablespoons
1 cup	Sourdough Starter (see recipe, page 80)	1⅓ cups
¼ cup	water	⅓ cup
3 cups	bread flour	4 cups
1 tablespoon	sugar	4 teaspoons
¾ teaspoon	salt	1 teaspoon
¼ teaspoon	ground sage	½ teaspoon
1 teaspoon	active dry yeast or bread machine yeast★★	1 teaspoon

DIRECTIONS

☞ Select the loaf size. In a small saucepan cook the broccoli, corn, and onion in hot oil for 2 to 3 minutes or until tender, stirring occasionally. Cool slightly.

☞ Add the vegetable mixture and remaining ingredients to the machine according to the manufacturer's directions. Select the basic white bread cycle.

☞ **★NOTE:** For the 1½-pound loaf, the bread machine pan must have a capacity of 10 cups or more. For the 2-pound loaf, the bread machine pan must have a capacity of 12 cups or more.

☞ **★★NOTE:** Our Test Kitchen recommends ½ cup broccoli, ⅓ cup corn, 2 tablespoons onion, 2 tablespoons oil, and 1 teaspoon yeast for either size recipe.

If the Gold Rush '49ers—famous for sourdough bread—stopped first in Texas, they may never have moved farther west. This slightly spicy cheese bread is as good as gold (well, almost).

TEX-MEX SOURDOUGH BREAD

DIRECTIONS

☞ Select the loaf size. Add the ingredients to the machine according to the manufacturer's directions, adding the cheese with the starter. Select the basic white bread cycle.

☞ *NOTE:* For the 1½-pound loaf, the bread machine pan must have a capacity of 10 cups or more. For the 2-pound loaf, the bread machine pan must have a capacity of 12 cups or more.

Did you know?

There really was a Monterey Jack—David Jacks, a nineteenth century cheesemaker who lived in Monterey, along California's central coast. His mild cheese took inspiration from similar ones made by the local missionary fathers. Today Jack cheese is sold plain and in flavors like pepper Jack, with jalapeño peppers; dill; and garlic.

Prep time: 15 minutes
Nutrition facts per slice: 146 calories, 3 g total fat (2 g saturated fat), 6 mg cholesterol, 115 mg sodium, 23 g carbohydrate, 1 g fiber, 5 g protein.

1½-POUND* (16 slices)	INGREDIENTS	2-POUND* (22 slices)
¾ cup	Sourdough Starter (see recipe, page 80)	1 cup
1 cup	shredded Monterey Jack cheese with jalapeño peppers	1⅓ cups
⅓ cup	water	½ cup
2 tablespoons	chopped, drained roasted red sweet peppers	3 tablespoons
1 tablespoon	margarine or butter	4 teaspoons
2⅔ cups	bread flour	3½ cups
⅓ cup	yellow cornmeal	½ cup
2 teaspoons	sugar	1 tablespoon
½ teaspoon	salt	¾ teaspoon
½ teaspoon	chili powder	¾ teaspoon
1 teaspoon	active dry yeast or bread machine yeast	1¼ teaspoons

93

FINNISH SOURDOUGH RYE BREAD

With a nod to peasant influences, this rustic country loaf is good with smoked cheeses and meats. The starter contains beer (if you choose), creating a real zippy bread.

Prep time: 10 minutes **Stand time:** 2 days

Nutrition facts per slice: 98 calories, 1 g total fat (0 g saturated fat), 0 mg cholesterol, 101 mg sodium, 19 g carbohydrate, 1 g fiber, 3 g protein.

1½-POUND★ (16 slices)	INGREDIENTS	2-POUND★ (22 slices)
1 cup	beer or water	1⅓ cups
½ cup	rye flour	⅔ cup
2 teaspoons	shortening or cooking oil	1 tablespoon
2 cups	bread flour	2⅔ cups
½ cup	rye flour	⅔ cup
1 tablespoon	gluten flour	2 tablespoons
2 teaspoons	brown sugar	1 tablespoon
¾ teaspoon	salt	1 teaspoon
1 teaspoon	active dry yeast or bread machine yeast	1¼ teaspoons

DIRECTIONS

☞ *To make starter:* Select the loaf size. In a medium mixing bowl stir the beer or water into the ½ or ⅔ cup rye flour just until smooth. Cover with plastic wrap. Let stand at room temperature (75° to 85°) for 2 days or until the mixture bubbles and has a slightly fermented aroma, stirring 2 or 3 times every day.

☞ *To finish the bread:* Add the starter and the remaining ingredients to machine according to the manufacturer's directions. If available, select the whole grain cycle, or select the basic white bread cycle.

☞ **★NOTE:** For the 1½-pound loaf, the bread machine pan must have a capacity of 10 cups or more. For the 2-pound loaf, the bread machine pan must have a capacity of 12 cups or more.

94

With whole wheat flour and wheat germ added for good measure, this bread will fit the bill for those who only turn to hearty, textural breads for their daily bread.

DIRECTIONS

☞ Select the loaf size. Add the ingredients to the machine according to the manufacturer's directions. If available, select the whole grain cycle, or select the basic white bread cycle.

☞ *NOTE: For the 1½-pound loaf, the bread machine pan must have a capacity of 10 cups or more. For the 2-pound loaf, the bread machine pan must have a capacity of 12 cups or more.

☞ **NOTE: Our Test Kitchen recommends 2 tablespoons gluten flour for either size recipe.

SOURDOUGH WHEAT BREAD

Prep time: 10 minutes

Nutrition facts per slice: 134 calories, 2 g total fat (0 g saturated fat), 0 mg cholesterol, 104 mg sodium, 25 g carbohydrate, 3 g fiber, 5 g protein.

1½-POUND* (16 slices)	INGREDIENTS	2-POUND* (22 slices)
1¼ cups	Sourdough Starter (see recipe, page 80)	1½ cups
¼ cup	milk or water	⅔ cup
1 tablespoon	cooking oil	2 tablespoons
2 cups	whole wheat flour	2⅓ cups
1 cup	bread flour	1⅓ cups
¼ cup	toasted wheat germ	⅓ cup
2 tablespoons	gluten flour**	2 tablespoons
1 tablespoon	brown sugar	4 teaspoons
¾ teaspoon	salt	1 teaspoon
1 teaspoon	active dry yeast or bread machine yeast	1½ teaspoons

95

RUSTIC ITALIAN BREAD

Prep time: 20 minutes   **Stand time:** 24 hours   **Rise time:** 30 minutes
Bake time: 25 minutes

Nutrition facts per slice: 109 calories, 2 g total fat (0 g saturated fat), 0 mg cholesterol,
103 mg sodium, 20 g carbohydrate, 1 g fiber, 3 g protein.

1½-POUND* (16 slices)	INGREDIENTS	2-POUND* (22 slices)
1 teaspoon	active dry yeast or bread machine yeast	1¼ teaspoons
⅓ cup	warm water (105° to 115°)	½ cup
¾ cup	bread flour	1 cup
¼ cup	milk	⅓ cup
1 teaspoon	sugar	1½ teaspoons
⅓ cup	water	½ cup
4 teaspoons	olive oil	2 tablespoons
¾ teaspoon	dried rosemary, crushed	1 teaspoon
1 teaspoon	bottled minced roasted garlic	1½ teaspoons
¾ teaspoon	salt	1 teaspoon
2¼ cups	bread flour	3½ cups
	Yellow cornmeal	
1½ teaspoons	bread flour	2 teaspoons

DIRECTIONS

☞ *To make starter:* Select the loaf size. Dissolve the yeast in the ⅓ or ½ cup warm water. Stir in the ¾ or 1 cup bread flour, milk, and sugar. Beat with a wire whisk or rotary beater just until smooth. Cover with plastic wrap. Let stand at room temperature (75° to 85°) for 24 hours or until mixture has a slightly fermented aroma, stirring 2 or 3 times. (Or, refrigerate for up to 4 days.)

☞ *To finish the bread:* Add the starter mixture and the next 6 ingredients to the machine according to the manufacturer's directions. Select dough cycle. When cycle is complete, remove dough from machine. Punch down. Cover and let rest for 10 minutes.

☞ *For the 1½-pound recipe:* On a lightly floured surface, shape dough into a ball. Place on a lightly greased baking sheet sprinkled with the cornmeal; flatten slightly to an 8-inch round loaf. Lightly rub top with the 1½ teaspoons bread flour. With a very sharp knife, make several cuts about ¼ inch deep on top of loaf. Cover; let rise in a warm place for 30 to 45 minutes or until nearly double. Bake in a 400° oven about 25 minutes or until loaf sounds hollow when lightly tapped. Remove from baking sheet; cool on a wire rack.

☞ *For the 2-pound recipe:* Prepare as above, except divide dough in half. Shape each half into a 6-inch round loaf. Continue as above, rubbing tops with the 2 teaspoons bread flour.

☞ ***NOTE:*** For the 1½-pound loaf, the bread machine pan must have a capacity of 10 cups or more. For the 2-pound loaf, the bread machine pan must have a capacity of 12 cups or more.

TARRAGON SOURDOUGH BREAD

This recipe fulfills all the requirements of a great bread—flavorful, high-rising, and golden brown. Tarragon gives it a Gallic connection, as the long-leafed herb is a favorite in French cooking.

Prep time: 10 minutes

Nutrition facts per slice: 125 calories, 2 g total fat (1 g saturated fat), 13 mg cholesterol, 144 mg sodium, 21 g carbohydrate, 1 g fiber, 5 g protein.

DIRECTIONS

☞ Select the loaf size. Add the ingredients to the machine according to the manufacturer's directions. Select the basic white bread cycle.

☞ *NOTE: For the 1½-pound loaf, the bread machine pan must have a capacity of 10 cups or more. For the 2-pound loaf, the bread machine pan must have a capacity of 12 cups or more.

☞ **NOTE: Our Test Kitchen recommends 1 egg for either size recipe.

1½-POUND★ (18 slices)	INGREDIENTS	2-POUND★ (24 slices)
¾ cup	Sourdough Starter (see recipe, page 80)	1 cup
¾ cup	cream-style cottage cheese	1 cup
1	egg**	1
2 tablespoons	water	3 tablespoons
2 tablespoons	margarine or butter, cut up	3 tablespoons
3 cups	bread flour	4 cups
2 teaspoons	sugar	1 tablespoon
1¼ teaspoons	dried tarragon, crushed, or	1½ teaspoons
4 teaspoons	snipped fresh tarragon	2 tablespoons
¾ teaspoon	salt	1 teaspoon
1 teaspoon	active dry yeast or bread machine yeast	1¼ teaspoons

98

Tart and tangy, this beloved bread is flavored with a hint of onion. Millet, a protein-rich cereal grass found in health-food stores, adds nutrition and crunch to every slice.

MILLET & ONION SOURDOUGH BREAD

Prep time: 15 minutes

Nutrition facts per slice: 125 calories, 2 g total fat (0 g saturated fat), 0 mg cholesterol, 82 mg sodium, 23 g carbohydrate, 1 g fiber, 4 g protein.

DIRECTIONS

☞ Select the loaf size. In a small saucepan cook onion and garlic in hot oil until onion is tender, stirring occasionally. Cool slightly.

☞ Add the onion mixture and the remaining ingredients to the machine according to the manufacturer's directions. Select the basic white bread cycle.

☞ ***NOTE:** For the 1½-pound loaf, the bread machine pan must have a capacity of 10 cups or more. For the 2-pound loaf, the bread machine pan must have a capacity of 12 cups or more.

☞ ****NOTE:** Our Test Kitchen recommends 1 clove garlic, 2 tablespoons oil, and 1 teaspoon yeast for either size recipe.

1½-POUND★ (20 slices)	INGREDIENTS	2-POUND★ (27 slices)
1 cup	chopped onion	1¼ cups
1 clove	garlic, minced★★	1 clove
2 tablespoons	olive oil or cooking oil★★	2 tablespoons
1¼ cups	Sourdough Starter (see recipe, page 80)	1½ cups
¼ cup	milk or water	½ cup
3 cups	bread flour	4 cups
¼ cup	millet	⅓ cup
1 tablespoon	sugar	4 teaspoons
¾ teaspoon	salt	1 teaspoon
1 teaspoon	active dry yeast or bread machine yeast★★	1 teaspoon

Did you know?

If you think millet is for the birds because it's used in birdseed, you should also know that other cultures prize it for its hardiness as a crop and its heartiness as a food. Particularly in India, but also in China and Africa, millet is used for breads, cereals, and sides. Look for these tiny yellow kernels in natural food markets. Store millet airtight in a cool spot up to two years.

99

CORNMEAL SOURDOUGH LOAF

One bite and you'll be hooked on this delicious combination of tangy sourdough and honey. It's a great basic bread for any use.

Prep time: 10 minutes

Nutrition facts per slice: 161 calories, 2 g total fat (0 g saturated fat), 1 mg cholesterol, 122 mg sodium, 30 g carbohydrate, 1 g fiber, 5 g protein.

1½-POUND★ (16 slices)	INGREDIENTS	2-POUND★ (22 slices)
1¼ cups	Sourdough Starter (see recipe, page 80)	1⅔ cups
½ cup	milk	⅔ cup
2 tablespoons	honey	3 tablespoons
2 tablespoons	margarine or butter, cut up	3 tablespoons
2½ cups	bread flour	3⅓ cups
½ cup	cracked wheat	⅔ cup
½ cup	yellow cornmeal	⅔ cup
2 tablespoons	gluten flour★★	2 tablespoons
¾ teaspoon	salt	1 teaspoon
1¼ teaspoons	active dry yeast or bread machine yeast	1½ teaspoons

DIRECTIONS

☞ Select the loaf size. Add the ingredients to the machine according to the manufacturer's directions. If available, select the whole grain cycle, or select the basic white bread cycle.

☞ ★**NOTE:** For the 1½-pound loaf, the bread machine pan must have a capacity of 10 cups or more. For the 2-pound loaf, the bread machine pan must have a capacity of 12 cups or more.

☞ ★★**NOTE:** Our Test Kitchen recommends 2 tablespoons gluten flour for either size recipe.

100

The sharp flavors of robust sourdough bread blend well with the aromatic flavors of three members of the onion family—leeks, onions, and shallots.

DIRECTIONS

☞ Select the loaf size. In a small saucepan cook the leek or green onions, onion, and shallot in hot oil until tender, stirring occasionally. Cool slightly.

☞ Add the leek mixture and the remaining ingredients to the machine according to the manufacturer's directions. Select the basic white bread cycle.

☞ *NOTE: For the 1½-pound loaf, the bread machine pan must have a capacity of 10 cups or more. For the 2-pound loaf, the bread machine pan must have a capacity of 12 cups or more.

HOT TIP

It's the volatile oils released when you cut an onion—whether it's a leek, green onion, yellow onion, or shallot—that make you teary. You can minimize this unpleasant effect by using a sharp knife (always a good idea). A dull knife will mash an onion rather than cut it, sending more irritating vapors into the air and into your eyes, while a sharp knife makes quick, clean cuts.

TRIPLE ONION SOURDOUGH BREAD

Prep time: 20 minutes

Nutrition facts per slice: 125 calories, 2 g total fat (0 g saturated fat), 0 mg cholesterol, 91 mg sodium, 23 g carbohydrate, 1 g fiber, 4 g protein.

1½-POUND* (18 slices)	INGREDIENTS	2-POUND* (24 slices)
⅓ cup	sliced leek or green onions	½ cup
¼ cup	chopped onion	⅓ cup
1 tablespoon	chopped shallot	2 tablespoons
2 tablespoons	olive oil or cooking oil	3 tablespoons
1¼ cups	Sourdough Starter (see recipe, page 80)	1½ cups
¼ cup	water	⅓ cup
3 cups	bread flour	4 cups
¾ teaspoon	salt	1 teaspoon
½ teaspoon	sugar	¾ teaspoon
1 teaspoon	active dry yeast or bread machine yeast	1¼ teaspoons

101

CREAM CHEESE SOURDOUGH BREAD

For a true sandwich meister, rye is the undisputed king of breads. Inheriting the throne is this tasty rendition, tart from the starter and rich with cream cheese.

Prep time: 15 minutes

Nutrition facts per slice: 133 calories, 2 g total fat (1 g saturated fat), 4 mg cholesterol, 114 mg sodium, 24 g carbohydrate, 2 g fiber, 4 g protein.

1½-POUND★ (16 slices)	INGREDIENTS	2-POUND★ (22 slices)
1 cup	Sourdough Starter (see recipe, page 80)	1¼ cups
⅓ cup	milk	½ cup
2 ounces	cream cheese, softened	3 ounces
2 teaspoons	cooking oil	1 tablespoon
2 teaspoons	honey	1 tablespoon
1¾ cups	bread flour	2½ cups
1¼ cups	rye flour	1½ cups
3 tablespoons	snipped fresh chives	¼ cup
2 tablespoons	gluten flour★★	2 tablespoons
¾ teaspoon	salt	1 teaspoon
¾ teaspoon	caraway seed	1 teaspoon
1 teaspoon	active dry yeast or bread machine yeast	1¼ teaspoons

DIRECTIONS

☞ Select the loaf size. Add the ingredients to the machine according to the manufacturer's directions. If available, select the whole grain cycle, or select the basic white bread cycle.

☞ ★**NOTE:** For the 1½-pound loaf, the bread machine pan must have a capacity of 10 cups or more. For the 2-pound loaf, the bread machine pan must have a capacity of 12 cups or more.

☞ ★★**NOTE:** Our Test Kitchen recommends 2 tablespoons gluten flour for either size recipe.

102

This cheese-laced sourdough has an unmistakable garlic flavor and is guaranteed to become a family favorite. It's good on its own or with our Pesto-Cream Cheese Spread (see recipe, page 117).

GARLIC SOURDOUGH BREAD

DIRECTIONS

☞ Select the loaf size. Add the ingredients to the machine according to the manufacturer's directions. Select the basic white bread cycle.

☞ **NOTE:** For the 1½-pound loaf, the bread machine pan must have a capacity of 10 cups or more. For the 2-pound loaf, the bread machine pan must have a capacity of 12 cups or more.

☞ ★★**NOTE:** Our Test Kitchen recommends 1 tablespoon honey for either size recipe.

Good Advice!

Most recipes call for minced garlic cloves—the tear-shape segments that form a bulb of garlic. A stainless steel garlic press will do the job, or you can mince cloves with a knife this way: Smash the clove lightly with the flat side of the knife to loosen the papery skin. Peel, then chop or mince as needed.

Prep time: 10 minutes
Nutrition facts per slice: 119 calories, 2 g total fat (1 g saturated fat), 2 mg cholesterol, 128 mg sodium, 21 g carbohydrate, 1 g fiber, 4 g protein.

1½-POUND★ (20 slices)	INGREDIENTS	2-POUND★ (27 slices)
1¼ cups	Sourdough Starter (see recipe, page 80)	1½ cups
2 tablespoons	milk	½ cup
1 tablespoon	cooking oil	2 tablespoons
1 tablespoon	honey★★	1 tablespoon
3 cups	bread flour	4 cups
½ cup	grated Parmesan cheese	⅔ cup
2 cloves	garlic, minced	3 cloves
¾ teaspoon	salt	1 teaspoon
1 teaspoon	active dry yeast or bread machine yeast	1½ teaspoons

105

PUMPERNICKEL SOURDOUGH BREAD

Coffee, molasses, and cocoa contribute the dark color to this German-style bread. Sliced and topped with smoked ham and baby Swiss, it becomes an exceptional sandwich.

Prep time: 15 minutes

Nutrition facts per slice: 122 calories, 1 g total fat (0 g saturated fat), 0 mg cholesterol, 102 mg sodium, 24 g carbohydrate, 2 g fiber, 4 g protein.

1½-POUND★ (16 slices)	INGREDIENTS	2-POUND★ (22 slices)
¾ teaspoon	instant coffee crystals	1 teaspoon
¼ cup	water	⅓ cup
1 cup	Rye Sourdough Starter (see recipe, page 81)	1⅓ cups
3 tablespoons	mild-flavored molasses	¼ cup
1 tablespoon	cooking oil	4 teaspoons
1¾ cups	bread flour	2⅓ cups
¾ cup	rye flour	1 cup
½ cup	whole wheat flour	⅔ cup
4 teaspoons	gluten flour	2 tablespoon:
4 teaspoons	unsweetened cocoa powder	2 tablespoon:
1½ teaspoons	caraway or fennel seed	2 teaspoons
¾ teaspoon	salt	1 teaspoon
1 teaspoon	active dry yeast or bread machine yeast	1¼ teaspoon:

DIRECTIONS

☞ Select the loaf size. Dissolve the coffee crystals in the water. Add the coffee mixture and the remaining ingredients to the machine according to the manufacturer's directions. If available, select the whole grain cycle, or select the basic white bread cycle.

☞ ★**NOTE:** For the 1½-pound loaf, the bread machine pan must have a capacity of 10 cups or more. For the 2-pound loaf, the bread machine pan must have a capacity of 12 cups or more.

May We Suggest?

Cocoa powder, along with coffee and rye flour, gives this bread its traditional dark color. Use pure unsweetened cocoa powder. Instant cocoa mix or presweetened cocoa powder, drink mixes made of ground cocoa plus sugar and other flavorings, will give different results.

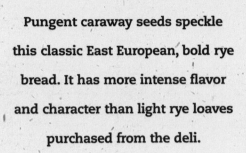

Pungent caraway seeds speckle this classic East European, bold rye bread. It has more intense flavor and character than light rye loaves purchased from the deli.

CARAWAY RYE SOURDOUGH BREAD

Prep time: 15 minutes **Stand time (starter):** 3 days
Nutrition facts per slice: 108 calories, 2 g total fat (0 g saturated fat), 12 mg cholesterol, 94 mg sodium, 20 g carbohydrate, 1 g fiber, 4 g protein.

DIRECTIONS

☞ *To make starter:* Select loaf size. Dissolve the ¾ or 1 teaspoon yeast in the warm water. Stir in the ½ or ⅔ cup rye flour just until smooth. Cover with plastic wrap. Let stand at room temperature (75° to 85°) for 3 days or until mixture has a slightly fermented aroma, stirring 2 or 3 times every day.

☞ *To finish the bread:* Add the starter mixture and the remaining ingredients to machine according to the manufacturer's directions. If available, select the whole grain cycle, or select the basic white bread cycle.

☞ **★NOTE:** For the 1½-pound loaf, the bread machine pan must have a capacity of 10 cups or more. For the 2-pound loaf, the bread machine pan must have a capacity of 12 cups or more.

☞ **★★NOTE:** Our Test Kitchen recommends 1 egg and 2 tablespoons molasses for either size recipe.

1½-POUND★ (18 slices)	INGREDIENTS	2-POUND★ (24 slices)
¾ teaspoon	active dry yeast or bread machine yeast	1 teaspoon
1 cup	warm water (105° to 115°)	1¼ cups
½ cup	rye flour	⅔ cup
1	egg★★	1
2 tablespoons	mild-flavored molasses★★	2 tablespoons
1 tablespoon	olive oil or cooking oil	4 teaspoons
2¼ cups	bread flour	3 cups
¾ cup	rye flour	1 cup
4 teaspoons	gluten flour	2 tablespoons
1 tablespoon	caraway seed	4 teaspoons
¾ teaspoon	salt	1 teaspoon
1 teaspoon	active dry yeast or bread machine yeast	1¼ teaspoons

BREAD MACHINE BAKING

HOLIDAY

{ **SPICED APPLE BRAID** }

see recipe, page 110

RAISIN GINGER BREAD

Recreate the loving memories of your mother's kitchen with the smells of this classic loaf. Serve up thick slices spread with our mouth watering Lemon Butter (see recipe, page 116).

Prep time: 15 minutes

Nutrition facts per slice: 115 calories, 3 g total fat (1 g saturated fat), 11 mg cholesterol, 109 mg sodium, 20 g carbohydrate, 1 g fiber, 3 g protein.

1½-POUND★ (20 slices)	INGREDIENTS	2-POUND★ (27 slices)
¾ cup	milk	1 cup
1	egg★★	1
3 tablespoons	margarine or butter, cut up	¼ cup
2 tablespoons	mild-flavored molasses	3 tablespoons
3 cups	bread flour	4 cups
¾ teaspoon	salt	1 teaspoon
¾ teaspoon	ground cinnamon	1 teaspoon
¾ teaspoon	ground ginger	1 teaspoon
¼ teaspoon	ground cloves	½ teaspoon
1 teaspoon	active dry yeast or bread machine yeast	1¼ teaspoons
½ cup	dark raisins	⅔ cup

DIRECTIONS

☞ Select the loaf size. Add the ingredients to the machine according to the manufacturer's directions. Select the basic white bread cycle. If desired, serve loaf with Lemon Butter.

☞ ★**NOTE:** For the 1½-pound loaf, the bread machine pan must have a capacity of 10 cups or more. For the 2-pound loaf, the bread machine pan must have a capacity of 12 cups or more.

☞ ★★**NOTE:** Our Test Kitchen recommends 1 egg for either size recipe.

That's a fact!

Light molasses, produced from the first boiling of the juices of sugarcane, has a mild flavor and pale color. Dark molasses, from the second boiling, is less sweet, but more robust. You can use either in a recipe, but substituting one for the other will result in a mild versus robust molasses flavor.

The golden pumpkin color of this loaf, combined with its mild ginger flavor and dates, makes it a special breakfast or snack. Slice and spread with a little Orange-Ginger Butter (see recipe, page 116).

GINGER PUMPKIN BREAD

DIRECTIONS

☞ Select the loaf size. Add the ingredients to the machine according to the manufacturer's directions. Select the basic white bread cycle.

☞ *NOTE: For the 1½-pound loaf, the bread machine pan must have a capacity of 10 cups or more. For the 2-pound loaf, the bread machine pan must have a capacity of 12 cups or more.

☞ **NOTE: Our Test Kitchen recommends 1 egg for either size recipe.

Prep time: 15 minutes

Nutrition facts per slice: 139 calories, 2 g total fat (1 g saturated fat), 14 mg cholesterol, 126 mg sodium, 25 g carbohydrate, 1 g fiber, 4 g protein.

1½-POUND★ (16 slices)	INGREDIENTS	2-POUND★ (22 slices)
½ cup	milk	⅔ cup
½ cup	canned pumpkin	⅔ cup
1	egg★★	1
2 tablespoons	margarine or butter, cut up	3 tablespoons
3 cups	bread flour	4 cups
1 tablespoon	brown sugar	2 tablespoons
¾ teaspoon	salt	1 teaspoon
¼ teaspoon	ground nutmeg	½ teaspoon
1 teaspoon	active dry yeast or bread machine yeast	1¼ teaspoons
½ cup	snipped pitted dates	⅔ cup
2 tablespoons	finely chopped crystallized ginger	3 tablespoons

109

SPICED APPLE BRAID

(Pictured on page 107.)

Prep time: 25 minutes   **Rise time:** 45 minutes   **Bake time:** 30 minutes

Nutrition facts per slice: 194 calories, 5 g total fat (1 g saturated fat), 14 mg cholesterol, 159 mg sodium, 34 g carbohydrate, 1 g fiber, 4 g protein.

1½-POUND (16 slices)	INGREDIENTS	2-POUND (22 slices)
⅓ cup	milk	½ cup
⅓ cup	apple juice	½ cup
⅓ cup	margarine or butter, cut up	½ cup
1	egg*	1
3 cups	bread flour	4 cups
3 tablespoons	sugar	¼ cup
¾ teaspoon	salt	1 teaspoon
1¼ teaspoons	active dry yeast or bread machine yeast	1½ teaspoons
one 14-ounce jar	spiced apple rings, drained*	one 14-ounce jar
1	slightly beaten egg white	1
1 tablespoon	water	1 tablespoon
	Powdered Sugar Glaze	

110

DIRECTIONS

☞ Select the loaf size. Add first 8 ingredients to machine according to the manufacturer's directions. Select the dough cycle. When cycle is complete, remove dough. Punch down. Cover and let rest for 10 minutes.

☞ Meanwhile, for filling, place apples in blender container. Cover; blend until nearly smooth. Mix egg white and water; set aside.

☞ *For the 1½-pound recipe:* On a lightly floured surface, roll dough into a 16×12-inch rectangle. Cut into three 16×4-inch strips. Spread about ¼ cup filling down center of each strip. Brush some egg white mixture on edges. Bring long edges together over filling and pinch to seal. To shape, line up the filled ropes, seams down, 1 inch apart on a greased baking sheet. Starting in middle, loosely braid by bringing left rope under center rope. Bring right rope under new center rope. Repeat to end. On other end, braid by bringing outside ropes alternately over center rope to center. Press ends together; tuck under. Brush with more egg white mixture. Cover; let rise for 45 to 60 minutes or until nearly double. Brush with remaining egg white mixture. Bake in a 350° oven about 30 minutes or until bread sounds hollow when tapped. If necessary, cover loosely with foil last 10 to 15 minutes to prevent overbrowning. Remove; cool on wire rack. Drizzle with Powdered Sugar Glaze.

☞ *For the 2-pound recipe:* Prepare as above, except divide dough in half. Roll each half into a 12-inch square. Cut each into three 12×4-inch strips. Fill each strip with about 2 tablespoons filling; form 2 braids using 3 filled ropes for each. Continue as above.

☞ *Powdered Sugar Glaze:* Mix 1 cup sifted powdered sugar and ½ teaspoon vanilla. Stir in enough milk (3 to 4 teaspoons) to make a glaze of drizzling consistency.

☞ ***NOTE:** Our Test Kitchen recommends 1 egg and 1 jar apple rings for either size recipe.

PEAR LOAF

Not all fresh foods hibernate in wintertime. Showcase one of the season's best—juicy pears—in this holiday-worthy bread. Apple juice or pear nectar lends sweetness.

DIRECTIONS

☞ Select the loaf size. Add the ingredients to the machine according to the manufacturer's directions, adding the pear with the liquid. Select the basic white bread cycle.

☞ **★NOTE:** Our Test Kitchen recommends ⅓ cup apple juice or pear nectar for either size.

☞ **★★NOTE:** Choose a firm, ripe pear. You may need to adjust the flour or juice if the pear is unripe or if it is very ripe and juicy.

HOT TIP

A pear is ripe when it yields to slight pressure at the stem end. If too firm, ripen pears in a paper bag for a day or two. To peel a pear, trim off stem and blossom ends, then remove the skin with a small paring knife. To chop, halve the peeled pear and scoop out the core. Slice each half, stack the slices, cut lengthwise, then crosswise. Use right away or the flesh will discolor.

Prep time: 15 minutes

Nutrition facts per slice: 134 calories, 3 g total fat (0 g saturated fat), 1 mg cholesterol, 116 mg sodium, 23 g carbohydrate, 1 g fiber, 4 g protein.

1½-POUND (16 slices)	INGREDIENTS	2-POUND (22 slices)
½ cup	milk	⅔ cup
⅓ cup	apple juice or pear nectar★	⅓ cup
¾ cup	chopped peeled pear★★	1 cup
4 teaspoons	margarine or butter	2 tablespoons
3 cups	bread flour	4 cups
2 tablespoons	brown sugar	3 tablespoons
¾ teaspoon	salt	1 teaspoon
½ teaspoon	finely shredded lemon peel	¾ teaspoon
1 teaspoon	active dry yeast or bread machine yeast	1¼ teaspoons
⅓ cup	chopped almonds, toasted	½ cup

111

APPLE EGGNOG BREAD

Combine fresh apples and creamy eggnog to make this tender, moist holiday loaf. For a finishing touch, nothing tops the Eggnog Glaze.

How sweet it is!

Prep time: 15 minutes

Nutrition facts per slice: 155 calories, 3 g total fat (0 g saturated fat), 13 mg cholesterol, 127 mg sodium, 28 g carbohydrate, 1 g fiber, 4 g protein.

1½-POUND★ (16 slices)	INGREDIENTS	2-POUND★ (22 slices)
½ cup	canned or dairy eggnog	¾ cup
¼ cup	water★★	¼ cup
½ cup	chopped peeled apple	¾ cup
1	egg★★	1
2 tablespoons	margarine or butter, cut up	3 tablespoons
¼ teaspoon	rum extract	½ teaspoon
3 cups	bread flour	4 cups
2 tablespoons	sugar	3 tablespoons
¾ teaspoon	salt	1 teaspoon
¼ teaspoon	ground nutmeg	½ teaspoon
1¼ teaspoons	active dry yeast or bread machine yeast	1½ teaspoons
	Eggnog Glaze	

DIRECTIONS

☞ Select loaf size. Add all the ingredients, except Eggnog Glaze, to the machine according to the manufacturer's directions, adding the apple with the liquid. Select the basic white bread cycle. Drizzle the cooled loaf with Eggnog Glaze.

☞ *Eggnog Glaze:* In a small bowl stir together 1 cup sifted powdered sugar and enough canned or dairy eggnog (1 to 2 tablespoons) to make a glaze of drizzling consistency.

☞ ★**NOTE:** For the 1½-pound loaf, the bread machine pan must have a capacity of 10 cups or more. For the 2-pound loaf, the bread machine pan must have a capacity of 12 cups or more.

☞ ★★**NOTE:** Our Test Kitchen recommends ¼ cup water and 1 egg for either size recipe.

Fill your kitchen with the ultimate of holiday aromas—mincemeat. Traditionally used as a filling for pies, tarts, and cookies, mincemeat jazzes up this spiced oat bread.

DIRECTIONS

☞ Select the loaf size. Add the ingredients to the machine according to the manufacturer's directions. Select the basic white bread cycle.

☞ *NOTE: For the 1½-pound loaf, the bread machine pan must have a capacity of 10 cups or more. For the 2-pound loaf, the bread machine pan must have a capacity of 12 cups or more.

☞ **NOTE: Our Test Kitchen recommends ¼ teaspoon cinnamon for either size recipe.

Did you know?

Despite its name, mincemeat—that luscious holiday pie filling—is most often meat-free. But this wasn't always true. Originally, beef suet and ground meat were part of the recipe, devised as a way to preserve meat. Now the combination of ingredients is usually chopped apples, raisins, spices, and sometimes rum or brandy.

MINCEMEAT LOAF

Prep time: 10 minutes

Nutrition facts per slice: 125 calories, 1 g total fat (0 g saturated fat), 0 mg cholesterol, 136 mg sodium, 24 g carbohydrate, 1 g fiber, 3 g protein.

1½-POUND* (16 slices)	INGREDIENTS	2-POUND* (22 slices)
¾ cup	water	1 cup
½ cup	mincemeat	⅔ cup
1 tablespoon	margarine or butter	4 teaspoons
3 cups	bread flour	4 cups
⅓ cup	regular or quick-cooking rolled oats	½ cup
1 tablespoon	brown sugar	4 teaspoons
¾ teaspoon	salt	1 teaspoon
¼ teaspoon	ground cinnamon**	¼ teaspoon
1¼ teaspoons	active dry yeast or bread machine yeast	1½ teaspoons

113

TWISTED CRANBERRY BREAD

DIRECTIONS

☞ Select the loaf size. Add first 8 ingredients to the machine according to manufacturer's directions. Select the dough cycle. When the cycle is complete, remove dough from machine. Punch down. Cover and let rest for 10 minutes.

☞ *For the 1½-pound recipe:* On a lightly floured surface, roll dough into a 14×10-inch rectangle. Brush with melted margarine or butter and sprinkle with Cranberry Filling. Starting from a long side, roll up into a spiral; seal edge. Place on a greased baking sheet. Cut roll in half lengthwise; turn cut sides up. Loosely weave halves together, keeping cut sides up. Press ends together. Cover and let rise in a warm place about 30 minutes or until nearly double.

☞ Bake in a 375° oven for 25 minutes. If necessary, loosely cover with foil the last 10 minutes to prevent overbrowning. Remove from baking sheet; cool on a wire rack. Drizzle with Orange Glaze.

☞ *For the 2-pound recipe:* Prepare as above, except divide dough in half. Roll each half into a 12×8-inch rectangle. Brush each rectangle with half of the melted margarine or butter and sprinkle each with half of the Cranberry Filling. Form 2 loaves on 2 greased baking sheets. Continue as above.

☞ *Cranberry Filling:* In a small mixing bowl stir together ½ cup finely chopped fresh cranberries, ¼ cup packed brown sugar, 2 tablespoons finely chopped pecans, 1½ teaspoons finely shredded orange peel, and ½ teaspoon ground allspice.

☞ *Orange Glaze:* In a small mixing bowl stir together ½ cup sifted powdered sugar and enough orange juice (1 to 3 teaspoons) to make a glaze of drizzling consistency.

Prep time: 30 minutes   **Rise time:** 30 minutes   **Bake time:** 25 minutes
Nutrition facts per slice: 138 calories, 3 g total fat (1 g saturated fat), 12 mg cholesterol, 117 mg sodium, 24 g carbohydrate, 1 g fiber, 4 g protein.

1½-POUND (18 slices)	INGREDIENTS	2-POUND (24 slices)
½ cup	milk	¾ cup
¼ cup	water	⅓ cup
1	egg(s)	2
2 tablespoons	margarine or butter, cut up	3 tablespoons
3 cups	bread flour	4 cups
2 tablespoons	sugar	3 tablespoons
¾ teaspoon	salt	1 teaspoon
1¼ teaspoons	active dry yeast or bread machine yeast	1½ teaspoons
2 teaspoons	margarine or butter, melted	1 tablespoon
	Cranberry Filling	
	Orange Glaze	

115

FLAVORED BUTTERS & SPREADS

Peach-Nut Butter

Place 1 cup pecans or almonds in blender container or food processor bowl. Cover; blend or process until finely chopped. Transfer to a small bowl.

Place ½ cup butter or margarine, cut up and softened, and ½ cup peach preserves in the blender container or food processor bowl. Cover and blend until combined, stopping to scrape down the sides as necessary. Add preserves mixture to the nuts in the bowl. Mix well. Cover and chill for at least 1 hour before serving. Makes 1½ cups (twenty-four 1-tablespoon servings).

Nutrition facts per tablespoon: 85 cal., 7 g total fat (3 g sat. fat), 10 mg chol., 40 mg sodium, 6 g carbo., 0 g fiber, 1 g pro.

Strawberry-Nut Butter

Prepare Peach-Nut Butter as directed above, except use 1 cup blanched almonds as the desired nuts. Cover and blend or process almonds until ground. Substitute strawberry preserves for the peach preserves. If desired, add 4 drops red food coloring to the preserves mixture while blending. Makes 1½ cups (twenty-four 1-tablespoon servings.)

Nutrition facts per tablespoon: 83 cal., 7 g total fat (3 g sat. fat), 10 mg chol., 40 mg sodium, 6 g carbo., 1 g fiber, 1 g pro.

Lemon Butter

In a small mixing bowl beat ½ cup softened butter or margarine, 1 tablespoon powered sugar, ½ teaspoon finely shredded lemon peel, and 1 teaspoon lemon juice with an electric

Pair your favorite muffin or bread with one of these easy-to-make flavored butters or spreads. Each recipe makes enough so you can enjoy some now and save some for later. Store leftovers, covered, up to 2 weeks in the refrigerator or up to 2 months in the freezer.

mixer until smooth. Cover and chill. Let butter stand at room temperature about 30 minutes before serving. Makes ⅔ cup (ten 1-tablespoon servings). *Note:* For *Orange Butter,* substitute orange peel and juice for the lemon peel and juice.

Nutrition facts per tablespoon: 82 cal., 9 g total fat (6 g sat. fat), 25 mg chol., 93 mg sodium, 1 g carbo., 0 g fiber, 0 g pro.

Orange-Ginger Butter

In a small saucepan heat and stir ½ cup orange marmalade just until melted. In a medium bowl beat ½ cup butter or margarine until fluffy. Beat in the melted marmalade, 1 tablespoon balsamic

vinegar or cider vinegar, and 1 tablespoon finely chopped crystallized ginger. Cover and chill at least 1 hour before serving. Makes about 1 cup (sixteen 1-tablespoon servings).

Nutrition facts per tablespoon: 78 cal., 5 g total fat (4 g sat. fat), 15 mg chol., 60 mg sodium, 8 g carbo., 1 g fiber, 0 g pro.

Pepper Butter

Prepare Orange-Ginger Butter as directed except substitute hot pepper jelly for the marmalade and omit the ginger. Makes about 1 cup (sixteen 1-tablespoon servings).

Nutrition facts per tablespoon: 77 cal., 6 g total fat (4 g sat. fat), 15 mg chol., 60 mg sodium, 7 g carbo., 0 g fiber, 0 g pro.

Cream Cheese Butter

In a small mixing bowl beat two 3-ounce packages softened cream cheese, ¼ cup softened butter, and 1 teaspoon vanilla until light and fluffy. Gradually add 1¼ cups sifted powdered sugar, beating well. Cover and chill. Let stand at room temperature 30 minutes before serving. Makes about 1 cup (sixteen 1-tablespoon servings).

Nutrition facts per tablespoon: 93 cal., 7 g total fat (4 g sat. fat), 19 mg chol., 61 mg sodium, 8 g carbo., 0 g fiber, 1 g pro.

Chocolate-Cashew Spread

In a small heavy saucepan melt 2 ounces semisweet chocolate over low heat, stirring constantly until chocolate begins to melt. Immediately remove the chocolate from heat; stir until smooth. Cool slightly.

Place 1 cup roasted unsalted cashews or toasted blanched almonds in a food processor bowl or blender container. Cover and process or blend until nuts are very finely chopped, stopping and scraping the sides as necessary. Add ¼ cup cut-up butter; process or blend until nearly smooth. Transfer mixture to a bowl; stir in the melted chocolate. Serve at room temperature. Makes 1 cup (sixteen 1-tablespoon servings).

Nutrition facts per tablespoon: 91 cal., 8 g total fat (3 g sat. fat), 8 mg chol., 30 mg sodium, 5 g carbo., 1 g fiber, 2 g pro.

Spiced Peach Spread

In a small saucepan combine 1 cup dried snipped peaches, ½ cup water, ¼ cup sugar, and ½ teaspoon apple pie spice or pumpkin pie spice. Bring to boiling over medium heat; reduce heat. Simmer, covered, for 20 minutes or until peaches are very soft. Place in a food processor bowl or blender container. Cover; process or blend until nearly smooth. To store, cover and refrigerate up to 1 week. Makes 1 cup (sixteen 1-tablespoon servings).

Nutrition facts per tablespoon: 36 cal., 0 g total fat (0 g sat. fat), 0 mg chol., 1 mg sodium, 9 g carbo., 1 g fiber, 0 g pro.

Nut 'n' Honey Butter

In a small bowl stir together ½ cup finely chopped toasted pecans or almonds, ½ cup softened butter or margarine, and 1 teaspoon honey. If not serving immediately, cover and chill. Bring to room temperature before serving. Makes 1 cup (sixteen 1-tablespoon servings).

Nutrition facts per tablespoon: 74 cal., 8 g total fat (4 g sat. fat), 15 mg chol., 58 mg sodium, 1 g carbo., 0 g fiber, 1 g pro.

Jumpin' Ginger Butter

In a small mixing bowl stir together ½ cup softened butter or margarine,

2 tablespoons sliced green onion, 1 tablespoon grated fresh gingerroot, 1 teaspoon minced garlic, and 1 teaspoon soy sauce. Cover; chill mixture until almost firm, allowing about 1 hour in the refrigerator or 20 minutes in the freezer.

On plastic wrap or waxed paper, shape the chilled mixture with a knife into two 4-inch-long logs. Fold wrap over logs and push logs into round shapes, using one hand to keep the plastic wrap taut while the other hand does the shaping. Wrap logs in the plastic wrap. If necessary, chill again and roll logs until smooth. Rewrap the logs; chill until serving time. Store in the refrigerator up to 1 week. To serve, cut the logs into ¼-inch-thick slices. Makes ½ cup (eight 1-tablespoon servings).

Nutrition facts per tablespoon: 102 cal., 11 g total fat (7 g sat. fat), 31 mg chol., 159 mg sodium, 0 g carbo., 0 g fiber, 0 g pro.

Herb Butter

In a small bowl place ½ cup butter or margarine, softened; and ½ teaspoon each dried thyme and marjoram, crushed, or 1 teaspoon dried basil, crushed. Stir until combined. Makes ½ cup (eight 1-tablespoon servings).

Nutrition facts per tablespoon: 100 cal., 11 g total fat (7 g sat. fat), 31 mg chol., 116 mg sodium, 0 g carbo., 0 g fiber, 0 g pro.

Herbed Feta Spread

In a small mixing bowl combine one 8-ounce package reduced-fat cream cheese, one 4-ounce package crumbled garlic-and-herb feta cheese, 1 tablespoon milk, and freshly ground pepper to taste. Beat with an electric mixer on medium

speed until mixture is well combined and of desired spreading consistency.

Line a 1½-cup mold or bowl with plastic wrap. Spoon cheese mixture into mold; spread evenly in mold, removing any air bubbles. Cover the top with plastic wrap and chill until ready to serve, up to 3 days. To serve, unwrap and invert molded cheese mixture onto serving platter. Carefully remove the plastic wrap. If desired, garnish with snipped fresh herbs and/or fresh herb sprigs. Makes about 1½ cups (twenty-four 1-tablespoon servings).

Nutrition facts per tablespoon: 37 cal., 3 g total fat (2 g sat. fat), 12 mg chol., 91 mg sodium, 1 g carbo., 0 g fiber, 2 g pro.

Parmesan-Garlic Butter

In a bowl beat ½ cup softened butter or margarine, ⅓ cup grated parmesan cheese, and ¼ teaspoon garlic powder with an electric mixer until smooth. Stir in 2 tablespoons snipped fresh parsley or 2 teaspoons dried parsley flakes. Cover and chill. Bring to room temperature before serving. Makes ⅔ cup (ten 1-tablespoon servings).

Nutrition facts per tablespoon: 96 cal., 10 g total fat (6 g sat. fat), 27 mg chol., 155 mg sodium, 0 g carbo., 0 g fiber, 2 g pro.

Pesto-Cream Cheese Spread

In an airtight container or bowl combine one 8-ounce package softened cream cheese and one 7-ounce container refrigerated pesto sauce. Stir together just until combined. Cover and chill until ready to serve, or up to 1 week. (To tote, pack in storage container on ice.) Let stand for 30 minutes for easier spreading. Stir spread before using. Makes 1½ cups (twenty-four 1-tablespoon servings).

Nutrition facts per tablespoon: 76 cal., 7 g total fat (2 g sat. fat), 11 mg chol., 73 mg sodium, 1 g carbo., 0 g fiber, 1 g pro.

CHOCOLATE ORANGE BRAID

Prep time: 35 minutes   **Rise time:** 1 hour   **Bake time:** 35 minutes

Nutrition facts per slice: 120 calories, 3 g total fat (1 g saturated fat), 9 mg cholesterol, 96 mg sodium, 21 g carbohydrate, 0 g fiber, 3 g protein.

1½-POUND (24 slices)	INGREDIENTS	2-POUND (30 slices)
¾ cup	milk	1 cup
1	egg(s)	2
¼ cup	margarine or butter	⅓ cup
2 tablespoons	water	3 tablespoons
3 cups	bread flour	4 cups
⅓ cup	sugar	½ cup
⅓ cup	unsweetened cocoa powder	½ cup
1 tablespoon	finely shredded orange peel	4 teaspoons
¾ teaspoon	salt	1 teaspoon
1¼ teaspoons	active dry yeast or bread machine yeast	1½ teaspoons
	Chocolate Powdered Sugar Glaze	

DIRECTIONS

☞ Select loaf size. Add all ingredients, except the Chocolate Powdered Sugar Glaze, to the machine according to the manufacturer's directions. Select dough cycle. When cycle is complete, remove dough from machine. Punch down. Cover and let rest 10 minutes.

☞ *For the 1½-pound recipe:* Divide dough into thirds. On a lightly floured surface, roll each portion into a 16-inch-long rope. To shape, line up the ropes, 1 inch apart, on a lightly greased baking sheet. Starting in the middle, loosely braid by bringing the left rope under the center rope. Bring the right rope under the new center rope. Repeat to end. On the other end, braid by bringing the outside ropes alternately over the center rope to center. Press ends together; tuck under. Cover and let rise in a warm place about 1 hour or until nearly double.

☞ Bake in a 325° oven for 35 to 40 minutes or until braid sounds hollow when lightly tapped. If necessary, loosely cover with foil the last 10 to 15 minutes to prevent overbrowning. Remove from baking sheet; cool on a rack. Drizzle with Chocolate Powdered Sugar Glaze.

☞ *For the 2-pound recipe:* Prepare as above, except divide the dough into 6 portions. Roll each portion of dough into a 16-inch-long rope; form 2 braids, using 3 ropes for each. Continue as above.

☞ *Chocolate Powdered Sugar Glaze:* In a small mixing bowl stir together 1 cup sifted powdered sugar, 1 tablespoon unsweetened cocoa powder, and ½ teaspoon vanilla. Stir in enough milk (1 to 2 tablespoons) to make a glaze of drizzling consistency.

WHITE CHOCOLATE CRANBERRY LOAF

The sensational combination of white chocolate with cranberries produces a taste so sublime, it's simply irresistible. Make this bread a sweet beginning—or ending—to your day.

DIRECTIONS

☞ Select the loaf size. Add the ingredients to the machine according to the manufacturer's directions. Select the basic white bread cycle.

☞ *NOTE: For the 1½-pound loaf, the bread machine pan must have a capacity of 10 cups or more. For the 2-pound loaf, the bread machine pan must have a capacity of 12 cups or more.

☞ **NOTE: Our Test Kitchen recommends 1 egg and 2 tablespoons sugar for either size recipe.

That's a fact!

Are white baking bars and white chocolate the same? Bakers use them interchangeably. Both products contain cocoa butter, sugar, milk, and vanilla or vanillan, but white baking bars are less costly than white chocolate and less temperamental. Neither are true chocolate, because they lack chocolate liquor, a byproduct of processed cocoa beans.

Prep time: 15 minutes

Nutrition facts per slice: 129 calories, 3 g total fat (1 g saturated fat), 14 mg cholesterol, 109 mg sodium, 22 g carbohydrate, 1 g fiber, 4 g protein.

1½-POUND★ (18 slices)	INGREDIENTS	2-POUND★ (22 slices)
¾ cup	milk	1 cup
1	egg★★	1
2 tablespoons	water	3 tablespoons
1 tablespoon	margarine or butter	4 teaspoons
1 teaspoon	vanilla	1½ teaspoons
3 cups	bread flour	4 cups
2 tablespoons	sugar★★	2 tablespoons
¾ teaspoon	salt	1 teaspoon
1 teaspoon	active dry yeast or bread machine yeast	1¼ teaspoons
2 ounces	white baking bar, chopped	3 ounces
⅓ cup	dried cranberries	½ cup

119

CANDY CANE LOAF

Kids will love this whimsical loaf. Twist together two ropes of dough —one is coated in red sugar— and gently curve into a cane shape. Spread with peppermint icing—yum!

Prep time: 25 minutes   **Rise time:** 1 hour   **Bake time:** 25 minutes
Nutrition facts per slice: 154 calories, 3 g total fat (1 g saturated fat), 12 mg cholesterol, 125 mg sodium, 27 g carbohydrate, 1 g fiber, 3 g protein.

1½-POUND (18 slices)	INGREDIENTS	2-POUND (24 slices)
⅓ cup	milk	½ cup
¼ cup	water*	¼ cup
1	egg(s)	2
¼ cup	margarine or butter, cut up	⅓ cup
3 cups	bread flour	4 cups
¼ cup	sugar	⅓ cup
¾ teaspoon	salt	1 teaspoon
2 teaspoons	active dry yeast or bread machine yeast	2½ teaspoons
3 tablespoons	red-colored sugar	¼ cup
	Peppermint Powdered Sugar Icing	

120

DIRECTIONS

☞ Select loaf size. Add the first 8 ingredients to the machine according to manufacturer's directions. Select the dough cycle. When cycle is complete, remove dough from machine. Punch down. Cover and let rest 10 minutes.

☞ Divide 1½-pound dough in half. On a lightly floured surface, roll each half into an 18-inch-long rope. (Divide 2-pound dough in half; roll each half into a 24-inch-long rope.) Roll 1 of the ropes in red sugar. (If the sugar does not stick, spray the dough lightly with nonstick coating and reroll in sugar.) Line up both ropes, 1 inch apart, on a greased baking sheet. Twist the ropes together; press ends together. Curve one end to form a cane shape. Cover and let rise in a warm place about 1 hour or until nearly double.

☞ Bake in a 350° oven about 25 minutes or until bread sounds hollow when tapped. Remove; cool. Frost the plain portion with Peppermint Powdered Sugar Icing.

☞ *Peppermint Powdered Sugar Icing:* Combine 1 cup sifted powdered sugar, 1 tablespoon milk, and a few drops peppermint or almond extract. Stir in a little milk, if needed, to make an icing of spreading consistency.

☞ ***NOTE:** Our Test Kitchen recommends ¼ cup water for either size recipe.

Similar to many sweets sold in the Christmas markets of southern Germany, this fruit- and nut-studded loaf tastes great with coffee or traditional Glüh-wein (glew-vighn), a mulled wine.

BAVARIAN CHRISTMAS BREAD

DIRECTIONS

☞ Select the loaf size. Add all ingredients, exept the Powdered Sugar Icing, to machine according to manufacturer's directions. Select the basic white bread cycle. If desired, drizzle cooled loaf with Powdered Sugar Icing.

☞ *Powdered Sugar Icing:* In a small mixing bowl stir together ⅔ cup sifted powdered sugar and ½ teaspoon vanilla. Stir in enough milk (2 to 3 teaspoons) to make an icing of drizzling consistency.

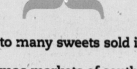

Did you know?

Kirschwasser (or kirsch) is a crystal-clear brandy infused with the flavor of cherries. The German name means "cherry water." The neighboring regions of France, Germany, and Switzerland have perfected the art of distilling this fine fruit spirit. Enjoy kirschwasser as an after-dinner digestive or in recipes.

Prep time: 15 minutes

Nutrition facts per slice: 150 calories, 4 g total fat (1 g saturated fat), 1 mg cholesterol, 123 mg sodium, 25 g carbohydrate, 1 g fiber, 4 g protein.

1½-POUND (16 slices)	INGREDIENTS 	2-POUND (22 slices)
¾ cup	milk	1 cup
¼ cup	water	⅓ cup
2 tablespoons	margarine or butter, cut up	3 tablespoons
1 tablespoon	kirsch or milk	2 tablespoons
3 cups	bread flour	4 cups
2 tablespoons	sugar	3 tablespoons
¾ teaspoon	salt	1 teaspoon
½ teaspoon	ground mace	¾ teaspoon
¼ teaspoon	ground cardamom	½ teaspoon
1 teaspoon	active dry yeast or bread machine yeast	1¼ teaspoons
½ cup	snipped pitted prunes or dark raisins	⅔ cup
⅓ cup	chopped hazelnuts	½ cup
	Powdered Sugar Icing (optional)	

CHERRY CHRISTMAS COFFEE BREAD

DIRECTIONS

☞ Select the recipe size. Add the first 9 ingredients to the machine according to the manufacturer's directions. Select the dough cycle. When cycle is complete, remove dough from machine. Punch down. Cover and let rest for 10 minutes.

☞ Meanwhile, for filling, in a bowl combine ½ or ⅔ cup sugar, 1 or 2 tablespoons bread flour, and 1 or 1½ teaspoons cinnamon. With a pastry blender, cut in 3 tablespoons or ¼ cup margarine or butter until crumbly. Set aside.

☞ *For the 1½-pound recipe:* Divide the dough in half. On a lightly floured surface, roll 1 half into a 12×6-inch rectangle. Sprinkle the rectangle with half of the filling, then fold in half to make a 12×3-inch rectangle. Cut into twelve 3×1-inch strips.

☞ Twist the strips. Arrange twisted strips on a greased large baking sheet to form a tree shape. Use 10 strips for the lower branches, placing cut ends toward the center, and one strip for the base. Cut remaining strip in half; use for top branches. Repeat with remaining dough, forming a second tree shape on another baking sheet. Cover; let rise in a warm place about 30 minutes or until nearly double.

☞ Bake in a 375° oven for 12 to 15 minutes or until golden brown. Remove from baking sheets; cool on wire racks. Drizzle with Powdered Sugar Glaze. Garnish with cherries.

☞ *For the 2-pound recipe:* Prepare and shape as above, except divide the dough and filling into thirds and form 3 tree shapes.

☞ *Powdered Sugar Glaze:* In a small bowl stir together 1 cup sifted powdered sugar and ½ teaspoon vanilla. Stir in enough milk (3 to 4 teaspoons) to make a glaze of drizzling consistency.

☞ ***NOTE:** Our Test Kitchen recommends 1 egg for either size recipe.

Prep time: 40 minutes   **Rise time:** 30 minutes   **Bake time:** 12 minutes
Nutrition facts per serving: 257 calories, 6 g total fat (1 g saturated fat), 14 mg cholesterol, 170 mg sodium, 46 g carbohydrate, 1 g fiber, 5 g protein.

1½-POUND (16 servings)	INGREDIENTS	2-POUND (24 servings)
¾ cup	milk	1 cup
¼ cup	water	⅓ cup
1	egg*	1
¼ cup	margarine or butter, cut up	⅓ cup
3½ cups	bread flour	4⅔ cups
¼ cup	sugar	⅓ cup
¾ teaspoon	salt	1 teaspoon
1 teaspoon	active dry yeast or bread machine yeast	1¼ teaspoons
1 cup	dried tart cherries	1⅓ cups
½ cup	sugar	⅔ cup
1 tablespoon	bread flour	2 tablespoons
1 teaspoon	ground cinnamon	1½ teaspoons
3 tablespoons	margarine or butter	¼ cup
	Powdered Sugar Glaze	
	Halved candied red and green cherries	

123

ST. LUCIA BUNS

In December the Swedes honor the Italian Saint Lucia in a celebration. The elaborate festivities always include these saffron and raisin buns.

Prep time: 40 minutes **Rise time:** 30 minutes **Bake time:** 10 minutes
Nutrition facts per bun: 196 calories, 6 g total fat (1 g saturated fat), 37 mg cholesterol, 198 mg sodium, 30 g carbohydrate, 1 g fiber, 6 g protein.

1½-POUND (12 buns)	INGREDIENTS	2-POUND (16 buns)
¾ cup	milk	1 cup
1	egg(s)	2
¼ cup	margarine or butter, cut up	⅓ cup
3 cups	bread flour	4 cups
3 tablespoons	packed brown sugar	¼ cup
1½ teaspoons	finely shredded orange peel	2 teaspoons
¾ teaspoon	salt	1 teaspoon
⅛ teaspoon	thread saffron, crushed	¼ teaspoon
1 teaspoon	active dry yeast or bread machine yeast	1½ teaspoons
1	beaten egg	1
1 tablespoon	water	1 tablespoon
12	raisins	16
	Granulated sugar	

DIRECTIONS

☞ Select the recipe size. Add the first 9 ingredients to the machine according to the manufacturer's directions. Select the dough cycle. When cycle is complete, remove dough from machine. Punch down. Cover and let rest for 10 minutes.

☞ Divide the 1½-pound dough into 24 portions (divide the 2-pound dough into 32 portions). On a lightly floured surface, roll each portion into a smooth 10-inch-long rope. Form each rope into an "S" shape and curve each end into a coil. Cross 2 of these "S"-shape ropes to form an X. Repeat with the remaining "S"-shape ropes. Place ropes on a greased large baking sheet. Cover and let rise in a warm place about 30 minutes or until nearly double.

☞ In a small bowl combine the beaten egg and water; brush over buns. Place 1 raisin in the center of each coil. Sprinkle the buns with granulated sugar. Bake in a 375° oven about 10 minutes or until golden brown. Remove from baking sheet; cool on a wire rack.

DIRECTIONS

☞ Select recipe size. Add first 8 ingredients to the machine according to manufacturer's directions. Select the dough cycle. When cycle is complete, remove dough from machine. Punch down. Cover and let rest 10 minutes.

☞ Meanwhile, for filling, in a small mixing bowl combine the ¼ or ⅓ cup sugar and cinnamon. Add the candied fruits and almonds; toss gently to coat. Set aside.

☞ *For the 1½-pound recipe:* On a lightly floured surface, roll dough into a 20×12-inch rectangle. Spread with the softened margarine or butter and sprinkle with the filling. Starting from a long side, roll up into a spiral. Moisten edge; pinch firmly to seal. Place, seam down, on a greased, foil-lined baking sheet. Bring the ends together to form a ring. Moisten ends; pinch together to seal ring. Flatten slightly. Using a sharp knife, make 12 cuts around the edge, cutting about two-thirds of the way to the center.

☞ Cover and let rise in a warm place for 40 to 50 minutes or until nearly double. Bake in a 350° oven for 25 to 30 minutes or until bread sounds hollow when lightly tapped. If necessary, loosely cover with foil last 15 minutes to prevent overbrowning. Remove from baking sheet; cool on a wire rack. Drizzle with Orange Icing.

☞ *For the 2-pound recipe:* Prepare as above, except divide dough in half. Roll each half into a 15×10-inch rectangle. Spread each rectangle with half of the softened margarine or butter and sprinkle each with half of the filling. Form 2 rings on 2 greased, foil-lined baking sheets; make 10 cuts around the edge of each ring. Continue as above.

☞ *Orange Icing:* Stir together 1 cup sifted powdered sugar and ¼ teaspoon vanilla. Stir in enough orange juice (3 to 4 teaspoons) to make an icing of drizzling consistency.

☞ **★NOTE:** Our Test Kitchen recommends ¼ cup water and 2 teaspoons cinnamon for either size recipe.

THREE KINGS' RING

Prep time: 30 minutes   **Rise time:** 40 minutes   **Bake time:** 25 minutes
Nutrition facts per serving: 316 calories, 9 g total fat (1 g saturated fat), 19 mg cholesterol, 201 mg sodium, 54 g carbohydrate, 1 g fiber, 6 g protein.

1½-POUND (12 servings)	INGREDIENTS	2-POUND (20 servings)
½ cup	milk	⅔ cup
¼ cup	water*	¼ cup
1	egg(s)	2
2 tablespoons	margarine or butter, cut up	3 tablespoons
3 cups	bread flour	4 cups
⅓ cup	sugar	½ cup
¾ teaspoon	salt	1 teaspoon
1½ teaspoons	active dry yeast or bread machine yeast	2 teaspoons
¼ cup	sugar	⅓ cup
2 teaspoons	ground cinnamon*	2 teaspoons
¾ cup	diced mixed candied fruits and peels	1 cup
½ cup	chopped almonds, toasted	⅔ cup
3 tablespoons	margarine or butter, softened	¼ cup
	Orange Icing	

125

PANETTONE

Italians serve panettone (pronounced pahn-EHT-tohn)—a fruit-loaded bread—at Christmas and other special occasions. A sweet wine, such as sauterne, is a nice accompaniment.

Prep time: 20 minutes   **Rise time:** 40 minutes   **Bake time:** 35 minutes
Nutrition facts per serving: 155 calories, 4 g total fat (1 g saturated fat), 14 mg cholesterol, 127 mg sodium, 26 g carbohydrate, 1 g fiber, 4 g protein.

1½-POUND (16 servings)	INGREDIENTS	2-POUND (22 servings)
⅔ cup	milk	¾ cup
¼ cup	water	⅓ cup
1	egg*	1
2 tablespoons	butter or margarine, cut up	3 tablespoons
1 tablespoon	honey	4 teaspoons
1 teaspoon	vanilla	1½ teaspoons
3 cups	bread flour	4 cups
1½ teaspoons	anise seed, crushed	2 teaspoons
¾ teaspoon	salt	1 teaspoon
¼ teaspoon	ground cloves	½ teaspoon
1¼ teaspoons	active dry yeast or bread machine yeast	1½ teaspoons
¼ cup	dark raisins	⅓ cup
¼ cup	dried currants	⅓ cup
¼ cup	diced candied citron	⅓ cup
¼ cup	chopped pecans or walnuts	⅓ cup

DIRECTIONS

☞ Select the recipe size. Add the ingredients to the machine according to manufacturer's directions. Select the dough cycle. When cycle is complete, remove dough from machine. Punch down. Cover and let rest 10 minutes.

☞ On a lightly floured surface, roll dough into a 22-inch-long rope. Place in a greased 10-inch fluted tube pan. Cover; let rise in a warm place for 40 to 50 minutes or until nearly double. Bake in a 350° oven for 35 to 40 minutes or until bread sounds hollow when lightly tapped. Remove from pan; cool on a rack.

☞ ***NOTE:** Our Test Kitchen recommends 1 egg for either size recipe.

Good Advice!

The tall, cylindrical metal mold for panettone measures about 7½ inches in diameter by 4 inches high, but you can substitute an extra-deep cake pan. New from Italy are the ovenproof paper panettone molds used by professional bakers that serve as pan and gift box in one. Kitchenware stores and some catalogs carry both types of molds, particularly at Christmas.

This wreath does a typical wreath one better because it not only looks and smells wonderful, it also is fully edible. Pass the Herb Butter (see recipe, page 117) for a change of taste.

DIRECTIONS

☞ Select the recipe size. Add the first 9 ingredients to the machine according to the manufacturer's directions. Select the dough cycle. When cycle is complete, remove dough from machine. Punch down. Cover and let rest for 10 minutes.

☞ *For the 1½-pound recipe:* Divide the dough in half. On a lightly floured surface, roll each half into a 25-inch-long rope. Line up ropes 1 inch apart. Loosely twist the ropes together. Bring ends together to form a ring. Moisten ends; pinch together to seal ring. Transfer to a lightly greased large baking sheet. Cover and let rise in a warm place about 45 minutes or until nearly double. Combine egg yolk and 1 tablespoon water; brush over ring. Bake in a 350° oven for 20 to 30 minutes or until golden brown. Remove from baking sheet; cool on a wire rack.

☞ *For the 2-pound recipe:* Prepare as above, except divide dough into fourths. Roll each fourth into a 20-inch-long rope. Form 2 rings; transfer to 2 lightly greased baking sheets. Continue as above.

☞ ***NOTE:** Our Test Kitchen recommends 2 eggs for either size recipe.

SEEDED CHALLAH WREATH

Prep time: 30 minutes   **Rise time:** 45 minutes   **Bake time:** 20 minutes
Nutrition facts per serving: 132 calories, 3 g total fat (1 g saturated fat), 40 mg cholesterol, 110 mg sodium, 21 g carbohydrate, 1 g fiber, 4 g protein.

1½-POUND (16 servings)	INGREDIENTS	2-POUND (22 servings)
¾ cup	water	1 cup
2	eggs*	2
2 tablespoons	cooking oil	3 tablespoons
2¼ cups	bread flour	2½ cups
1 cup	whole wheat flour	1½ cups
2 tablespoons	brown sugar	3 tablespoons
1 tablespoon	poppy, flax, or dill seed	4 teaspoons
¾ teaspoon	salt	1 teaspoon
1 teaspoon	active dry yeast or bread machine yeast	1¼ teaspoons
1	egg yolk	1
1 tablespoon	water	1 tablespoon

127

FESTIVE 5-SPICE BREAD

Rich with sour cream and chockful of dried fruits, this 5-spice scented loaf is perfect for gift-giving. Package in tinted cellophane, tie with colorful ribbon, and it's a wrap!

Prep time: 15 minutes

Nutrition facts per slice: 175 calories, 3 g total fat (1 g saturated fat), 3 mg cholesterol, 116 mg sodium, 34 g carbohydrate, 1 g fiber, 4 g protein.

DIRECTIONS

☞ Select loaf size. Add ingredients, except the glaze, to machine according to manufacturer's directions. Select basic white bread cycle.

☞ *Powdered Sugar Glaze:* In a small bowl stir together 1 cup sifted powdered sugar and 1 teaspoon vanilla. Stir in enough milk (4 to 6 teaspoons) to make a glaze of drizzling consistency.

1½-POUND (16 slices)	INGREDIENTS	2-POUND (22 slices)
½ cup	dairy sour cream	⅔ cup
½ cup	water	⅔ cup
1 tablespoon	margarine or butter	4 teaspoons
1 teaspoon	vanilla	1½ teaspoons
3 cups	bread flour	4 cups
3 tablespoons	sugar	¼ cup
¾ teaspoon	salt	1 teaspoon
½ teaspoon	5-spice powder	¾ teaspoon
1¼ teaspoons	active dry yeast or bread machine yeast	1½ teaspoons
¾ cup	snipped mixed dried berries and cherries	1 cup
	Powdered Sugar Glaze	

That's a fact!

While the number "five" figures prominently in the name of Chinese five-spice powder, some blends have up to six or seven spices, or as few as four. A typical mix includes ground anise seed, star anise, clove, cinnamon, and Szechwan peppercorns. Chinese markets stock it, as do most supermarkets.

DIRECTIONS

☞ Select loaf size. Add first 7 ingredients to the machine according to manufacturer's directions. Select dough cycle. When cycle is complete, remove dough from machine. Punch down. Cover; let rest 10 minutes.

☞ *For the 1½-pound recipe:* Set aside one-fourth of the dough. Shape remaining dough into a ball; place in a greased 2-quart casserole. Combine egg yolk and 1 tablespoon water; brush lightly over loaf.

☞ Divide reserved dough into fourths; roll each portion into a 10-inch-long rope. Twist 2 ropes together; place slightly off center across top of loaf, tucking ends under. Repeat with the remaining 2 ropes, placing parallel to first twist on top of loaf. Cover; let rise in a warm place about 30 minutes or until nearly double. Brush with more egg yolk mixture.

☞ Bake in a 325° oven for 40 to 45 minutes or until bread sounds hollow when lightly tapped. If necessary, loosely cover with foil last 10 to 15 minutes to prevent overbrowning. Remove from casserole; cool on a wire rack.

☞ *For the 2-pound recipe:* Prepare as above, except divide dough into thirds. Shape 2 portions into balls; place each portion into a greased 1-quart casserole. Brush with egg yolk mixture. Divide remaining portion into 8 pieces; shape into 8-inch-long ropes. Form 4 twisted ropes, placing 2 on top of each loaf. Continue as directed above.

ITALIAN HOLIDAY LOAF

Prep time: 40 minutes **Rise time:** 30 minutes **Bake time:** 40 minutes

Nutrition facts per slice: 136 calories, 4 g total fat (1 g saturated fat), 27 mg cholesterol, 139 mg sodium, 21 g carbohydrate, 1 g fiber, 4 g protein.

1½-POUND (16 slices)	INGREDIENTS	2-POUND (22 slices)
⅔ cup	water	¾ cup
1	egg(s)	2
¼ cup	margarine or butter, cut up	⅓ cup
3 cups	bread flour	4 cups
3 tablespoons	sugar	¼ cup
¾ teaspoon	salt	1 teaspoon
1 teaspoon	active dry yeast or bread machine yeast	1¼ teaspoons
1	egg yolk	1
1 tablespoon	water	1 tablespoon

129

ALMOND FILLED HEARTS

Prep time: 50 minutes   **Rise time:** 30 minutes   **Bake time:** 12 minutes

Nutrition facts per heart: 324 calories, 10 g total fat (2 g saturated fat), 44 mg cholesterol, 206 mg sodium, 49 g carbohydrate, 1 g fiber, 10 g protein.

1½-POUND (10 hearts)	INGREDIENTS	2-POUND (12 hearts)
⅔ cup	milk	1 cup
1	egg*	1
2 tablespoons	margarine or butter, cut up	3 tablespoons
3 cups	bread flour	4 cups
2 tablespoons	granulated sugar	3 tablespoons
¾ teaspoon	salt	1 teaspoon
1¼ teaspoons	active dry yeast or bread machine yeast	1½ teaspoons
	Almond Filling	
	Milk (optional)	
	Red-colored or plain coarse sugar (optional)	

DIRECTIONS

☞ Select the recipe size. Add the first 7 ingredients to the machine according to the manufacturer's directions. Select the dough cycle. When cycle is complete, remove dough from machine. Punch down. Cover and let rest for 10 minutes.

☞ *For the 1½-pound recipe:* On a lightly floured surface, roll dough into a 22½×10-inch rectangle. Cut into ten 10×2¼-inch strips. Divide Almond Filling into 10 portions; roll each portion into a 9½-inch-long rope. Place a rope lengthwise down center of each strip of dough. Fold dough in half lengthwise to enclose filling; moisten edges of dough; seal. Place, seams down, on greased large baking sheets. Form each filled strip into a heart shape; moisten ends and pinch together at base of heart to seal.

☞ Cover and let rise in a warm place for 30 to 40 minutes or until nearly double. If desired, brush with a little milk and sprinkle with coarse sugar. Bake in a 350° oven for 12 to 15 minutes or until golden. Remove from baking sheets; cool on wire racks.

☞ *For the 2-pound recipe:* Prepare as above, except roll dough into a 27×10-inch rectangle. Cut into twelve 10×2¼-inch strips. Divide the Almond Filling into 12 portions. Continue as above.

☞ *Almond Filling:* In a medium mixing bowl beat together one 8-ounce can almond paste, crumbled; ¼ cup granulated sugar; 1 tablespoon all-purpose flour; and 1 egg yolk until smooth. (Or, combine the ingredients in a food processor bowl. Cover and process until the mixture clings together.)

☞ **★NOTE:** Our Test Kitchen recommends 1 egg for either size recipe.

HOLIDAY CREAM-FILLED BUNS

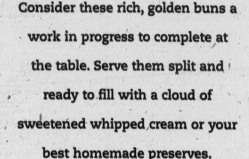

Consider these rich, golden buns a work in progress to complete at the table. Serve them split and ready to fill with a cloud of sweetened whipped cream or your best homemade preserves.

Prep time: 30 minutes **Rise time:** 20 minutes **Bake time:** 15 minutes

Nutrition facts per bun: 229 calories, 8 g total fat (3 g saturated fat), 13 mg cholesterol, 192 mg sodium, 33 g carbohydrate, 1 g fiber, 5 g protein.

1½-POUND (12 buns)	INGREDIENTS	2-POUND (16 buns)
⅔ cup	milk	¾ cup
¼ cup	water	⅓ cup
¼ cup	margarine or butter, cut up	⅓ cup
3 cups	bread flour	4 cups
⅓ cup	granulated sugar	½ cup
¾ teaspoon	salt	1 teaspoon
1¼ teaspoons	active dry yeast or bread machine yeast	1½ teaspoons
	Sifted powdered sugar	
	Cream Filling or seedless red raspberry or strawberry jam	

DIRECTIONS

☞ Select the recipe size. Add the first 7 ingredients to the machine according to the manufacturer's directions. Select the dough cycle. When cycle is complete, remove dough from machine. Punch down. Cover and let rest for 10 minutes.

☞ Divide the 1½-pound dough into 12 portions (divide the 2-pound dough into 16 portions). Using lightly floured hands, shape each portion into a smooth ball, tucking ends under. Place about 2 inches apart on a greased large baking sheet. Cover and let rise in a warm place for 20 to 30 minutes or until nearly double.

☞ Bake in a 375° oven about 15 minutes or until golden brown. Immediately sprinkle tops lightly with powdered sugar. Remove from baking sheet; cool on wire racks.

☞ To serve, cut a slit in each bun. Fill each with about 1 teaspoon Cream Filling or jam.

☞ *Cream Filling:* In a chilled bowl combine ⅓ cup whipping cream and 1 tablespoon sugar. Beat with chilled beaters of an electric mixer on medium speed or with a rotary beater until soft peaks form. By hand, fold in ⅓ cup dairy sour cream.

DIRECTIONS

☞ Select recipe size. Add first 8 ingredients to the machine according to manufacturer's directions. Select the dough cycle. When cycle is complete, remove dough from machine. Punch down. Cover and let rest 10 minutes.

☞ Meanwhile, for filling, in a small bowl stir together the candied fruits and 3 tablespoons or ¼ cup sugar.

☞ *For the 1½-pound recipe:* On a lightly floured surface, roll dough into a 16×12-inch rectangle. Brush with melted margarine or butter and sprinkle with filling. Starting from a short side, roll up into a spiral; seal edge. With a sharp knife, diagonally cut the roll into 12 slices. Set aside the 2 end slices. On a greased large baking sheet, arrange remaining slices, cut sides down, in a circle with pointed ends out, overlapping slices slightly and leaving a 4-inch circle in the center. Place the 2 end pieces in the center. Cover and let rise in a warm place for 30 to 40 minutes or until nearly double. Combine the egg yolk and 1 teaspoon water; brush over circle.

☞ Bake in a 350° oven about 25 minutes or until bread sounds hollow when lightly tapped. If necessary, loosely cover with foil last 10 minutes to prevent overbrowning. Remove from baking sheet; cool on a wire rack. Drizzle with Powdered Sugar Icing.

☞ *For the 2-pound recipe:* Prepare as above, except divide dough in half. Roll each half into a 12-inch square. Brush each square with half of the melted margarine and sprinkle each with half of the filling. Form 2 circles on 2 greased large baking sheets, leaving 3-inch circles in centers. Continue as above.

☞ *Powdered Sugar Icing:* Stir together 1 cup sifted powdered sugar and ½ teaspoon vanilla. Stir in enough milk (1 to 2 tablespoons) to make an icing of drizzling consistency.

☞ *★NOTE:* Our Test Kitchen recommends 1 egg for either size recipe.

POINSETTIA BREAD

Prep time: 25 minutes   **Rise time:** 30 minutes   **Bake time:** 25 minutes
Nutrition facts per serving: 209 calories, 6 g total fat (1 g saturated fat), 27 mg cholesterol, 161 mg sodium, 35 g carbohydrate, 1 g fiber, 4 g protein.

1½-POUND (16 servings)	INGREDIENTS	2-POUND (24 servings)
⅔ cup	milk	1 cup
1	egg★	1
¼ cup	margarine or butter, cut up	⅓ cup
2 tablespoons	water	¼ cup
3 cups	bread flour	4 cups
¼ cup	sugar	⅓ cup
¾ teaspoon	salt	1 teaspoon
2 teaspoons	active dry yeast or bread machine yeast	2½ teaspoons
½ cup	mixed candied fruits and peels, finely chopped	¾ cup
3 tablespoons	sugar	¼ cup
2 tablespoons	margarine or butter, melted	3 tablespoons
1	egg yolk	1
1 teaspoon	water	1 teaspoon
	Powdered Sugar Icing	

133

FRUITED CHRISTMAS WREATH

Prep time: 40 minutes **Rise time:** 30 minutes **Bake time:** 25 minutes

Nutrition facts per serving: 343 calories, 12 g total fat (2 g saturated fat), 19 mg cholesterol, 225 mg sodium, 55 g carbohydrate, 1 g fiber, 6 g protein.

1½-POUND (12 servings)	INGREDIENTS	2-POUND (16 servings)
¾ cup	milk*	¾ cup
1	egg(s)	2
¼ cup	margarine or butter	⅓ cup
3 cups	bread flour	4 cups
¼ cup	sugar	⅓ cup
¾ teaspoon	salt	1 teaspoon
¼ teaspoon	ground nutmeg	½ teaspoon
1¼ teaspoons	active dry yeast or bread machine yeast	1½ teaspoons
2 tablespoons	margarine or butter, melted*	2 tablespoons
	Fruit Filling	
	Powdered Sugar Glaze	

134

DIRECTIONS

☞ Select the recipe size. Add the first 8 ingredients to the machine according to the manufacturer's directions. Select the dough cycle. When cycle is complete, remove dough from machine. Punch down. Cover and let rest for 10 minutes.

☞ Divide the 1½-pound dough in half. On a lightly floured surface, roll each half into a 10-inch circle. (Divide 2-pound dough in half; roll each half into a 12-inch circle.) Place a circle of dough on a greased 12-inch pizza pan. Brush with some melted margarine or butter and spread with the Fruit Filling. Top with second circle of dough. Place a 2-inch-diameter glass, upright, in the center of the dough to use as a guide (the center remains intact). Cut the 1½-pound dough, cutting from the edge of dough just to the bottom of the glass, into 12 wedges (cut 2-pound dough into 16 wedges). Remove glass. Twist each wedge 2 times. Brush with remaining melted margarine. Cover; let rise in a warm place for 30 to 40 minutes or until nearly double.

☞ Bake in a 350° oven for 25 to 30 minutes or until golden and bread sounds hollow when lightly tapped. If necessary, loosely cover with foil last 10 minutes to prevent overbrowning. Remove from pan; cool slightly on a rack. Drizzle with Powdered Sugar Glaze.

☞ *Fruit Filling:* In a small saucepan combine one 6-ounce package mixed dried fruit bits and ½ cup orange juice. Bring to boiling; remove from heat. Cover and let stand for 10 minutes; drain. Stir in ¾ cup chopped pecans, ¼ cup sugar, and ½ teaspoon ground cinnamon. Transfer to small bowl; cover and chill until needed.

☞ *Powdered Sugar Glaze:* In a small mixing bowl stir together 1 cup sifted powdered sugar and enough milk (1 to 2 tablespoons) to make a glaze of drizzling consistency.

☞ ***NOTE:** Our Test Kitchen recommends ¾ cup milk and 2 tablespoons melted margarine or butter for either size recipe.

DIRECTIONS

☞ Select recipe size. Add first 8 ingredients to the machine according to manufacturer's directions. Select the dough cycle. When cycle is complete, remove dough from machine. Punch down. Cover and let rest 10 minutes.

☞ Meanwhile, for filling, combine the cranberries, granulated sugar, and the 2 or 3 tablespoons water. Bring to boiling; reduce heat. Cook, stirring often, for 2 to 3 minutes or until cranberry skins pop and mixture thickens slightly. Combine cornstarch and the 1 tablespoon or 4 teaspoons water; stir into mixture. Cook and stir until mixture is very thick and just begins to bubble. Remove from heat. Stir in orange marmalade; transfer to small bowl. Cover surface with plastic wrap; cool.

☞ *For the 1½-pound recipe:* Divide dough in half. On a lightly floured surface, roll 1 half into a 12-inch circle; cut circle into 8 wedges. Spread about 2 teaspoons filling onto each wedge. Starting at the wide end of each wedge, loosely roll toward the point. Arrange wedges, points down, on a greased large baking sheet to form a wreath shape. Repeat with the remaining dough, forming a wreath shape on another baking sheet. Cover; let rise in a warm place for 30 to 45 minutes or until nearly double. Bake in a 350° oven for 15 to 20 minutes or until golden brown. Remove; cool slightly on wire racks. Drizzle with Powdered Sugar Glaze. Sprinkle with nuts.

☞ *For the 2-pound recipe:* Prepare as above, except divide dough into thirds and roll into 10-inch circles. Cut each circle into 8 wedges; fill and roll up wedges. Form 2 wreaths on 2 greased large baking sheets, using 12 wedges for each wreath. Continue as above.

☞ *Powdered Sugar Glaze:* Stir together 1 cup sifted powdered sugar and ½ teaspoon vanilla. Stir in enough milk (3 to 4 teaspoons) to make a glaze of drizzling consistency.

☞ *NOTE: Our Test Kitchen recommends 1 egg for either size recipe.

CRANBERRY ORANGE WREATH

Prep time: 35 minutes **Rise time:** 30 minutes **Bake time:** 15 minutes

Nutrition facts per serving: 185 calories, 3 g total fat (1 g saturated fat), 14 mg cholesterol, 135 mg sodium, 35 g carbohydrate, 1 g fiber, 4 g protein.

1½-POUND (16 servings)	INGREDIENTS	2-POUND (24 servings)
⅓ cup	milk	½ cup
⅓ cup	water	½ cup
1	egg*	1
3 tablespoons	margarine or butter, cut up	¼ cup
3 cups	bread flour	4 cups
⅓ cup	packed brown sugar	½ cup
¾ teaspoon	salt	1 teaspoon
1 teaspoon	active dry yeast or bread machine yeast	1¼ teaspoons
¾ cup	cranberries	1 cup
2 tablespoons	granulated sugar	3 tablespoons
2 tablespoons	water	3 tablespoons
1 tablespoon	cornstarch	4 teaspoons
1 tablespoon	cold water	4 teaspoons
¼ cup	orange marmalade	⅓ cup
	Powdered Sugar Glaze	
	Chopped almonds, toasted	

135

CORNUCOPIA ROLLS

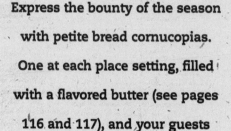

Express the bounty of the season with petite bread cornucopias. One at each place setting, filled with a flavored butter (see pages 116 and 117), and your guests will be charmed.

Prep time: 40 minutes **Rise time:** 20 minutes **Bake time:** 15 minutes
Nutrition facts per roll: 111 calories, 3 g total fat (1 g saturated fat), 2 mg cholesterol, 116 mg sodium, 17 g carbohydrate, 1 g fiber, 4 g protein.

1½-POUND (18 rolls)	INGREDIENTS	2-POUND (24 rolls)
1 cup	water	1⅓ cups
2 tablespoons	milk	3 tablespoons
2 tablespoons	olive oil or cooking oil	3 tablespoons
2½ cups	bread flour	3⅓ cups
½ cup	yellow cornmeal	⅔ cup
½ cup	grated Parmesan cheese	⅔ cup
½ teaspoon	salt	¾ teaspoon
1 teaspoon	active dry yeast or bread machine yeast	1¼ teaspoons
1	slightly beaten egg white	1
1 tablespoon	water	1 tablespoon

DIRECTIONS

☞ Select recipe size. Add first 8 ingredients to the machine according to manufacturer's directions. Select the dough cycle. When cycle is complete, remove dough from machine. Punch down. Cover and let rest 10 minutes.

☞ Meanwhile, cut eighteen (or twenty-four) 9-inch squares from heavy foil. Fold each square in half diagonally to form a triangle. Hold triangle with long side at bottom. Roll a lower corner over to meet top point, forming a cone. Bring other lower corner around front of cone.

☞ Divide the 1½-pound dough into 18 portions (divide the 2-pound dough into 24 portions). On a lightly floured surface, roll each portion into a 16-inch-long rope. Wrap each rope around a foil cone, starting at the lower point and coiling dough around the cone to completely cover foil. Place on greased large baking sheets.

☞ Combine egg white and 1 tablespoon water; brush over rolls. Cover and let rise in a warm place about 20 minutes or until nearly double. Bake in a 350° oven for 15 to 20 minutes or until golden brown. Remove foil cones; cool rolls on wire racks.

Moist and tender, with the nutty taste of wheat germ, these flavorful rolls are sure to be a hit at your Thanksgiving table. Serve warm with Orange-Ginger Butter (see recipe, page 116).

SWEET POTATO PULL-APART ROLLS

DIRECTIONS

☞ Select the recipe size. Add the first 10 ingredients to the machine according to the manufacturer's directions. Select the dough cycle. When cycle is complete, remove dough from machine. Punch down. Cover and let rest for 10 minutes.

☞ *For the 1½-pound recipe:* Divide dough into 16 portions. Shape each portion into a smooth ball. Divide balls between 2 lightly greased 8×1½-inch round baking pans. Cover and let rise in a warm place about 30 minutes or until nearly double. Combine egg white and water; brush over rolls. Sprinkle with additional wheat germ. Bake in a 375° oven about 18 minutes or until lightly browned. Cool in pans for 10 minutes. Remove rolls from pans; cool slightly on wire racks.

☞ *For the 2-pound recipe:* Prepare as above, except divide dough into 24 portions. Shape into smooth balls; divide between 2 lightly greased 9×1½-inch round baking pans. Continue as above.

☞ **★NOTE:** Our Test Kitchen recommends 1 egg for either size recipe.

Prep time: 50 minutes   **Rise time:** 30 minutes   **Bake time:** 18 minutes
Nutrition facts per roll: 144 calories, 3 g total fat (1 g saturated fat), 14 mg cholesterol, 138 mg sodium, 24 g carbohydrate, 1 g fiber, 6 g protein.

1½-POUND (16 rolls)	INGREDIENTS	2-POUND (24 rolls)
¾ cup	mashed, drained, canned sweet potatoes	1 cup
½ cup	milk	¾ cup
1	egg★	1
2 tablespoons	margarine or butter, cut up	3 tablespoons
2½ cups	bread flour	3⅓ cups
½ cup	whole wheat flour	⅔ cup
½ cup	toasted wheat germ	⅔ cup
1 tablespoon	brown sugar	4 teaspoons
¾ teaspoon	salt	1 teaspoon
1¼ teaspoons	active dry yeast or bread machine yeast	1½ teaspoons
1	slightly beaten egg white	1
1 tablespoon	water	1 tablespoon
	Toasted wheat germ	

137

Offer these pretty rosettes as dessert or a breakfast treat on special occasions. For a pretty touch, use a decorator's bag fitted with a large star tip to fill the rosettes with lemon curd.

LEMON CURD ROSETTES

DIRECTIONS

☞ Select the recipe size. Add the first 8 ingredients to the machine according to the manufacturer's directions. Select the dough cycle. When cycle is complete, remove dough from machine. Punch down. Cover and let rest for 10 minutes.

☞ Divide the 1½-pound dough into 24 portions (divide the 2-pound dough into 32 portions). On a lightly floured surface, roll each portion into a 12-inch-long rope. Tie each rope into a loose knot. Tuck the top end under the roll; bring the bottom end up and tuck into center of roll. Place 3 inches apart on greased baking sheets. Cover and let rise in a warm place about 30 minutes or until nearly double. Combine 1 egg yolk and 1 tablespoon water; brush over rolls.

☞ Bake in a 375° oven for 10 to 12 minutes or until golden. Remove from baking sheets; cool on wire racks. Spoon about ½ teaspoon lemon curd into the center of each roll.

Prep time: 55 minutes **Rise time:** 30 minutes **Bake time:** 10 minutes

Nutrition facts per roll: 97 calories, 2 g total fat (1 g saturated fat), 28 mg cholesterol, 109 mg sodium, 16 g carbohydrate, 0 g fiber, 3 g protein.

1½-POUND (24 rolls)	INGREDIENTS	2-POUND (32 rolls)
¾ cup	water	1 cup
2	egg yolks	3
3 tablespoons	margarine or butter, cut up	¼ cup
3 cups	bread flour	4 cups
¼ cup	sugar	⅓ cup
1 teaspoon	salt	1¼ teaspoons
¾ teaspoon	ground cardamom	1 teaspoon
1½ teaspoons	active dry yeast or bread machine yeast	2 teaspoons
1	egg yolk	1
1 tablespoon	water	1 tablespoon
⅓ cup	lemon curd	½ cup

139

EASTER DATE BREAD

Prep time: 25 minutes **Rise time:** 45 minutes **Bake time:** 25 minutes
Nutrition facts per slice: 158 calories, 6 g total fat (2 g saturated fat), 14 mg cholesterol, 93 mg sodium, 24 g carbohydrate, 1 g fiber, 3 g protein.

1½-POUND (24 slices)	INGREDIENTS	2-POUND (36 slices)
½ cup	milk	⅔ cup
¼ cup	water	⅓ cup
1	egg(s)	2
¼ cup	butter or margarine, cut up	⅓ cup
3 cups	bread flour	4 cups
¼ cup	granulated sugar	⅓ cup
¾ teaspoon	salt	1 teaspoon
¾ teaspoon	finely shredded lemon peel	1 teaspoon
1½ teaspoons	active dry yeast or bread machine yeast	1¾ teaspoons
1 cup	ground walnuts	1⅓ cups
¾ cup	snipped pitted dates	1 cup
¼ cup	granulated sugar	⅓ cup
¼ cup	currant jelly	6 tablespoons
	Milk (optional)	
	Sifted powdered sugar	

DIRECTIONS

☞ Select the loaf size. Add first 9 ingredients to the machine according to manufacturer's directions. Select the dough cycle. When cycle is complete, remove dough from machine. Punch down. Cover; let rest for 10 minutes.

☞ Meanwhile, for filling, in a medium bowl combine the walnuts, dates, and ¼ or ⅓ cup sugar. Set aside.

☞ *For the 1½-pound recipe:* Divide dough in half. On a lightly floured surface, roll each half into a 16×10-inch rectangle. Spread each rectangle with 2 tablespoons jelly to within ½ inch of the edges. Sprinkle each with half of the filling. Starting from a long side, loosely roll up into a spiral. (If rolled too tightly, the filling may cause the dough to crack during baking.) Moisten edge; pinch firmly to seal. Place, seams down, on a greased large baking sheet, tucking ends under.

☞ Cover and let rise in a warm place for 45 to 60 minutes or until nearly double. If desired, brush with milk. Bake in a 350° oven for 25 to 30 minutes or until bread sounds hollow when lightly tapped. If necessary, loosely cover with foil last 10 to 15 minutes to prevent overbrowning. Remove from baking sheet; cool on a wire rack. Sprinkle with powdered sugar.

☞ *For the 2-pound recipe:* Prepare as above, except divide the dough into thirds. Roll each portion into a 14×10-inch rectangle. Spread each rectangle with 2 tablespoons jelly and sprinkle each with one-third of the filling. Continue as above, using 2 greased large baking sheets.

A golden sweet yeast loaf is an Old World tradition that can't be improved upon—unless you use a bread machine to make it! This one reveals a lovely swirl of raisins and nuts when sliced.

RUMANIAN EASTER BREAD

Prep time: 30 minutes   **Rise time:** 30 minutes   **Bake time:** 30 minutes
Nutrition facts per slice: 204 calories, 9 g total fat (1 g saturated fat), 18 mg cholesterol, 99 mg sodium, 29 g carbohydrate, 1 g fiber, 4 g protein.

DIRECTIONS

☞ Select loaf size. Add first 8 ingredients to the machine according to manufacturer's directions. Select dough cycle. When cycle is complete, remove dough from machine. Punch down. Cover; let rest 10 minutes.

☞ Meanwhile, for filling, in a medium saucepan combine ¾ or 1 cup sugar and ½ or ⅔ cup water; bring to boiling. Boil gently, uncovered, for 5 minutes. Remove from heat; stir in pecans, raisins, lemon peel, and cinnamon. Cool to room temperature.

☞ Divide 1½-pound dough in half. On a floured surface, roll each half into a 10×8-inch rectangle. (Divide 2-pound dough in half; roll each half into a 12×10-inch rectangle.) Spread each with half of filling. Starting from a short side, roll into a spiral; seal edge and ends. Place, seams down, on a greased large baking sheet.

☞ Cover; let rise in a warm place 30 minutes or until nearly double. Combine 1 beaten egg and 1 tablespoon milk; brush over loaves. Bake in a 350° oven for 30 to 35 minutes or until bread sounds hollow when tapped. If necessary, cover with foil last 10 minutes to prevent overbrowning. Remove from baking sheet; cool.

☞ *NOTE: Our Test Kitchen recommends 1 egg for either size recipe.

1½-POUND (24 slices)	INGREDIENTS	2-POUND (32 slices)
½ cup	milk	⅔ cup
¼ cup	water	⅓ cup
1	egg*	1
¼ cup	margarine or butter	⅓ cup
3 cups	bread flour	4 cups
⅓ cup	sugar	½ cup
¾ teaspoon	salt	1 teaspoon
1 teaspoon	active dry yeast or bread machine yeast	1¼ teaspoons
¾ cup	sugar	1 cup
½ cup	water	⅔ cup
2 cups	ground pecans	2½ cups
1 cup	golden raisins	1⅓ cups
1 teaspoon	finely shredded lemon peel	1¼ teaspoons
¾ teaspoon	ground cinnamon	1 teaspoon
1	beaten egg	1
1 tablespoon	milk	1 tablespoon

141

EASTER RABBITS

Prep time: 40 minutes **Rise time:** 35 minutes **Bake time:** 10 minutes
Nutrition facts per roll: 156 calories, 4 g total fat (1 g saturated fat), 16 mg cholesterol, 159 mg sodium, 26 g carbohydrate, 1 g fiber, 5 g protein.

1½-POUND (14 rolls)	INGREDIENTS	2-POUND (21 rolls)
¾ cup	milk	1 cup
1	egg*	1
3 tablespoons	margarine or butter, cut up	¼ cup
3 cups	bread flour	4 cups
¼ cup	sugar	⅓ cup
¾ teaspoon	salt	1 teaspoon
¼ teaspoon	ground nutmeg*	¼ teaspoon
1¼ teaspoons	active dry yeast or bread machine yeast	1½ teaspoons
1	slightly beaten egg white	1
1 tablespoon	water	1 tablespoon

DIRECTIONS

☞ Select the recipe size. Add the first 8 ingredients to the machine according to the manufacturer's directions. Select the dough cycle. When cycle is complete, remove dough from machine. Punch down. Cover and let rest for 10 minutes.

☞ On a lightly floured surface, roll the 1½-pound dough into a 14×8-inch rectangle. Cut lengthwise into fifteen 14-inch-long strips, each about ½ inch wide. Reserve 1 strip to form tails. (Roll the 2-pound dough into a 14×12-inch rectangle; cut lengthwise into twenty-three 14-inch-long strips, each about ½ inch wide. Reserve 2 strips to form tails.) Gently roll the strips into smooth ropes.

☞ On lightly greased baking sheets, shape each rabbit by crossing 1 end of a rope over the other to form a loop, overlapping about 2 inches from each end. Twist the ends of rope once at the point where dough overlaps. Shape ends into points to resemble ears. Shape small portions from reserved strip(s) into smooth balls for tails. Place a ball on top of dough at bottom of each loop, moistening if necessary to get tail to stick.

☞ Cover and let rise in a warm place for 35 to 45 minutes or until nearly double. In a small bowl combine egg white and water; brush over rabbits. Bake in a 375° oven about 10 minutes or until golden brown. Remove from baking sheets; cool on wire racks.

☞ **NOTE:** Our Test Kitchen recommends 1 egg and ¼ teaspoon nutmeg for either size recipe.

CURRANT BREAD

This bread is reminiscent of the Welsh bread called Bara Brith. It is speckled with currants and spices and traditionally served on holidays and at harvest festivals.

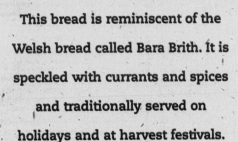

Prep time: 10 minutes
Nutrition facts per slice: 128 calories, 2 g total fat (0 g saturated fat), 13 mg cholesterol, 99 mg sodium, 25 g carbohydrate, 1 g fiber, 4 g protein.

DIRECTIONS

☞ Select the loaf size. Add the ingredients to the machine according to the manufacturer's directions. Select the basic white bread cycle.

☞ **★NOTE:** For the 1½-pound loaf, the bread machine pan must have a capacity of 10 cups or more. For the 2-pound loaf, the bread machine pan must have a capacity of 12 cups or more.

☞ **★★NOTE:** Our Test Kitchen recommends ¾ cup milk and 1 egg for either size recipe.

1½-POUND★ (18 slices)	INGREDIENTS	2-POUND★ (24 slices)
¾ cup	milk★★	¾ cup
¼ cup	water	½ cup
1	egg★★	1
1 tablespoon	shortening or cooking oil	4 teaspoons
3 cups	bread flour	4 cups
3 tablespoons	packed brown sugar	¼ cup
¾ teaspoon	salt	1 teaspoon
¾ teaspoon	ground cinnamon or pumpkin pie spice	1 teaspoon
1 teaspoon	active dry yeast or bread machine yeast	1¼ teaspoons
1 cup	dried currants or dark raisins	1⅓ cups

HOT TIP

Save time, dishes, and steps by measuring several liquid ingredients—milk and water, for example—at once in the same measuring cup, then transfer all to the bread machine.

144

These yummy, golden brown sweet rolls are like doughnuts, but are filled with either chocolate or fruit preserves. During Hanukkah, Israeli vendors sell sufganyot by the basketfuls.

SUFGANYOT

Prep time: 45 minutes **Cook time:** 2 minutes per batch
Nutrition facts per doughnut: 164 calories, 5 g total fat (1 g saturated fat), 13 mg cholesterol, 72 mg sodium, 26 g carbohydrate, 1 g fiber, 4 g protein.

DIRECTIONS

☞ Select the recipe size. Add the first 9 ingredients to the machine according to the manufacturer's directions. Select the dough cycle. When cycle is complete, remove dough from machine. Punch down. Cover and let rest for 10 minutes.

☞ Divide the 1½-pound dough in half (divide the 2-pound dough into thirds). On a lightly floured surface, roll each portion to ¼-inch thickness. Cut dough with a floured 2½-inch biscuit cutter, dipping cutter into flour between cuts. Reroll and cut trimmings. Place about ½ teaspoon chocolate spread or fruit preserves onto the center of half of the circles. Lightly moisten edges of circles; top with remaining circles. Press edges together with fingers or tines of a fork to seal.

☞ Fry doughnuts, 2 or 3 at a time, in deep hot oil (365°) about 2 minutes or until golden brown, turning once. Using a slotted spoon, remove from oil and drain on paper towels. Sprinkle with powdered sugar. Transfer to wire racks to cool.

☞ *NOTE: Our Test Kitchen recommends 1 egg and ½ teaspoon vanilla for either size recipe.

1½-POUND (16 doughnuts)	INGREDIENTS	2-POUND (22 doughnuts)
¾ cup	water	1 cup
1	egg*	1
4 teaspoons	cooking oil	2 tablespoons
½ teaspoon	vanilla*	½ teaspoon
3 cups	bread flour	4 cups
¼ cup	granulated sugar	⅓ cup
½ teaspoon	salt	¾ teaspoon
¼ teaspoon	ground cinnamon	½ teaspoon
1¼ teaspoons	active dry yeast or bread machine yeast	1½ teaspoons
¼ cup	chocolate hazelnut spread or fruit preserves, such as seedless red raspberry or blackberry	⅓ cup
	Cooking oil for deep-fat frying	
	Sifted powdered sugar	

145

ST. PATRICK'S SHAMROCK

DIRECTIONS

☞ Select the recipe size. Add the first 8 ingredients to the machine according to the manufacturer's directions. Select the dough cycle. When cycle is complete, remove dough from machine. Punch down. Cover and let rest 10 minutes.

☞ Meanwhile, for filling, in a medium mixing bowl beat together cream cheese, ¼ or ⅓ cup granulated sugar, egg yolk, and vanilla.

☞ On a lightly floured surface, roll the 1½-pound dough into a 15×10-inch rectangle. Cut into three 10×5-inch strips. (Roll the 2-pound dough into a 15-inch square; cut into three 15×5-inch strips.) Spread one-third of the filling down center of each strip; moisten edges. Bring long edges together over filling and pinch to seal.

☞ On a well-greased baking sheet, shape one rope into a loop, attaching one end about 2 inches above the other end to form one leaf and stem of shamrock. Shape remaining ropes into loops; attach one on either side of first loop near the stem. Cover and let rise in a warm place about 30 minutes or until nearly double. In a small bowl combine egg white and 1 tablespoon water; brush over shamrock. Sprinkle with green sugar.

☞ Bake in a 350° oven for 25 to 30 minutes or until bread sounds hollow when lightly tapped. Remove from baking sheet; cool on a wire rack for 1 hour. Store in the refrigerator.

☞ **NOTE:** Our Test Kitchen recommends 1 egg for either size recipe. Also, for the filling, use 1 egg yolk for either size.

Prep time: 35 minutes **Rise time:** 30 minutes **Bake time:** 25 minutes
Nutrition facts per serving: 199 calories, 8 g total fat (3 g saturated fat), 39 mg cholesterol, 180 mg sodium, 27 g carbohydrate, 1 g fiber, 5 g protein.

1½-POUND (16 servings)	INGREDIENTS	2-POUND (22 servings)
¾ cup	milk	1 cup
2 tablespoons	water	3 tablespoons
1	egg*	1
¼ cup	margarine or butter, cut up	⅓ cup
3 cups	bread flour	4 cups
¼ cup	granulated sugar	⅓ cup
¾ teaspoon	salt	1 teaspoon
1¼ teaspoons	active dry yeast or bread machine yeast	1½ teaspoons
two 3-ounce packages	cream cheese, softened	one 8-ounce package
¼ cup	granulated sugar	⅓ cup
1	egg yolk*	1
½ teaspoon	vanilla	1 teaspoon
1	slightly beaten egg white	1
1 tablespoon	water	1 tablespoon
1 tablespoon	green-colored coarse sugar	4 teaspoons

Reminiscent of native loaves from the Alsace region of France, this version uses smoked meats instead of dried fruits. Flecked with ham and black pepper, it can serve as a savory hors d'oeuvre.

SAVORY KUGELHOPF

DIRECTIONS

☞ Select the loaf size. Add the ingredients to the machine according to the manufacturer's directions. Select the basic white bread cycle.

☞ ***NOTE:** For the 1½-pound loaf, the bread machine pan must have a capacity of 10 cups or more. For the 2-pound loaf, the bread machine pan must have a capacity of 12 cups or more.

☞ ****NOTE:** Our Test Kitchen recommends ¾ cup half-and-half, cream, or milk; 1 egg; and ¼ teaspoon pepper for either size recipe.

☞ *****NOTE:** To make ⅔ cup crisp-cooked bacon, start with about 8 slices. To make ¾ cup crisp-cooked bacon, start with about 10 slices.

Prep time: 15 minutes

Nutrition facts per slice: 137 calories, 4 g total fat (1 g saturated fat), 21 mg cholesterol, 196 mg sodium, 20 g carbohydrate, 1 g fiber, 5 g protein.

1½-POUND★ (16 slices)	INGREDIENTS	2-POUND★ (22 slices)
¾ cup	half-and-half, light cream, or milk**	¾ cup
¼ cup	water	⅓ cup
1	egg**	1
2 tablespoons	margarine or butter, cut up	3 tablespoons
3 cups	bread flour	4 cups
1 tablespoon	sugar	4 teaspoons
¾ teaspoon	salt	1 teaspoon
¼ teaspoon	coarsely ground black pepper**	¼ teaspoon
1 teaspoon	active dry yeast or bread machine yeast	1¼ teaspoons
⅔ cup	finely diced cooked ham or crumbled crisp-cooked bacon***	¾ cup

Did you know?

Although generally thought of as Austrian, kugelhopf is also claimed by bakers from Alsace, Germany and Poland. You may know it by one of its many spellings—kugelhopf, gugelhupf, sugelhupf, and its many versions—and types—sweet, savory, with eggs and without. Enjoyed by many, kugelhopf's origination and variations really don't matter when you take one delicious bite.

SWEET

{ CHOCOLATE CHERRY BREAD }

see recipe, page 150

CHOCOLATE CHERRY BREAD

(Pictured on page 149.)

Bread? Dessert? Does it matter what you call it when chocolate and cherries co-star in one luscious loaf? This is the best antidote for a midafternoon slump.

Prep time: 15 minutes
Nutrition facts per slice: 113 calories, 2 g total fat (0 g saturated fat), 11 mg cholesterol, 95 mg sodium, 20 g carbohydrate, 1 g fiber, 3 g protein.

1½-POUND★ (20 slices)	INGREDIENTS	2-POUND★ (27 slices)
¾ cup	milk	1 cup
1	egg★★	1
2 tablespoons	water	3 tablespoons
1 tablespoon	margarine or butter	4 teaspoons
¼ teaspoon	almond extract★★	¼ teaspoon
3 cups	bread flour	4 cups
2 tablespoons	sugar	3 tablespoons
¾ teaspoon	salt	1 teaspoon
1 teaspoon	active dry yeast or bread machine yeast	1¼ teaspoons
⅓ cup	dried cherries, snipped	½ cup
⅓ cup	semisweet chocolate pieces, chilled	½ cup

DIRECTIONS

☞ Select the loaf size. Add the ingredients to the machine according to the manufacturer's directions. Select the basic white bread cycle.

☞ ★**NOTE:** For the 1½-pound loaf, the bread machine pan must have a capacity of 10 cups or more. For the 2-pound loaf, the bread machine pan must have a capacity of 12 cups or more.

☞ ★★**NOTE:** Our Test Kitchen recommends 1 egg and ¼ teaspoon almond extract for either size recipe.

HOT TIP

Depending on the brand, bread machines often will produce different end products. For example, in one bread machine, our Test Kitchen found that chilled chocolate chips would create a swirled bread (pictured on page 149) while another bread machine created an unswirled, solidly-colored bread. Either way, this bread tastes delicious.

MACADAMIA WHITE CHOCOLATE BREAD

Buttery-tasting macadamia nuts combine with divine white chocolate to create the ultimate of breads. For a special touch, it's finished off with a drizzle of white and dark chocolate glazes.

DIRECTIONS

☞ Select loaf size. Add first 10 ingredients to the machine according to the manufacturer's directions. Select the basic white bread cycle. Drizzle the cooled loaf with White Chocolate Glaze, then Dark Chocolate Glaze.

☞ *White Chocolate Glaze:* Heat 1 ounce white baking bar, cut up, and 1 teaspoon shortening over low heat until melted.

☞ *Dark Chocolate Glaze:* Heat 1 ounce semisweet chocolate, cut up, and 1 teaspoon shortening over low heat until melted.

☞ ***NOTE:** For the 1½-pound loaf, the bread machine pan must have a capacity of 10 cups or more. For the 2-pound loaf, the bread machine pan must have a capacity of 12 cups or more.

☞ ****NOTE:** Our Test Kitchen recommends 2 tablespoons margarine or butter and 2 tablespoons sugar for either size recipe.

Prep time: 15 minutes
Nutrition facts per slice: 173 calories, 7 g total fat (2 g saturated fat), 14 mg cholesterol, 118 mg sodium, 23 g carbohydrate, 1 g fiber, 4 g protein.

1½-POUND★ (18 slices)	INGREDIENTS	2-POUND★ (24 slices)
⅔ cup	milk	¾ cup
1	egg(s)	2
2 tablespoons	water	¼ cup
2 tablespoons	margarine or butter**	2 tablespoons
3 cups	bread flour	4 cups
2 tablespoons	sugar**	2 tablespoons
¾ teaspoon	salt	1 teaspoon
1 teaspoon	active dry yeast or bread machine yeast	1¼ teaspoons
½ cup	chopped macadamia nuts	⅔ cup
2 ounces	white baking bar, chopped	3 ounces
	White Chocolate Glaze	
	Dark Chocolate Glaze	

151

CHERRY ALMOND BREAD

The fun pink color of this sweet bread comes from maraschino cherry juice. Top off slices with a dab of Cream Cheese Butter (see page 116)—a delectable combo!

Prep time: 15 minutes
Nutrition facts per slice: 116 calories, 2 g total fat (0 g saturated fat), 1 mg cholesterol, 105 mg sodium, 20 g carbohydrate, 1 g fiber, 4 g protein.

1½-POUND (18 slices)	INGREDIENTS	2-POUND (24 slices)
¾ cup	milk	1 cup
½ cup	maraschino cherries, halved	⅔ cup
¼ cup	maraschino cherry juice	⅓ cup
4 teaspoons	margarine or butter	2 tablespoons
¼ teaspoon	almond extract*	¼ teaspoon
3 cups	bread flour	4 cups
¼ cup	chopped almonds	⅓ cup
1 tablespoon	sugar	4 teaspoons
¾ teaspoon	salt	1 teaspoon
1 teaspoon	active dry yeast or bread machine yeast	1¼ teaspoons

DIRECTIONS

☞ Select the loaf size. Add the ingredients to the machine according to the manufacturer's directions, adding the cherries with the milk and the almonds with the flour. Select the basic white bread cycle.

☞ ***NOTE:** Our Test Kitchen recommends ¼ teaspoon almond extract for either size recipe.

That's a fact!

Sorry, kids. Maraschino cherries do not sprout from the rims of your parents' cocktails. They really do grow on trees. The name comes from *marasca*, Italian for the variety of cherry whose juice is fermented to make maraschino cordial. The preserved cherries that garnish drinks, cakes, cookies, and breads taste like the cordial, but are nonalcoholic.

152

CHOCOLATE HAZELNUT LOAF

This blue-ribbon recipe combines the wonderful flavors of chocolate and hazelnut. Look for the secret ingredient—chocolate hazelnut spread—next to the peanut butter in the supermarket.

Prep time: 15 minutes

Nutrition facts per slice: 143 calories, 4 g total fat (0 g saturated fat), 14 mg cholesterol, 312 mg sodium, 23 g carbohydrate, 1 g fiber, 4 g protein.

1½-POUND★ (16 slices)	INGREDIENTS	2-POUND★ (22 slices)
½ cup	milk	⅔ cup
¼ cup	water	⅓ cup
¼ cup	chocolate hazelnut spread	⅓ cup
1	egg★★	1
3 cups	bread flour	4 cups
2 tablespoons	sugar	3 tablespoons
¾ teaspoon	salt	1 teaspoon
1¼ teaspoons	active dry yeast or bread machine yeast	1½ teaspoons
⅓ cup	chopped hazelnuts, toasted	½ cup
	Chocolate hazelnut spread (optional)	

DIRECTIONS

☞ Select loaf size. Add ingredients, except the optional chocolate hazelnut spread, to machine according to manufacturer's directions. Select basic white bread cycle. If desired, serve cooled loaf with additional chocolate hazelnut spread.

☞ ★**NOTE:** For the 1½-pound loaf, the bread machine pan must have a capacity of 10 cups or more. For the 2-pound loaf, the bread machine pan must have a capacity of 12 cups or more.

☞ ★★**NOTE:** Our Test Kitchen recommends 1 egg for either size recipe.

Good Advice!

Toasting hazelnuts not only deepens their rich flavor, but also loosens their bitter, paper-thin brown skin so you can more easily remove it. Toast nuts on a baking sheet in a 350° oven for 10 to 15 minutes, stirring once or twice, until the nuts are aromatic. Place toasted nuts on a clean kitchen towel and rub off the skin (some skins may remain).

154

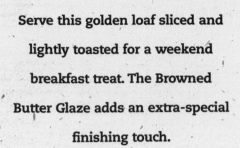

Serve this golden loaf sliced and lightly toasted for a weekend breakfast treat. The Browned Butter Glaze adds an extra-special finishing touch.

LEMON BREAKFAST BREAD

Prep time: 15 minutes

Nutrition facts per slice: 157 calories, 4 g total fat (1 g saturated fat), 14 mg cholesterol, 133 mg sodium, 27 g carbohydrate, 1 g fiber, 4 g protein.

DIRECTIONS

☞ Select the loaf size. Add all ingredients, except the Browned Butter Glaze, to machine according to the manufacturer's directions. Select the basic white bread cycle. Drizzle the cooled loaf with Browned Butter Glaze.

☞ *Browned Butter Glaze:* In a small saucepan heat 1 tablespoon butter until golden brown. Stir in 1 cup sifted powdered sugar and ½ teaspoon vanilla. Stir in enough milk (about 1 tablespoon) to make a glaze of drizzling consistency. Use immediately (glaze will appear thin, but it sets up quickly when drizzled on loaf).

☞ ***NOTE:** For the 1½-pound loaf, the bread machine pan must have a capacity of 10 cups or more. For the 2-pound loaf, the bread machine pan must have a capacity of 12 cups or more.

☞ ****NOTE:** To get ½ or ⅔ cup mashed potato, peel and cut up 1 medium to large potato. In a small saucepan cook potato in boiling water for 15 to 18 minutes or until tender. Drain. Mash with a potato masher; cool to room temperature. Measure the amount needed.

☞ *****NOTE:** Our Test Kitchen recommends 1 egg for either size recipe.

1½-POUND★ (18 slices)	INGREDIENTS	2-POUND★ (24 slices)
½ cup	milk	⅔ cup
½ cup	mashed cooked potato★★	⅔ cup
⅓ cup	water	½ cup
¼ cup	margarine or butter, cut up	⅓ cup
1	egg★★★	1
3 cups	bread flour	4 cups
¼ cup	sugar	⅓ cup
1 teaspoon	finely shredded lemon peel	1½ teaspoons
¾ teaspoon	salt	1 teaspoon
1 teaspoon	active dry yeast or bread machine yeast	1¼ teaspoons
	Browned Butter Glaze	

155

CHOCOLATE CRANBERRY NUT BREAD

You don't have to wait until the winter holidays for cranberries. Fortunately dried cranberries are available year-round. Look for them in the produce section or dried fruit section of the supermarket.

Prep time: 15 minutes

Nutrition facts per slice: 175 calories, 6 g total fat (1 g saturated fat), 14 mg cholesterol, 127 mg sodium, 27 g carbohydrate, 1 g fiber, 5 g protein.

1½-POUND★ (16 slices)	INGREDIENTS	2-POUND★ (22 slices)
⅔ cup	milk★★	⅔ cup
1	egg(s)	2
¼ cup	water	⅓ cup
2 tablespoons	honey	3 tablespoons
2 tablespoons	margarine or butter★★	2 tablespoons
3 cups	bread flour	4 cups
¾ teaspoon	salt	1 teaspoon
1¼ teaspoons	active dry yeast or bread machine yeast	1½ teaspoons
½ cup	chopped hazelnuts	⅔ cup
½ cup	dried cranberries	⅔ cup
⅓ cup	miniature semisweet chocolate pieces	½ cup

DIRECTIONS

☞ Select the loaf size. Add the ingredients to the machine according to the manufacturer's directions. Select the basic white bread cycle.

☞ ★**NOTE:** For the 1½-pound loaf, the bread machine pan must have a capacity of 10 cups or more. For the 2-pound loaf, the bread machine pan must have a capacity of 12 cups or more.

☞ ★★**NOTE:** Our Test Kitchen recommends ⅔ cup milk and 2 tablespoons margarine or butter for either size recipe.

WALNUT CHERRY BREAD

Dried cherries and walnuts give this bread texture, while shredded orange peel adds a citrus flavor. Orange-Ginger Butter (see recipe, page 116) is a great serve-along.

DIRECTIONS

☞ Select the loaf size. Add the ingredients to the machine according to the manufacturer's directions. Select the basic white bread cycle.

May We Suggest?

Did you know that nuts can be "toasted" in the microwave oven? Place ½ to 1 cup nuts in a 2-cup measure. Cook, uncovered, on 100 percent power (high) until light brown, stirring after 2 minutes, then every 30 seconds. Cook nuts from 2 to 4 minutes, watching carefully. Nuts will continue to toast as they stand.

Prep time: 15 minutes

Nutrition facts per slice: 164 calories, 4 g total fat (0 g saturated fat), 1 mg cholesterol, 110 mg sodium, 28 g carbohydrate, 1 g fiber, 4 g protein.

1½-POUND (16 slices)	INGREDIENTS	2-POUND (22 slices)
¾ cup	milk	1 cup
¼ cup	water	⅓ cup
¼ cup	light-colored corn syrup	⅓ cup
2 tablespoons	walnut oil or cooking oil	3 tablespoons
3 cups	bread flour	4 cups
1 teaspoon	finely shredded orange peel or lemon peel	1½ teaspoons
¾ teaspoon	salt	1 teaspoon
1¼ teaspoons	active dry yeast or bread machine yeast	1½ teaspoons
¾ cup	snipped dried tart cherries or cranberries	1 cup
⅓ cup	chopped walnuts, toasted	½ cup

157

CHOCOLATE MALT BREAD

The rich malt and chocolate flavor of this loaf makes it a real crowd-pleaser. Try it toasted for breakfast or top it with peanut butter and sliced banana for a great lunchtime sandwich.

Prep time: 10 minutes
Nutrition facts per slice: 121 calories, 2 g total fat (0 g saturated fat), 13 mg cholesterol, 118 mg sodium, 23 g carbohydrate, 1 g fiber, 4 g protein.

1½-POUND★ (18 slices)	INGREDIENTS	2-POUND★ (24 slices)
½ cup	milk	¾ cup
1	egg★★	1
3 tablespoons	water	¼ cup
4 teaspoons	margarine or butter	2 tablespoons
3 cups	bread flour	4 cups
⅓ cup	instant chocolate malted milk powder	½ cup
2 tablespoons	sugar	3 tablespoons
¾ teaspoon	salt	1 teaspoon
1 teaspoon	active dry yeast or bread machine yeast	1¼ teaspoons

DIRECTIONS

☞ Select the loaf size. Add the ingredients to the machine according to the manufacturer's directions. Select the basic white bread cycle.

☞ ★NOTE: For the 1½-pound loaf, the bread machine pan must have a capacity of 10 cups or more. For the 2-pound loaf, the bread machine pan must have a capacity of 12 cups or more.

☞ ★★NOTE: Our Test Kitchen recommends 1 egg for either size recipe.

Did you know?

Malt powder is made of a grain, which typically is barley, that is soaked, sprouted, dried, and then ground into a powder that tastes slightly sweet. The powder is used in making vinegar and malted milk powder, brewing beer, distilling liquor, and as an additive to foods.

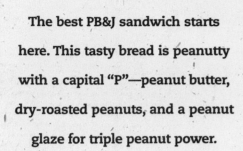

The best PB&J sandwich starts here. This tasty bread is peanutty with a capital "P"—peanut butter, dry-roasted peanuts, and a peanut glaze for triple peanut power.

PEANUT BUTTER HONEY BREAD

DIRECTIONS

☞ Select the loaf size. Add all ingredients, except the Peanut Butter Glaze, to the machine according to the manufacturer's directions. Select the basic white bread cycle. Drizzle cooled loaf with Peanut Butter Glaze.

☞ *Peanut Butter Glaze:* In a small mixing bowl stir together 1 cup sifted powdered sugar and 2 tablespoons peanut butter. Stir in enough milk (1 to 2 tablespoons) to make a glaze of drizzling consistency.

☞ **★NOTE:** For the 1½-pound loaf, the bread machine pan must have a capacity of 10 cups or more. For the 2-pound loaf, the bread machine pan must have a capacity of 12 cups or more.

☞ **★★NOTE:** Our Test Kitchen recommends 1 egg for either size recipe.

Prep time: 15 minutes
Nutrition facts per slice: 192 calories, 5 g total fat (1 g saturated fat), 14 mg cholesterol, 162 mg sodium, 31 g carbohydrate, 1 g fiber, 6 g protein.

1½-POUND★ (16 slices)	INGREDIENTS	2-POUND★ (22 slices)
½ cup	milk	¾ cup
¼ cup	water	⅓ cup
¼ cup	peanut butter	⅓ cup
1	egg★★	1
3 tablespoons	honey	¼ cup
3 cups	bread flour	4 cups
¾ teaspoon	salt	1 teaspoon
1¼ teaspoons	active dry yeast or bread machine yeast	1½ teaspoons
⅓ cup	chopped dry-roasted peanuts	½ cup
	Peanut Butter Glaze	

159

Vibrant green pistachios dot this light, moist, chocolatey loaf. The yummy chocolate glaze is not mandatory, of course, but is highly recommended! Sprinkle with additional pistachios, if you like.

CHOCOLATE PISTACHIO BREAD

DIRECTIONS

☞ Select loaf size. Add first 11 ingredients to the machine according to the manufacturer's directions. Select the basic white bread cycle. Drizzle the cooled loaf with Chocolate Glaze. If desired, sprinkle with additional chopped pistachio nuts.

☞ *Chocolate Glaze:* In a small mixing bowl stir together ½ cup sifted powdered sugar, 1 tablespoon unsweetened cocoa powder, and ¼ teaspoon vanilla. Stir in enough milk (1 to 2 teaspoons) to make a glaze of drizzling consistency.

☞ ***NOTE:** For the 1½-pound loaf, the bread machine pan must have a capacity of 10 cups or more. For the 2-pound loaf, the bread machine pan must have a capacity of 12 cups or more.

☞ ****NOTE:** Our Test Kitchen recommends 1 egg for either size recipe.

Prep time: 15 minutes

Nutrition facts per slice: 130 calories, 3 g total fat (1 g saturated fat), 11 mg cholesterol, 98 mg sodium, 21 g carbohydrate, 1 g fiber, 4 g protein.

1½-POUND★ (20 slices)	INGREDIENTS	2-POUND★ (27 slices)
¾ cup	milk	1 cup
1	egg★★	1
3 tablespoons	water	¼ cup
4 teaspoons	margarine or butter	2 tablespoons
1 teaspoon	vanilla	1½ teaspoons
3 cups	bread flour	4 cups
3 tablespoons	sugar	¼ cup
2 tablespoons	unsweetened cocoa powder	3 tablespoons
¾ teaspoon	salt	1 teaspoon
1 teaspoon	active dry yeast or bread machine yeast	1¼ teaspoons
½ cup	chopped pistachio nuts	⅔ cup
	Chocolate Glaze	
	Chopped pistachio nuts (optional)	

161

CHOCOLATE STRAWBERRY BREAD

If your weakness is chocolate, you will adore this bread. It features the tastes of cocoa, semisweet chocolate pieces, and strawberry flavors, What more could you ask for?

Prep time: 10 minutes

Nutrition facts per slice: 145 calories, 3 g total fat (1 g saturated fat), 14 mg cholesterol, 127 mg sodium, 25 g carbohydrate, 1 g fiber, 4 g protein.

1½-POUND★ (16 slices)	INGREDIENTS	2-POUND★ (22 slices)
⅔ cup	milk	¾ cup
¼ cup	water	⅓ cup
¼ cup	strawberry preserves	⅓ cup
1	egg★★	1
2 tablespoons	margarine or butter, cut up	3 tablespoons
½ teaspoon	strawberry extract	¾ teaspoon
3 cups	bread flour	4 cups
2 tablespoons	unsweetened cocoa powder	3 tablespoons
¾ teaspoon	salt	1 teaspoon
1 teaspoon	active dry yeast or bread machine yeast	1½ teaspoons
¼ cup	miniature semisweet chocolate pieces	⅓ cup

DIRECTIONS

☞ Select the loaf size. Add the ingredients to the machine according to the manufacturer's directions. Select the basic white bread cycle.

☞ ★**NOTE:** For the 1½-pound loaf, the bread machine pan must have a capacity of 10 cups or more. For the 2-pound loaf, the bread machine pan must have a capacity of 12 cups or more.

☞ ★★**NOTE:** Our Test Kitchen recommends 1 egg for either size recipe.

HOT TIP

When it comes to picking fruit spreads, mind your p's and j's. Jellies are very firm, translucent spreads made of fruit juices boiled with sugar. Jams are mashed fruit cooked with sugar until thick. Preserves resemble jams but have larger chunks of fruit.

CHOCOLATE CASHEW LOAF

Indulge your love of chocolate and cashews in this sweet and satisfying bread. Get creative—try in your favorite bread pudding recipe or as French toast topped with a fresh strawberry sauce.

DIRECTIONS

☞ Select the loaf size. Add the ingredients to the machine according to the manufacturer's directions. Select the basic white bread cycle.

☞ **★NOTE:** For the 1½-pound loaf, the bread machine pan must have a capacity of 10 cups or more. For the 2-pound loaf, the bread machine pan must have a capacity of 12 cups or more.

☞ **★★NOTE:** Our Test Kitchen recommends 1 egg for either size recipe.

Prep time: 15 minutes

Nutrition facts per slice: 155 calories, 4 g total fat (1 g saturated fat), 14 mg cholesterol, 159 mg sodium, 24 g carbohydrate, 1 g fiber, 5 g protein.

1½-POUND★ (16 slices)	INGREDIENTS	2-POUND★ (22 slices)
¾ cup	milk	1 cup
1	egg★★	1
3 tablespoons	water	¼ cup
3 tablespoons	honey	¼ cup
4 teaspoons	margarine or butter	2 tablespoons
1 teaspoon	vanilla	1½ teaspoons
3 cups	bread flour	4 cups
2 tablespoons	unsweetened cocoa powder	3 tablespoons
¾ teaspoon	salt	1 teaspoon
1 teaspoon	active dry yeast or bread machine yeast	1¼ teaspoons
½ cup	coarsely chopped cashews	⅔ cup

163

SWEET LEMON TEA BREAD

Here's one tea bread that really lives up to its name. Not only is it a perfect partner to a cup of tea, but the ingredients include tea and other traditional accompaniments for tea.

Prep time: 10 minutes

Nutrition facts per slice: 112 calories, 2 g total fat (0 g saturated fat), 13 mg cholesterol, 113 mg sodium, 19 g carbohydrate, 1 g fiber, 3 g protein.

DIRECTIONS

☞ Select the loaf size. Add the ingredients to the machine according to the manufacturer's directions, adding the tea powder with the liquid. Select the basic white bread cycle.

☞ *NOTE: For the 1½-pound loaf, the bread machine pan must have a capacity of 10 cups or more. For the 2-pound loaf, the bread machine pan must have a capacity of 12 cups or more.

☞ **NOTE: Our Test Kitchen recommends 1 egg for either size recipe.

1½-POUND★ (18 slices)	INGREDIENTS	2-POUND★ (24 slices)
⅔ cup	milk	¾ cup
¼ cup	water	⅓ cup
2 tablespoons	instant tea powder	3 tablespoons
1	egg★★	1
2 tablespoons	margarine or butter, cut up	3 tablespoons
3 cups	bread flour	4 cups
3 tablespoons	sugar	¼ cup
2 teaspoons	finely shredded lemon peel	1 tablespoon
¾ teaspoon	salt	1 teaspoon
½ teaspoon	ground cardamom	¾ teaspoon
1 teaspoon	active dry yeast or bread machine yeast	1¼ teaspoons

164

This bread gets a double whammy of citrus with lemon and orange. The crowning glory is an orange glaze for extra citrus punch.

CITRUS LOAF

DIRECTIONS

☞ Select loaf size. Add all ingredients, except the Citrus Glaze, to the machine according to manufacturer's directions. Select the basic white bread cycle. Frost cooled loaf with Citrus Glaze.

☞ *Citrus Glaze:* In a small mixing bowl stir together 1 cup sifted powdered sugar and ½ teaspoon finely shredded orange peel. Stir in enough orange juice (3 to 4 teaspoons) to make a glaze of spreading consistency.

☞ ***NOTE:** For the 1½-pound loaf, the bread machine pan must have a capacity of 10 cups or more. For the 2-pound loaf, the bread machine pan must have a capacity of 12 cups or more.

☞ ****NOTE:** Our Test Kitchen recommends ⅔ cup water and 1 egg for either size recipe.

Prep time: 15 minutes

Nutrition facts per slice: 118 calories, 2 g total fat (0 g saturated fat), 11 mg cholesterol, 97 mg sodium, 22 g carbohydrate, 1 g fiber, 3 g protein.

1½-POUND★ (20 slices)	INGREDIENTS	2-POUND★ (27 slices)
⅔ cup	water★★	⅔ cup
⅓ cup	orange juice	½ cup
1	egg★★	1
2 tablespoons	margarine or butter, cut up	3 tablespoons
3 cups	bread flour	4 cups
3 tablespoons	sugar	¼ cup
1 teaspoon	finely shredded lemon peel	1½ teaspoons
¾ teaspoon	salt	1 teaspoon
½ teaspoon	finely shredded orange peel	1 teaspoon
1 teaspoon	active dry yeast or bread machine yeast	1¼ teaspoons
	Citrus Glaze	

165

POPPY SEED TEA BREAD

Sour cream adds richness, lemon peel supplies flavor, and poppy seeds lend a bit of crunchy texture. Sliced thin and cut into decorative shapes, it's worthy of placing on a special tea tray.

DIRECTIONS

☞ Select the loaf size. Add the ingredients to the machine according to the manufacturer's directions. Select the basic white bread cycle.

☞ *NOTE: For the 1½-pound loaf, the bread machine pan must have a capacity of 10 cups or more. For the 2-pound loaf, the bread machine pan must have a capacity of 12 cups or more.

☞ **NOTE: Our Test Kitchen recommends 1 egg for either size recipe.

Prep time: 15 minutes
Nutrition facts per slice: 151 calories, 5 g total fat (1 g saturated fat), 16 mg cholesterol, 137 mg sodium, 23 g carbohydrate, 1 g fiber, 4 g protein.

1½-POUND* (16 slices)	INGREDIENTS	2-POUND* (22 slices)
⅔ cup	milk	¾ cup
⅓ cup	dairy sour cream	½ cup
1	egg**	1
3 tablespoons	margarine or butter, cut up	¼ cup
3 cups	bread flour	4 cups
¼ cup	sugar	⅓ cup
2 tablespoons	poppy seed	3 tablespoons
1 tablespoon	finely shredded lemon peel	4 teaspoons
¾ teaspoon	salt	1 teaspoon
1 teaspoon	active dry yeast or bread machine yeast	1¼ teaspoons

167

LEMONY MOLASSES BREAD

This tart and sweet loaf has a delicate, golden brown crust and can rise to any occasion. Serve slices on a doily-lined plate and voila! It's an instant party!

Prep time: 15 minutes

Nutrition facts per slice: 146 calories, 5 g total fat (1 g saturated fat), 14 mg cholesterol, 127 mg sodium, 22 g carbohydrate, 1 g fiber, 4 g protein.

1½-POUND★ (16 slices)	INGREDIENTS	2-POUND★ (22 slices)
¾ cup	milk★★	¾ cup
1	egg(s)	2
2 tablespoons	water	3 tablespoons
2 tablespoons	mild-flavored molasses	3 tablespoons
2 tablespoons	margarine or butter★★	2 tablespoons
3 cups	bread flour	4 cups
1 teaspoon	finely shredded lemon peel	1½ teaspoons
¾ teaspoon	salt	1 teaspoon
1¼ teaspoons	active dry yeast or bread machine yeast★★	1¼ teaspoons
½ cup	chopped pecans, toasted	⅔ cup

DIRECTIONS

☞ Select the loaf size. Add the ingredients to the machine according to the manufacturer's directions. Select the basic white bread cycle.

☞ ★**NOTE:** For the 1½-pound loaf, the bread machine pan must have a capacity of 10 cups or more. For the 2-pound loaf, the bread machine pan must have a capacity of 12 cups or more.

☞ ★★**NOTE:** Our Test Kitchen recommends ¾ cup milk, 2 tablespoons margarine or butter, and 1¼ teaspoons yeast for either size recipe.

168

FIG & PINE NUT BREAD

Does Tuscany suddenly beckon? This bread is likely why. From out of a rustic Italian farm kitchen comes its earthy flavors of whole grains, sweet dried figs, and toasted pine nuts.

DIRECTIONS

☞ Select the loaf size. Add the ingredients to the machine according to the manufacturer's directions. If available, select the whole grain cycle, or select the basic white bread cycle.

☞ ★**NOTE:** For the 1½-pound loaf, the bread machine pan must have a capacity of 10 cups or more. For the 2-pound loaf, the bread machine pan must have a capacity of 12 cups or more.

☞ ★★**NOTE:** Our Test Kitchen recommends 1 egg for either size recipe.

May We Suggest?

Slightly sweet and spicy nutmeg is amazingly intense when freshly grated from the whole kernel with an inexpensive grater from the gadget section. Tinned steel nutmeg graters have one flat side and one curved grating side. Nutmeg mills work like a pepper mill: Drop in the whole nutmeg, turn the crank, and a blade shaves off ground spice.

Prep time: 15 minutes
Nutrition facts per slice: 160 calories, 4 g total fat (1 g saturated fat), 14 mg cholesterol, 136 mg sodium, 27 g carbohydrate, 2 g fiber, 5 g protein.

1½-POUND★ (16 slices)	INGREDIENTS	2-POUND★ (22 slices)
⅔ cup	milk	¾ cup
1	egg★★	1
3 tablespoons	margarine or butter, cut up	¼ cup
2 tablespoons	water	3 tablespoons
2 cups	bread flour	2⅔ cups
1 cup	whole wheat flour	1⅓ cups
3 tablespoons	sugar	¼ cup
¾ teaspoon	salt	1 teaspoon
⅛ teaspoon	ground nutmeg	¼ teaspoon
1 teaspoon	active dry yeast or bread machine yeast	1½ teaspoons
⅔ cup	dried figs, cut into thin strips	¾ cup
¼ cup	pine nuts, toasted	⅓ cup

169

APPLE BRICKLE BREAD

Celebrate fall harvest with this bread—the fresh tart apples combine with the sweet almond brickle to create a loaf that tastes a bit like candied apple.

Prep time: 15 minutes

Nutrition facts per slice: 127 calories, 3 g total fat (0 g saturated fat), 14 mg cholesterol, 130 mg sodium, 21 g carbohydrate, 1 g fiber, 4 g protein.

1½-POUND★ (18 slices)	INGREDIENTS	2-POUND★ (24 slices)
⅔ cup	milk★★	⅔ cup
½ cup	chopped peeled apple	⅔ cup
1	egg(s)	2
2 tablespoons	water★★	2 tablespoons
2 tablespoons	margarine or butter★★	2 tablespoons
3 cups	bread flour	4 cups
2 tablespoons	sugar	3 tablespoons
¾ teaspoon	salt	1 teaspoon
½ teaspoon	ground cinnamon	¾ teaspoon
1 teaspoon	active dry yeast or bread machine yeast	1¼ teaspoons
⅓ cup	almond brickle pieces	½ cup

DIRECTIONS

☞ Select the loaf size. Add the ingredients to the machine according to the manufacturer's directions, adding the apple with the milk. Select the basic white bread cycle.

☞ **★NOTE:** For the 1½-pound loaf, the bread machine pan must have a capacity of 10 cups or more. For the 2-pound loaf, the bread machine pan must have a capacity of 12 cups or more.

☞ **★★NOTE:** Our Test Kitchen recommends ⅔ cup milk, 2 tablespoons water, and 2 tablespoons margarine or butter for either size recipe.

170

Give your kids a sweet send-off to school with this bread topped with Nut 'n' Honey Butter (recipe on page 117). The sweetly spiced loaf is flavored with apple cider and applesauce.

DIRECTIONS

☞ Select the loaf size. Add the ingredients to the machine according to the manufacturer's directions. Select the basic white bread cycle.

☞ *NOTE: For the 1½-pound loaf, the bread machine pan must have a capacity of 10 cups or more. For the 2-pound loaf, the bread machine pan must have a capacity of 12 cups or more.

☞ **NOTE: Our Test Kitchen recommends ½ cup applesauce for either size recipe.

OATMEAL APPLESAUCE BREAD

Prep time: 10 minutes

Nutrition facts per slice: 108 calories, 1 g total fat (0 g saturated fat), 0 mg cholesterol, 98 mg sodium, 21 g carbohydrate, 1 g fiber, 3 g protein.

1½-POUND★ (18 slices)	INGREDIENTS	2-POUND★ (24 slices)
¾ cup	apple cider or apple juice	1 cup
½ cup	applesauce**	½ cup
1 tablespoon	margarine or butter	4 teaspoons
3 cups	bread flour	4 cups
⅓ cup	regular or quick-cooking rolled oats	½ cup
1 tablespoon	brown sugar	4 teaspoons
¾ teaspoon	salt	1 teaspoon
¼ teaspoon	apple pie spice	½ teaspoon
1 teaspoon	active dry yeast or bread machine yeast	1¼ teaspoons

APPLE BUTTER BREAD

Moist and delicious, this always-appealing bread has graced American dinner tables for generations. Try it toasted drizzled with honey for breakfast or with melted cheddar cheese for lunch.

Prep time: 10 minutes

Nutrition facts per slice: 123 calories, 2 g total fat (0 g saturated fat), 14 mg cholesterol, 120 mg sodium, 22 g carbohydrate, 1 g fiber, 4 g protein.

1½-POUND★ (16 slices)	INGREDIENTS	2-POUND★ (22 slices)
½ cup	milk	⅔ cup
⅓ cup	apple butter	½ cup
¼ cup	water	⅓ cup
1	egg★★	1
4 teaspoons	margarine or butter	2 tablespoons
3 cups	bread flour	4 cups
¾ teaspoon	salt	1 teaspoon
½ teaspoon	apple pie spice or ground allspice	¾ teaspoon
1 teaspoon	active dry yeast or bread machine yeast	1¼ teaspoons

DIRECTIONS

☞ Select the loaf size. Add the ingredients to the machine according to the manufacturer's directions. Select the basic white bread cycle.

☞ ★**NOTE:** For the 1½-pound loaf, the bread machine pan must have a capacity of 10 cups or more. For the 2-pound loaf, the bread machine pan must have a capacity of 12 cups or more.

☞ ★★**NOTE:** Our Test Kitchen recommends 1 egg for either size recipe.

HOT TIP

In a pinch, you can blend apple pie spice from spices you probably have on hand. For 1 teaspoon apple pie spice, combine ½ teaspoon ground cinnamon, ¼ teaspoon ground nutmeg, ⅛ teaspoon ground allspice, and a dash ground cloves or ginger.

172

APPLE WALNUT BREAD

Here's a twist to Mom's apple pie. If you love apples and nuts, try them in a new venue in an impressive sweet bread made moist with applesauce and munchy with chopped nuts.

DIRECTIONS

☞ Select the loaf size. Add the ingredients to the machine according to the manufacturer's directions. Select the basic white bread cycle.

☞ ***NOTE:** For the 1½-pound loaf, the bread machine pan must have a capacity of 10 cups or more. For the 2-pound loaf, the bread machine pan must have a capacity of 12 cups or more.

☞ ****NOTE:** Our Test Kitchen recommends ⅔ cup water, 2 tablespoons margarine or butter, and 1 teaspoon yeast for either size recipe.

Prep time: 15 minutes

Nutrition facts per slice: 128 calories, 4 g total fat (1 g saturated fat), 12 mg cholesterol, 108 mg sodium, 19 g carbohydrate, 1 g fiber, 4 g protein.

1½-POUND★ (18 slices)	INGREDIENTS	2-POUND★ (24 slices)
⅔ cup	water★★	⅔ cup
1	egg(s)	2
¼ cup	applesauce	⅓ cup
2 tablespoons	margarine or butter★★	2 tablespoons
3 cups	bread flour	4 cups
2 tablespoons	sugar	3 tablespoons
¾ teaspoon	salt	1 teaspoon
1 teaspoon	active dry yeast or bread machine yeast★★	1 teaspoon
½ cup	chopped walnuts	⅔ cup

173

BLUEBERRY MUFFIN BREAD

Become a hero to the blueberry muffin fans in your home. For an old-fashioned breakfast, serve toasted slices of this blueberry-studded bread with scrambled eggs and bacon.

Prep time: 10 minutes

Nutrition facts per slice: 140 calories, 2 g total fat (1 g saturated fat), 14 mg cholesterol, 127 mg sodium, 25 g carbohydrate, 1 g fiber, 4 g protein.

1½-POUND★ (16 slices)	INGREDIENTS	2-POUND★ (22 slices)
¾ cup	milk	1 cup
1	egg★★	1
3 tablespoons	water	¼ cup
2 tablespoons	margarine or butter, cut up	3 tablespoons
3 cups	bread flour	4 cups
3 tablespoons	sugar	¼ cup
¾ teaspoon	salt	1 teaspoon
¼ teaspoon	ground nutmeg	½ teaspoon
1 teaspoon	active dry yeast or bread machine yeast	1¼ teaspoons
⅓ cup	dried blueberries	½ cup
	Powdered Sugar Glaze (optional)	

DIRECTIONS

☞ Select loaf size. Add all ingredients, except the Powdered Sugar Glaze, to the machine according to manufacturer's directions. Select the basic white bread cycle. If desired, drizzle the cooled loaf with Powdered Sugar Glaze.

☞ *Powdered Sugar Glaze:* In a small mixing bowl stir together ½ cup sifted powdered sugar and enough milk (1 to 2 teaspoons) to make a glaze of drizzling consistency.

☞ ★**NOTE:** For the 1½-pound loaf, the bread machine pan must have a capacity of 10 cups or more. For the 2-pound loaf, the bread machine pan must have a capacity of 12 cups or more.

☞ ★★**NOTE:** Our Test Kitchen recommends 1 egg for either size recipe.

DOUGHNUTS

Make your own doughnuts? You bet! You'll think these glazed doughnuts are worth every minute it takes to make them once you take one warm and wonderful bite.

Prep time: 20 minutes **Rise time:** 45 minutes **Fry time:** 2 minutes per batch
Nutrition facts per doughnut: 166 calories, 7 g total fat (1 g saturated fat), 14 mg cholesterol, 102 mg sodium, 23 g carbohydrate, 1 g fiber, 4 g protein.

1½-POUND (16 doughnuts)	INGREDIENTS	2-POUND (22 doughnuts)
¾ cup	milk	1 cup
2 tablespoons	water*	2 tablespoons
1	egg(s)	2
3 tablespoons	margarine or butter, cut up	¼ cup
3 cups	bread flour	4 cups
¼ cup	sugar	⅓ cup
½ teaspoon	salt	¾ teaspoon
1½ teaspoons	active dry yeast or bread machine yeast	2 teaspoons
	Cooking oil or shortening for deep-fat frying	
	Powdered Sugar Icing	

DIRECTIONS

☞ Select recipe size. Add all ingredients, except the oil or shortening and Powdered Sugar Icing, to the bread machine according to the manufacturer's directions. Select dough cycle. When the cycle is complete, remove dough from machine. Punch down. Turn dough out onto a floured surface. Divide in half. Cover and let rest for 10 minutes.

☞ Roll each half of dough to ½-inch thickness. Cut with a floured doughnut cutter. Reroll and cut trimmings. Cover and let rise for 45 to 60 minutes or until light. Heat cooking oil to 365°. Carefully fry doughnuts, 2 or 3 at a time, about 2 minutes, turning once. Drain on paper towels. Glaze with Powdered Sugar Icing.

☞ *Powdered Sugar Icing:* In a medium bowl combine 1½ cups sifted powdered sugar, ½ teaspoon vanilla, and enough milk (2 to 3 tablespoons) to make of drizzling consistency.

☞ **★Note:** Our Test Kitchen recommends 2 tablespoons water for either size recipe.

176

MAPLE BRAN BREAKFAST BREAD

Jump start your day with the nutritious goodness of this flavor-packed loaf. Fiber-rich bran coupled with the natural sweetness of maple makes this a healthy and delicious choice.

DIRECTIONS

☞ Select the loaf size. Add the ingredients to the machine according to the manufacturer's directions, adding the bran cereal with the flour. Select the basic white bread cycle.

☞ **NOTE:** Our Test Kitchen recommends 2 tablespoons water and 2 teaspoons gluten flour for either size recipe.

Good Advice!

When life gives you leftover bread, make French toast! Here's one way: Stir together 2 beaten eggs, ½ cup of milk, and ½ teaspoon vanilla. Lay 3 or 4 thick, day-old bread slices in a dish and pour egg mixture over; let bread soak about 15 minutes, turning slices once. Drain. Brown bread in butter or oil in a hot skillet on both sides until golden. Serve with maple syrup.

Prep time: 15 minutes

Nutrition facts per slice: 123 calories, 3 g total fat (1 g saturated fat), 1 mg cholesterol, 145 mg sodium, 21 g carbohydrate, 2 g fiber, 4 g protein.

1½-POUND (16 slices)	INGREDIENTS	2-POUND (22 slices)
¾ cup	milk	1 cup
3 tablespoons	maple-flavored syrup or pure maple syrup	¼ cup
2 tablespoons	margarine or butter, cut up	3 tablespoons
2 tablespoons	water*	2 tablespoons
2½ cups	bread flour	3⅓ cups
¾ cup	whole bran cereal	1 cup
2 teaspoons	gluten flour*	2 teaspoons
¾ teaspoon	salt	1 teaspoon
1¼ teaspoons	active dry yeast or bread machine yeast	1½ teaspoons
¼ cup	chopped walnuts, toasted	⅓ cup

17

CRANBERRY GRANOLA BREAD

Bowl 'em over tomorrow morning! Instead of the same ordinary bowl of cold cereal, serve up slices of a granola-flecked fruit bread that also makes tasty toast.

Prep time: 15 minutes

Nutrition facts per slice: 154 calories, 3 g total fat (1 g saturated fat), 1 mg cholesterol, 140 mg sodium, 27 g carbohydrate, 2 g fiber, 5 g protein.

DIRECTIONS

☞ Select the loaf size. Add the ingredients to the machine according to the manufacturer's directions. Select the basic white bread cycle.

☞ **★NOTE:** Our Test Kitchen recommends 1 tablespoon margarine or butter for either size recipe.

1½-POUND (16 slices)	INGREDIENTS	2-POUND (22 slices)
1¼ cups	buttermilk	1⅔ cups
2 tablespoons	honey	3 tablespoons
1 tablespoon	margarine or butter*	1 tablespoon
1½ cups	bread flour	2 cups
1½ cups	whole wheat flour	2 cups
1 tablespoon	gluten flour	2 tablespoons
¾ teaspoon	salt	1 teaspoon
1 teaspoon	active dry yeast or bread machine yeast	1¼ teaspoons
⅔ cup	granola	¾ cup
½ cup	dried cranberries	¾ cup
¼ cup	chopped almonds, toasted	⅓ cup

That's a fact!

Hitting its height in popularity in the '70s, granola, a breakfast cereal, generally contains a variety of grains (usually oats), nuts, and dried fruit. It usually contains oil and honey and is toasted for a crunchy texture. Added to breads, granola boosts the fiber and nutrition.

BANANA CHOCOLATE CHIP BREAD

What better way to enjoy chocolate than combining it with the rich fruity flavor of banana? Save your ripe bananas and put them to good use in this mini chocolate chip-filled loaf.

DIRECTIONS

☞ Select the loaf size. Add the ingredients to the machine according to the manufacturer's directions. Select the basic white bread cycle.

☞ ***NOTE:** For the 1½-pound loaf, the bread machine pan must have a capacity of 10 cups or more. For the 2-pound loaf, the bread machine pan must have a capacity of 12 cups or more.

☞ ****NOTE:** Our Test Kitchen recommends ½ cup milk and 2 tablespoons margarine or butter for either size recipe.

Prep time: 15 minutes

Nutrition facts per slice: 145 calories, 3 g total fat (1 g saturated fat), 14 mg cholesterol, 126 mg sodium, 25 g carbohydrate, 1 g fiber, 4 g protein.

1½-POUND★ (16 slices)	INGREDIENTS	2-POUND★ (22 slices)
½ cup	milk★★	½ cup
½ cup	mashed ripe banana	⅔ cup
1	egg(s)	2
2 tablespoons	margarine or butter★★	2 tablespoons
3 cups	bread flour	4 cups
2 tablespoons	brown sugar	3 tablespoons
¾ teaspoon	salt	1 teaspoon
1 teaspoon	active dry yeast or bread machine yeast	1¼ teaspoons
⅓ cup	miniature semisweet chocolate pieces	½ cup

19

PINEAPPLE BANANA LOAF

Capture the flavors of the tropics in this sweet loaf. Banana and candied pineapple make it a family favorite, especially when spread with peanut butter or drizzled with honey.

Prep time: 15 minutes

Nutrition facts per slice: 117 calories, 2 g total fat (0 g saturated fat), 11 mg cholesterol, 97 mg sodium, 21 g carbohydrate, 1 g fiber, 3 g protein.

1½-POUND★ (20 slices)	INGREDIENTS	2-POUND★ (27 slices)
½ cup	buttermilk	⅔ cup
½ cup	mashed ripe banana	⅔ cup
1	egg★★	1
1 tablespoon	margarine or butter	4 teaspoons
1 teaspoon	vanilla	1½ teaspoons
3 cups	bread flour	4 cups
3 tablespoons	sugar	¼ cup
¾ teaspoon	salt	1 teaspoon
1 teaspoon	active dry yeast or bread machine yeast	1¼ teaspoons
¼ cup	chopped candied pineapple	⅓ cup
¼ cup	chopped pecans or walnuts, toasted	⅓ cup

DIRECTIONS

☞ Select the loaf size. Add the ingredients to the machine according to the manufacturer's directions. Select the basic white bread cycle.

☞ ★**NOTE:** For the 1½-pound loaf, the bread machine pan must have a capacity of 10 cups or more. For the 2-pound loaf, the bread machine pan must have a capacity of 12 cups or more.

☞ ★★**NOTE:** Our Test Kitchen recommends 1 egg for either size recipe.

Good Advice!

Bits of sticky candied fruit will sometimes clump together in a dough no matter how thoroughly it's kneaded. For more even distribution, first toss the chopped pieces in a little of the flour from the recipe, then add them with the rest of the ingredients as directed.

180

CARROT PINEAPPLE BREAD

Double your pleasure with the fusion of carrot and pineapple flavors. The cakelike appearance and cream cheese topping makes it so versatile—you may want to serve it for dessert.

DIRECTIONS

☞ Select loaf size. Add all ingredients, except the Cream Cheese Glaze, to the machine according to manufacturer's directions. Select basic white bread cycle. Spoon the Cream Cheese Glaze over cooled loaf, allowing some glaze to flow down sides of bread.

☞ *Cream Cheese Glaze:* In a small mixing bowl stir together one-fourth of an 8-ounce tub cream cheese and 1 tablespoon sugar. Stir in enough milk (4 to 5 teaspoons) to make a glaze of drizzling consistency.

☞ ***NOTE:** For the 1½-pound loaf, the bread machine pan must have a capacity of 10 cups or more. For the 2-pound loaf, the bread machine pan must have a capacity of 12 cups or more.

☞ ****NOTE:** Our Test Kitchen recommends one 8-ounce can pineapple and 2 tablespoons margarine or butter for either size recipe.

Prep time: 15 minutes

Nutrition facts per slice: 136 calories, 3 g total fat (1 g saturated fat), 17 mg cholesterol, 128 mg sodium, 22 g carbohydrate, 1 g fiber, 4 g protein.

1½-POUND★ (18 slices)	INGREDIENTS	2-POUND★ (24 slices)
one 8-ounce can	crushed pineapple (juice packed), undrained★★	one 8-ounce can
⅓ cup	finely shredded carrot	½ cup
1	egg(s)	2
2 tablespoons	margarine or butter★★	2 tablespoons
3 cups	bread flour	4 cups
2 tablespoons	sugar	3 tablespoons
¾ teaspoon	salt	1 teaspoon
½ teaspoon	ground ginger	¾ teaspoon
1 teaspoon	active dry yeast or bread machine yeast	1¼ teaspoons
	Cream Cheese Glaze	

181

HAWAIIAN ISLE BREAD

If eating at a kitchen island is all the island living you're doing these days, take a tropical trip via a moist, sweet bread with all the appropriate flavors—coconut, pineapple, and macadamia nuts.

Prep time: 20 minutes

Nutrition facts per slice: 161 calories, 3 g total fat (0 g saturated fat), 13 mg cholesterol, 111 mg sodium, 29 g carbohydrate, 1 g fiber, 4 g protein.

1½-POUND★ (18 slices)	INGREDIENTS	2-POUND★ (24 slices)
¾ cup	milk	1 cup
1	egg★★	1
2 tablespoons	water	3 tablespoons
1 tablespoon	margarine or butter	4 teaspoons
1 teaspoon	vanilla	1½ teaspoons
¼ teaspoon	coconut extract★★	¼ teaspoon
3 cups	bread flour	4 cups
2 tablespoons	sugar	3 tablespoons
¾ teaspoon	salt	1 teaspoon
1 teaspoon	active dry yeast or bread machine yeast	1¼ teaspoons
½ cup	coarsely chopped candied pineapple	⅔ cup
½ cup	coconut, toasted	⅔ cup
	Powdered Sugar Glaze	
2 tablespoons	chopped macadamia nuts★★	2 tablespoons

DIRECTIONS

☞ Select loaf size. Add first 12 ingredients to the machine according to the manufacturer's directions. Select the basic white bread cycle. Drizzle the cooled loaf with Powdered Sugar Glaze and sprinkle with macadamia nuts.

☞ *Powdered Sugar Glaze:* In a small mixing bowl stir together 1 cup sifted powdered sugar and ½ teaspoon vanilla. Stir in enough milk (3 to 4 teaspoons) to make a glaze of drizzling consistency.

☞ ★**NOTE:** For the 1½-pound loaf, the bread machine pan must have a capacity of 10 cups or more. For the 2-pound loaf, the bread machine pan must have a capacity of 12 cups or more.

☞ ★★**NOTE:** Our Test Kitchen recommends 1 egg, ¼ teaspoon coconut extract, and 2 tablespoons nuts for either size recipe.

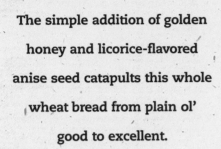

The simple addition of golden honey and licorice-flavored anise seed catapults this whole wheat bread from plain ol' good to excellent.

HONEY ANISE BREAD

DIRECTIONS

☞ Select the loaf size. Add the ingredients to the machine according to the manufacturer's directions. If available, select the whole grain cycle, or select the basic white bread cycle.

☞ **NOTE:** For the 1½-pound loaf, the bread machine pan must have a capacity of 10 cups or more. For the 2-pound loaf, the bread machine pan must have a capacity of 12 cups or more.

HOT TIP

If you've never tried anise seed, here's your chance. The anise seed comes from the anise plant, which is a member of the parsley family. The distinctive licorice flavor is enjoyed in candies as well as savory dishes. It is often used in Southeast Asian cuisine. Look for anise seed in the spice section of the supermarket.

Prep time: 10 minutes

Nutrition facts per slice: 110 calories, 2 g total fat (0 g saturated fat), 1 mg cholesterol, 117 mg sodium, 21 g carbohydrate, 2 g fiber, 4 g protein.

1½-POUND★ (16 slices)	INGREDIENTS	2-POUND★ (22 slices)
1 cup	milk	1¼ cups
2 tablespoons	honey	3 tablespoons
1 tablespoon	water	2 tablespoons
1 tablespoon	margarine or butter	2 tablespoons
1½ cups	bread flour	2 cups
1½ cups	whole wheat flour	2 cups
1 tablespoon	anise seed, crushed	4 teaspoons
2 teaspoons	gluten flour	1 tablespoon
¾ teaspoon	salt	1 teaspoon
1 teaspoon	active dry yeast or bread machine yeast	1¼ teaspoons

183

NEW ORLEANS BEIGNETS

The traditional French fritter or beignet is a puffy, deep-fried doughnutlike pastry. Try them topped—as they typically are in New Orleans—sprinkled with powdered sugar.

Prep time: 30 minutes **Cook time:** 1 minute per batch
Nutrition facts per beignet: 77 calories, 2 g total fat (1 g saturated fat), 7 mg cholesterol, 62 mg sodium, 12 g carbohydrate, 0 g fiber, 2 g protein.

1½-POUND (32 beignets)	INGREDIENTS	2-POUND (48 beignets)
⅔ cup	buttermilk	¾ cup
¼ cup	water	⅓ cup
1	egg*	1
1 tablespoon	margarine or butter	4 teaspoons
1 teaspoon	vanilla	1½ teaspoons
3 cups	bread flour	4 cups
¼ cup	sugar	⅓ cup
¾ teaspoon	salt	1 teaspoon
1¼ teaspoons	active dry yeast or bread machine yeast	1½ teaspoons
	Cooking oil for deep-fat frying	
	Sifted powdered sugar	

DIRECTIONS

☞ Select the recipe size. Add all ingredients, except the cooking oil and powdered sugar, to the machine according to manufacturer's directions. Select the dough cycle. When cycle is complete, remove dough from machine. Punch down. Cover; let rest for 10 minutes.

☞ Divide the 1½-pound dough in half (divide the 2-pound dough into thirds). On a lightly floured surface, roll each portion of dough into a 9-inch square. Cut each into sixteen 2¼-inch squares.

☞ Fry the dough squares, 2 or 3 at a time, in deep hot oil (375°) for 1 to 2 minutes or until golden brown, turning once. Using a slotted spoon, remove from oil and drain on paper towels. Sprinkle with powdered sugar. Transfer to wire racks to cool.

☞ **NOTE:** Our Test Kitchen recommends 1 egg for either size recipe.

CINNAMON RAISIN GRAHAM BREAD

Home is where the heart is—and nothing says "home" better than this blissful bread. Packed full of good-for-you raisins and flavored with graham flour, it's the ultimate old-fashioned bread.

Prep time: 10 minutes

Nutrition facts per slice: 124 calories, 2 g total fat (0 g saturated fat), 0 mg cholesterol, 118 mg sodium, 24 g carbohydrate, 2 g fiber, 4 g protein.

1½-POUND★ (16 slices)	INGREDIENTS	2-POUND★ (22 slices)
1 cup	water	1⅓ cups
3 tablespoons	honey	¼ cup
2 tablespoons	margarine or butter, cut up	3 tablespoons
2 cups	bread flour	2¾ cups
1 cup	graham (coarse whole wheat) flour	1¼ cups
1 tablespoon	gluten flour	4 teaspoons
¾ teaspoon	salt	1 teaspoon
¾ teaspoon	ground cinnamon	1 teaspoon
1 teaspoon	active dry yeast or bread machine yeast★★	1 teaspoon
⅓ cup	dark raisins	½ cup

DIRECTIONS

☞ Select the loaf size. Add the ingredients to the machine according to the manufacturer's directions. If available, select the whole grain cycle, or select the basic white bread cycle.

☞ ★**NOTE:** For the 1½-pound loaf, the bread machine pan must have a capacity of 10 cups or more. For the 2-pound loaf, the bread machine pan must have a capacity of 12 cups or more.

☞ ★★**NOTE:** Our Test Kitchen recommends 1 teaspoon yeast for either size recipe.

That's a fact!

Graham flour got its name from its developer, Rev. Sylvester Graham, a health advocate from Connecticut during the 1800s. Graham flour is whole wheat flour that is slightly coarser than regular ground whole wheat flour. You may use graham flour interchangeably with regular whole wheat flour in recipes.

186

You won't have to wait until the pears are ripe and juicy. This recipe utilizes sweet, juicy canned pears. Mash the drained pears well before adding them to the machine.

FRENCH PEAR BREAD

DIRECTIONS

☞ Select the loaf size. Add the ingredients to the machine according to the manufacturer's directions. Select the basic white bread cycle.

☞ ***NOTE:** For the 1½-pound loaf, the bread machine pan must have a capacity of 10 cups or more. For the 2-pound loaf, the bread machine pan must have a capacity of 12 cups or more.

☞ ****NOTE:** Our Test Kitchen recommends 1 egg for either size recipe.

Prep time: 10 minutes
Nutrition facts per slice: 89 calories, 1 g total fat (0 g saturated fat), 11 mg cholesterol, 84 mg sodium, 18 g carbohydrate, 1 g fiber, 3 g protein.

1½-POUND* (20 slices)	INGREDIENTS	2-POUND* (27 slices)
¾ cup	mashed, drained canned pears (juice packed)	1 cup
¼ cup	water	⅓ cup
1	egg**	1
1 tablespoon	honey	4 teaspoons
3 cups	bread flour	4 cups
¾ teaspoon	salt	1 teaspoon
⅛ teaspoon	pepper	¼ teaspoon
1 teaspoon	active dry yeast or bread machine yeast	1¼ teaspoons

187

FINNISH CARDAMOM LOAF

Cardamom, a member of the ginger family, gives this bread a spicy-sweet flavor. One taste and you'll appreciate why the Far East spice trade changed the Western world.

Prep time: 10 minutes

Nutrition facts per slice: 115 calories, 2 g total fat (1 g saturated fat), 13 mg cholesterol, 107 mg sodium, 19 g carbohydrate, 1 g fiber, 4 g protein.

1½-POUND★ (20 slices)	INGREDIENTS	2-POUND★ (27 slices)
¾ cup	evaporated milk	1 cup
¼ cup	water★★	¼ cup
1	egg★★	1
2 tablespoons	margarine or butter, cut up	3 tablespoons
3 cups	bread flour	4 cups
⅓ cup	sugar	½ cup
¾ teaspoon	salt	1 teaspoon
¾ teaspoon	ground cardamom	1 teaspoon
1 teaspoon	active dry yeast or bread machine yeast	1¼ teaspoons

DIRECTIONS

☞ Select the loaf size. Add the ingredients to the machine according to the manufacturer's directions. Select the basic white bread cycle.

☞ ★**NOTE:** For the 1½-pound loaf, the bread machine pan must have a capacity of 10 cups or more. For the 2-pound loaf, the bread machine pan must have a capacity of 12 cups or more.

☞ ★★**NOTE:** Our Test Kitchen recommends ¼ cup water and 1 egg for either size recipe.

HOT TIP

Spices, such as cardamom, are often available whole or ground. Ground spices lose their flavor fairly quickly (in about 6 months), so buying ground spices in small quantities makes sense. Whole spices can be stored longer and ground when needed. Keep spices in airtight containers in a cool, dark place.

CARAMEL CAPPUCCINO LOAF

Instant coffee and caramel ice-cream topping give this bread its appealing aroma and taste. It's sweet, but not too sweet, and will be popular with coffee fans.

DIRECTIONS

☞ Select the loaf size. Dissolve the coffee crystals in water. Add the coffee mixture and the remaining ingredients to the machine according to the manufacturer's directions. Select the basic white bread setting.

☞ *NOTE: For the 1½-pound loaf, the bread machine pan must have a capacity of 10 cups or more. For the 2-pound loaf, the bread machine pan must have a capacity of 12 cups or more.

☞ **NOTE: Our Test Kitchen recommends 1 egg for either size recipe.

Prep time: 10 minutes
Nutrition facts per slice: 102 calories, 2 g total fat (0 g saturated fat), 11 mg cholesterol, 114 mg sodium, 18 g carbohydrate, 1 g fiber, 3 g protein.

1½-POUND★ (20 slices)	INGREDIENTS	2-POUND★ (27 slices)
4 teaspoons	instant coffee crystals	2 tablespoons
¼ cup	water	⅓ cup
⅓ cup	milk	½ cup
¼ cup	caramel ice-cream topping	⅓ cup
1	egg**	1
2 tablespoons	margarine or butter, cut up	3 tablespoons
3 cups	bread flour	4 cups
¾ teaspoon	salt	1 teaspoon
1¼ teaspoons	active dry yeast or bread machine yeast	1½ teaspoons

189

PEANUT BUTTER SNACK BREAD

Die-hard peanut butter fans will appreciate this crunchy, flavorful loaf. Serve with a steaming cup of hot cocoa—morning, noon, or night.

Prep time: 15 minutes

Nutrition facts per slice: 184 calories, 7 g total fat (1 g saturated fat), 15 mg cholesterol, 194 mg sodium, 24 g carbohydrate, 1 g fiber, 7 g protein.

1½-POUND★ (16 slices)	INGREDIENTS	2-POUND★ (22 slices)
1 cup + 2 tablespoons	milk	1¼ cups
⅓ cup	peanut butter	½ cup
1	egg(s)	2
3 cups	bread flour	4 cups
2 tablespoons	sugar	3 tablespoons
¾ teaspoon	salt	1 teaspoon
1 teaspoon	active dry yeast or bread machine yeast	1¼ teaspoons
¾ cup	chopped peanuts	1 cup

DIRECTIONS

☞ Select the loaf size. Add the ingredients to the machine according to the manufacturer's directions. Select the basic white bread cycle.

☞ ★**NOTE:** For the 1½-pound loaf, the bread machine pan must have a capacity of 10 cups or more. For the 2-pound loaf, the bread machine pan must have a capacity of 12 cups or more.

Did you know?

Don't tell your kids, but peanut butter was invented by a doctor as a health food. A St. Louis physician first thought to grind peanuts to a tasty paste at the turn of the nineteenth century and told the world about it at the 1904 St. Louis World's Fair. Its popularity quickly soared as a sandwich spread, especially with grape jelly.

190

BLUEBERRY BLACK WALNUT BREAD

Black walnuts and dried blueberries create a taste sensation to behold. Vary the recipe another time by using dried cherries and English walnuts.

DIRECTIONS

☞ Select the loaf size. Add the ingredients to the machine according to the manufacturer's directions. Select the basic white bread cycle.

☞ **⋆NOTE:** For the 1½-pound loaf, the bread machine pan must have a capacity of 10 cups or more. For the 2-pound loaf, the bread machine pan must have a capacity of 12 cups or more.

☞ **⋆⋆NOTE:** Our Test Kitchen recommends 1 egg and 2 tablespoons margarine or butter for either size recipe.

Prep time: 15 minutes

Nutrition facts per slice: 135 calories, 4 g total fat (1 g saturated fat), 13 mg cholesterol, 115 mg sodium, 21 g carbohydrate, 1 g fiber, 4 g protein.

1½-POUND⋆ (18 slices)	INGREDIENTS	2-POUND⋆ (24 slices)
½ cup	milk	⅔ cup
½ cup	vanilla yogurt	⅔ cup
1	egg⋆⋆	1
2 tablespoons	margarine or butter⋆⋆	2 tablespoons
3 cups	bread flour	4 cups
¾ teaspoon	salt	1 teaspoon
1 teaspoon	active dry yeast or bread machine yeast	1¼ teaspoons
⅓ cup	dried blueberries	½ cup
⅓ cup	chopped black walnuts	½ cup

191

SHAPED

{ CHOCOLATE HAZELNUT RING }

see recipe, page 194

CHOCOLATE HAZELNUT RING

(Pictured on page 193.)

Prep time: 25 minutes **Rise time:** 45 minutes **Bake time:** 30 minutes
Nutrition facts per serving: 196 calories, 7 g total fat (1 g saturated fat), 14 mg cholesterol, 144 mg sodium, 28 g carbohydrate, 1 g fiber, 5 g protein.

1½-POUND (16 servings)	INGREDIENTS	2-POUND (22 servings)
⅔ cup	milk	¾ cup
1	egg*	1
3 tablespoons	margarine or butter, cut up	¼ cup
2 tablespoons	water	3 tablespoons
3 cups	bread flour	4 cups
¼ cup	sugar	⅓ cup
¾ teaspoon	salt	1 teaspoon
1¼ teaspoons	active dry yeast or bread machine yeast	1½ teaspoons
⅓ cup	chocolate hazelnut spread	½ cup
⅓ cup	chopped hazelnuts	½ cup
	Chocolate Hazelnut Icing	

DIRECTIONS

☞ Select recipe size. Add first 8 ingredients to machine according to the manufacturer's directions. Select dough cycle. When cycle is complete, remove dough from machine. Punch down. Cover; let rest for 10 minutes.

☞ On a lightly floured surface, roll the 1½-pound dough into a 15×10-inch rectangle (roll the 2-pound dough into an 18×10-inch rectangle). Spread with chocolate hazelnut spread and sprinkle with hazelnuts.

☞ Starting from a long side, roll up into a spiral; seal edge. Place, seam down, on a greased large baking sheet. Bring ends together to form a ring. Moisten ends; pinch together to seal ring. Using kitchen scissors or a sharp knife, cut from the outside edge toward center, leaving about 1 inch attached. Repeat around the edge at 1-inch intervals. Gently turn each slice slightly so the same side of all slices faces upward.

☞ Cover and let rise in a warm place for 45 to 60 minutes or until nearly double. Bake in a 350° oven for 30 to 35 minutes or until bread sounds hollow when lightly tapped (the center may be lighter in color). If necessary, loosely cover with foil last 10 minutes to prevent overbrowning. Remove from baking sheet; cool on a wire rack. Drizzle with Chocolate Hazelnut Icing.

☞ *Chocolate Hazelnut Icing:* In a microwave-safe container heat ¼ cup chocolate hazelnut spread on 100 percent power (high) for 30 to 60 seconds or until of drizzling consistency.

☞ ***NOTE:** Our Test Kitchen recommends 1 egg for either size recipe.

TRIPLE CHOCOLATE CRESCENTS

Just bite into these rolls flavored three times with chocolate and you'll understand why the botanical name of the cacao tree, *Theobroma cacao*, translates as "food of the gods."

DIRECTIONS

☞ Select recipe size. Add first 9 ingredients to the machine according to manufacturer's directions. Select the dough cycle. When cycle is complete, remove dough from machine. Punch down. Cover and let rest 10 minutes.

☞ *For the 1½-pound recipe:* Divide dough in half. On a lightly floured surface, roll each half into a 10-inch circle; cut circle into 10 wedges. Break each chocolate bar into 10 pieces; place 1 piece onto wide end of each wedge. Starting at the wide end of each wedge, roll up toward the point.

☞ Place rolls, points down, on greased baking sheets. Cover; let rise in a warm place for 20 to 30 minutes or until nearly double. Bake in a 375° oven for 12 to 15 minutes or until rolls sound hollow when lightly tapped. Remove from baking sheets; cool slightly on wire racks. Drizzle with Chocolate Glaze.

☞ *For the 2-pound recipe:* Prepare and shape as above, except divide the dough into thirds.

☞ *Chocolate Glaze:* In a bowl stir together 1 cup sifted powdered sugar, 2 tablespoons unsweetened cocoa powder, and ½ teaspoon vanilla. Stir in enough milk (1 to 2 tablespoons) to make a glaze of drizzling consistency.

☞ **★NOTE:** Our Test Kitchen recommends 1 egg for either size recipe.

Prep time: 25 minutes   **Rise time:** 20 minutes   **Bake time:** 12 minutes
Nutrition facts per roll: 161 calories, 5 g total fat (1 g saturated fat), 11 mg cholesterol, 119 mg sodium, 26 g carbohydrate, 1 g fiber, 4 g protein.

1½-POUND (20 rolls)	INGREDIENTS	2-POUND (30 rolls)
⅔ cup	milk	¾ cup
¼ cup	water	⅓ cup
¼ cup	margarine or butter, cut up	⅓ cup
1	egg★	1
3 cups	bread flour	4 cups
¼ cup	sugar	⅓ cup
¼ cup	unsweetened cocoa powder	⅓ cup
¾ teaspoon	salt	1 teaspoon
1½ teaspoons	active dry yeast or bread machine yeast	2 teaspoons
two 1½-ounce	milk chocolate bars	three 1½-ounce
	Chocolate Glaze	

195

CHOCOLATE PEANUT BUTTER TWISTS

Kids will enjoy helping make these twists. The combination of peanut butter, honey, and semisweet chocolate pieces makes for a very special morning or afternoon treat.

Prep time: 30 minutes   **Rise time:** 30 minutes   **Bake time:** 10 minutes
Nutrition facts per twist: 159 calories, 6 g total fat (1 g saturated fat), 12 mg cholesterol, 141 mg sodium, 22 g carbohydrate, 1 g fiber, 5 g protein.

1½-POUND (18 twists)	INGREDIENTS	2-POUND (24 twists)
½ cup	milk	⅔ cup
¼ cup	water	⅓ cup
1	egg*	1
3 tablespoons	margarine or butter, cut up	¼ cup
3 cups	bread flour	4 cups
2 tablespoons	sugar	3 tablespoons
¾ teaspoon	salt	1 teaspoon
1¼ teaspoons	active dry yeast or bread machine yeast	1½ teaspoons
⅓ cup	creamy peanut butter	½ cup
1 tablespoon	honey	2 tablespoons
⅓ cup	miniature semisweet chocolate pieces	½ cup

DIRECTIONS

☞ Select recipe size. Add first 8 ingredients to machine according to manufacturer's directions. Select dough cycle. When cycle is complete, remove dough from machine. Punch down. Cover; let rest for 10 minutes.

☞ Meanwhile, for filling, in a small bowl combine the peanut butter and honey.

☞ *For the 1½-pound recipe:* On a lightly floured surface, roll dough to an 18×12-inch rectangle. Spread with filling to within ½ inch of edges. Sprinkle with chocolate pieces, pressing lightly into dough. Starting from a long side, fold one-third of dough over center third. Fold remaining third over center, forming 3 equal layers. Moisten; seal edges. Cut crosswise into eighteen 1-inch-wide strips. Twist each strip twice.

☞ Place strips 2 inches apart on greased baking sheets, pressing ends down. Cover; let rise in a warm place about 30 minutes or until nearly double. Bake in a 350° oven 10 to 12 minutes or until golden. Remove from baking sheets; cool slightly on racks.

☞ *For the 2-pound recipe:* Prepare as above, except roll dough into a 24×12-inch rectangle; fill, fold, and cut dough crosswise into twenty-four 1-inch-wide strips.

☞ ***NOTE:** Our Test Kitchen recommends 1 egg for either size recipe.

CHOCOLATE MARZIPAN SWIRLS

DIRECTIONS

☞ Select the recipe size. Add the first 8 ingredients to the machine according to the manufacturer's directions. Select the dough cycle. When cycle is complete, remove dough from machine. Punch down. Cover and let rest for 10 minutes.

☞ *For the 1½-pound recipe:* On a lightly floured surface, roll dough into a 16×12-inch rectangle. Spread with the Almond Filling. Starting from a long side, roll into a spiral; seal edge. Cut into 16 slices. Place, cut sides down, in a greased 13×9×2-inch baking pan. Cover and let rise in a warm place about 45 minutes or until nearly double. Bake in a 375° oven about 20 minutes or until golden brown. Cool about 5 minutes; invert onto a wire rack. Drizzle with Powdered Sugar Glaze and sprinkle with almonds.

☞ *For the 2-pound recipe:* Prepare as above, except divide the dough in half. Roll each half into a 12×8-inch rectangle. Spread each rectangle with half of the Almond Filling; roll up. Cut each roll into 12 slices; place 24 slices in a greased 15×10×1-inch baking pan. Continue as above.

☞ *Almond Filling:* In a medium mixing bowl beat together one 8-ounce can almond paste, crumbled; ¼ cup sugar; 1 egg white; 2 tablespoons unsweetened cocoa powder; and 2 tablespoons milk until nearly smooth.

☞ *Powdered Sugar Glaze:* In a small mixing bowl stir together 1½ cups sifted powdered sugar and 1 teaspoon vanilla. Stir in enough milk (1 to 2 tablespoons) to make a glaze of drizzling consistency.

☞ ★**NOTE:** Our Test Kitchen recommends ¼ cup almonds for either size recipe.

Prep time: 30 minutes   **Rise time:** 45 minutes   **Bake time:** 20 minutes
Nutrition facts per roll: 270 calories, 9 g total fat (1 g saturated fat), 27 mg cholesterol, 151 mg sodium, 41 g carbohydrate, 1 g fiber, 7 g protein.

1½-POUND (16 rolls)	INGREDIENTS	2-POUND (24 rolls)
2	eggs	3
⅓ cup	milk	½ cup
¼ cup	water	⅓ cup
¼ cup	margarine or butter, cut up	⅓ cup
3 cups	bread flour	4 cups
3 tablespoons	sugar	¼ cup
¾ teaspoon	salt	1 teaspoon
1½ teaspoons	active dry yeast or bread machine yeast	2 teaspoons
	Almond Filling	
	Powdered Sugar Glaze	
¼ cup	sliced almonds, toasted★	¼ cup

197

MINI MAPLE BUNS

DIRECTIONS

☞ Select the recipe size. Add the first 8 ingredients to the machine according to the manufacturer's directions. Select the dough cycle. When cycle is complete, remove dough from machine. Punch down. Cover and let rest for 10 minutes.

☞ Meanwhile, for filling, in a small bowl stir together the brown sugar, softened margarine or butter, the 1 tablespoon or 4 teaspoons flour, and cinnamon.

☞ *For the 1½-pound recipe:* On a lightly floured surface, roll dough into a 14×12-inch rectangle. Spread with the filling to within ¼ inch of the edges. Cut the rectangle in half lengthwise to make two 12×7-inch rectangles. Starting from a long side, roll up each rectangle into a spiral; seal edge. Cut each into 16 slices. Place, cut sides down, 1 inch apart on greased large baking sheets. Cover and let rise in a warm place about 25 minutes or until nearly double. Brush rolls with a little additional milk. Bake in a 375° oven for 12 to 15 minutes or until golden brown.

☞ For icing, in a saucepan heat the 3 tablespoons or ¼ cup butter over medium-low heat for 7 to 10 minutes or until light brown. Remove from heat. Stir in powdered sugar and the 3 tablespoons or ¼ cup maple syrup. Stir in enough milk (2 to 3 teaspoons) to make an icing of drizzling consistency.

☞ Remove buns from baking sheets; cool slightly on wire racks. Drizzle with the icing.

☞ *For the 2-pound recipe:* Prepare and fill as above, except roll dough into a 16×14-inch rectangle. Cut in half lengthwise to make two 16×7-inch rectangles. Roll up; cut each into 20 slices. Continue as above.

☞ **★NOTE:** Our Test Kitchen recommends 1 egg for either size dough and 2 to 3 teaspoons milk for either icing.

Prep time: 15 minutes **Rise time:** 25 minutes **Bake time:** 12 minutes
Nutrition facts per bun: 137 calories, 6 g total fat (1 g saturated fat), 10 mg cholesterol, 102 mg sodium, 20 g carbohydrate, 0 g fiber, 2 g protein.

1½-POUND (32 buns)	INGREDIENTS	2-POUND (40 buns)
⅔ cup	milk	¾ cup
⅓ cup	maple-flavored syrup	½ cup
⅓ cup	margarine or butter, cut up	½ cup
1	egg★	1
3 cups	bread flour	4 cups
¾ teaspoon	salt	1 teaspoon
1¼ teaspoons	active dry yeast or bread machine yeast	1½ teaspoons
½ cup	finely chopped pecans	⅔ cup
¼ cup	packed brown sugar	⅓ cup
3 tablespoons	margarine or butter, softened	¼ cup
1 tablespoon	bread flour	4 teaspoons
2 teaspoons	ground cinnamon	1 tablespoon
3 tablespoons	butter	¼ cup
1½ cups	sifted powdered sugar	2 cups
3 tablespoons	maple-flavored syrup	¼ cup
2 to 3 teaspoons	milk★	2 to 3 teaspoons

COCONUT FILLED SWEET ROLLS

Prep time: 25 minutes   **Rise time:** 30 minutes   **Bake time:** 20 minutes
Nutrition facts per roll: 268 calories, 8 g total fat (3 g saturated fat), 19 mg cholesterol, 204 mg sodium, 45 g carbohydrate, 1 g fiber, 6 g protein.

1½-POUND (12 rolls)	INGREDIENTS	2-POUND (16 rolls)
¾ cup	milk	1 cup
1	egg*	1
3 tablespoons	margarine or butter, cut up	¼ cup
1 tablespoon	water*	1 tablespoon
3 cups	bread flour	4 cups
¼ cup	sugar	⅓ cup
¾ teaspoon	salt	1 teaspoon
1¼ teaspoons	active dry yeast or bread machine yeast	1½ teaspoons
¼ cup	sugar	⅓ cup
2 tablespoons	margarine or butter, melted	3 tablespoons
⅔ cup	coconut, toasted	¾ cup
	Powdered Sugar Glaze	
	Coconut, toasted	

DIRECTIONS

☞ Select the recipe size. Add the first 8 ingredients to the machine according to the manufacturer's directions. Select the dough cycle. When cycle is complete, remove dough from machine. Punch down. Cover and let rest for 10 minutes.

☞ Meanwhile, for filling, in a small mixing bowl stir together the ¼ or ⅓ cup sugar and the melted margarine or butter.

☞ *For the 1½-pound recipe:* On a lightly floured surface, roll the dough into a 12-inch circle. Spread with the filling and sprinkle with the ⅔ cup coconut. Cut into 12 wedges. Starting at wide end of each wedge, loosely roll toward the point. Place rolls, points down, in a greased 13×9×2-inch baking pan.

☞ Cover and let rise in a warm place about 30 minutes or until nearly double. Bake in a 350° oven for 20 to 25 minutes or until golden brown. Cool in pan on a wire rack for 2 minutes. Invert to remove from pan; turn right side up. Cool slightly. Drizzle rolls with Powdered Sugar Glaze. Sprinkle with additional coconut.

☞ *For the 2-pound recipe:* Prepare as above, except divide the dough in half and roll into 10-inch circles. Spread each circle with half of the filling and sprinkle each with half of the ¾ cup coconut. Cut each circle into 8 wedges. Roll up wedges; place in a greased 15×10×1-inch baking pan. Continue as above.

☞ *Powdered Sugar Glaze:* In a small bowl stir together 1 cup sifted powdered sugar and 1 teaspoon vanilla. Stir in enough milk (3 to 4 teaspoons) to make a glaze of drizzling consistency.

☞ ***NOTE:** Our Test Kitchen recommends 1 egg and 1 tablespoon water for either size recipe.

APPLE WALNUT BLUE CHEESE BURST

DIRECTIONS

☞ Select the recipe size. Add the first 8 ingredients to the machine according to the manufacturer's directions. Select the dough cycle. When cycle is complete, remove dough from machine. Punch down. Cover and let rest for 10 minutes.

☞ Meanwhile, for filling, in a medium mixing bowl combine the apples, blue cheese, walnuts, and brown sugar.

☞ *For the 1½-pound recipe:* On a lightly floured surface, roll the dough into an 18×12-inch rectangle. Spread with the filling. Starting from a long side, roll up into a spiral; seal edge. Place, seam down, on a greased large baking sheet. Bring ends together to form a ring. Moisten ends; pinch together to seal ring. Using kitchen scissors or a sharp knife, make a cut from the outside edge toward center, leaving about ½ inch attached. Repeat around the edge at 1- to 1½-inch intervals. Gently pull apart each slice.

☞ Cover and let rise in a warm place for 45 to 60 minutes or until nearly double. Bake in a 350° oven for 30 to 35 minutes or until bread sounds hollow when lightly tapped. If necessary, loosely cover with foil last 10 to 15 minutes to prevent overbrowning. Remove; cool on a wire rack.

☞ *For the 2-pound recipe:* Prepare as above, except roll the dough into a 20×16-inch rectangle. Fill and shape as directed above and place on a greased extra-large baking sheet.

Prep time: 25 minutes **Rise time:** 45 minutes **Bake time:** 30 minutes
Nutrition facts per serving: 179 calories, 7 g total fat (2 g saturated fat), 19 mg cholesterol, 239 mg sodium, 24 g carbohydrate, 1 g fiber, 6 g protein.

1½-POUND (16 servings)	INGREDIENTS	2-POUND (22 servings)
¾ cup	buttermilk	1 cup
1	egg(s)	2
¼ cup	margarine or butter, cut up	⅓ cup
2⅓ cups	bread flour	3¼ cups
⅔ cup	whole wheat flour	¾ cup
2 tablespoons	granulated sugar	3 tablespoons
¾ teaspoon	salt	1 teaspoon
1 teaspoon	active dry yeast or bread machine yeast	1¼ teaspoons
1 cup	chopped, peeled cooking apples	1½ cups
¾ cup	crumbled blue cheese	1 cup
⅓ cup	chopped walnuts, toasted	½ cup
2 tablespoons	brown sugar	3 tablespoons

201

WALNUT FILLED LOAVES

Offer up nourishment for the body and the soul with this special hand-rolled bread. The golden spiral loaves offer a brown sugar-sweetened walnut filling. The ultimate in comfort food.

Prep time: 35 minutes **Rise time:** 30 minutes **Bake time:** 30 minutes
Nutrition facts per slice: 133 calories, 7 g total fat (1 g saturated fat), 14 mg cholesterol, 75 mg sodium, 16 g carbohydrate, 1 g fiber, 3 g protein.

1½-POUND (32 slices)	INGREDIENTS	2-POUND (48 slices)
¾ cup	milk	1 cup
1	egg(s)	2
3 tablespoons	margarine or butter, cut up	¼ cup
3 cups	bread flour	4 cups
¼ cup	granulated sugar	⅓ cup
¾ teaspoon	salt	1 teaspoon
1 teaspoon	active dry yeast or bread machine yeast	1¼ teaspoons
2 cups	ground walnuts	3 cups
⅓ cup	packed brown sugar	½ cup
3 tablespoons	granulated sugar	¼ cup
1 tablespoon	margarine or butter, softened	2 tablespoons
4 teaspoons	milk	2 tablespoons
¼ teaspoon	vanilla	½ teaspoon
1	beaten egg	1
1 tablespoon	water	1 tablespoon

DIRECTIONS

☞ Select loaf size. Add first 7 ingredients to the machine according to the manufacturer's directions. Select dough cycle. When cycle is complete, remove dough from machine. Punch down. Cover; let rest for 10 minutes.

☞ For filling, stir together walnuts, brown sugar, and the 3 tablespoons or ¼ cup granulated sugar. Stir in softened margarine or butter, the 4 teaspoons or 2 tablespoons milk, and vanilla.

☞ *For the 1½-pound recipe:* Divide dough in half. On a lightly floured surface, roll each half into a 16×10-inch rectangle. Spread each rectangle with half of filling almost to the edges. Starting from a long side, loosely roll into a spiral. In a small bowl stir together 1 beaten egg and water. Moisten edge of dough with some egg mixture; pinch firmly to seal. Place loaves, seams down, on a greased large baking sheet, tucking ends under. Prick tops with a fork.

☞ Cover; let rise in a warm place about 30 minutes or until nearly double. Brush with remaining egg mixture. Bake in a 350° oven about 30 minutes or until bread sounds hollow when tapped. If necessary, loosely cover with foil last 15 minutes to prevent overbrowning. Remove from baking sheet; cool on racks.

☞ *For the 2-pound recipe:* Prepare and shape as above, except divide dough and filling into thirds. Use 2 greased large baking sheets.

202

BRUNCH BRAIDS

DIRECTIONS

☞ Select the recipe size. Add the first 8 ingredients to the machine according to the manufacturer's directions. Select the dough cycle. When the cycle is complete, remove dough from machine. Punch down. Cover and let rest for 10 minutes.

☞ Meanwhile, for filling, in a large skillet cook sausage or bacon until done; drain off fat. In a medium mixing bowl beat together the 6 or 8 eggs, 3 tablespoons or ¼ cup milk, ¼ teaspoon salt, and pepper; add to skillet. Cook over medium heat, without stirring, until mixture begins to set on the bottom and around the edge. Using a spatula, lift and fold the partially cooked eggs so the uncooked portion flows underneath. Continue cooking until eggs are cooked through, but are still glossy and moist. Remove from heat.

☞ *For the 1½-pound recipe:* On a lightly floured surface, roll dough into an 18×16-inch rectangle. Cut into six 8×6-inch rectangles. Transfer to greased baking sheets. Spoon about ⅓ cup filling down the center of each rectangle. On the long sides, make 2-inch cuts from the edges toward the center at 1-inch intervals. Alternately fold opposite strips of dough, at an angle, across the filling. Lightly press ends in the center together to seal.

☞ Cover and let rise in a warm place about 15 minutes or until nearly double. (Or, cover and let rise in the refrigerator for 2 to 24 hours. Before baking, remove from the refrigerator and let stand for 20 minutes.) Bake in a 350° oven about 15 minutes or until golden brown. Remove from baking sheets; transfer to wire racks. Serve warm.

☞ *For the 2-pound recipe:* Prepare and shape as above, except roll dough into a 24×16-inch rectangle; cut into eight 8×6-inch rectangles.

☞ ***NOTE:** Our Test Kitchen recommends 1 egg for either size dough and ¼ teaspoon salt and ⅛ teaspoon pepper for either size filling.

Prep time: 30 minutes   **Rise time:** 15 minutes   **Bake time:** 15 minutes
Nutrition facts per serving: 458 calories, 15 g total fat (4 g saturated fat), 262 mg cholesterol, 659 mg sodium, 59 g carbohydrate, 2 g fiber, 19 g protein.

1½-POUND (6 servings)	INGREDIENTS	2-POUND (8 servings)
½ cup	milk	⅔ cup
¼ cup	water	⅓ cup
1	egg*	1
2 tablespoons	margarine or butter, cut up	3 tablespoons
3 cups	bread flour	4 cups
3 tablespoons	sugar	¼ cup
¾ teaspoon	salt	1 teaspoon
1¼ teaspoons	active dry yeast or bread machine yeast	1½ teaspoons
6 ounces	spicy bulk pork sausage or	8 ounces
6 slices	bacon, chopped	8 slices
6	eggs	8
3 tablespoons	milk	¼ cup
¼ teaspoon	salt*	¼ teaspoon
⅛ teaspoon	pepper*	⅛ teaspoon

205

MIXED BERRY COFFEE CAKE

Prep time: 25 minutes **Rise time:** 30 minutes **Bake time:** 25 minutes

Nutrition facts per serving: 189 calories, 3 g total fat (1 g saturated fat), 19 mg cholesterol, 167 mg sodium, 35 g carbohydrate, 2 g fiber, 5 g protein.

1½-POUND (12 servings)	INGREDIENTS	2-POUND (16 servings)
½ cup	milk	⅔ cup
¼ cup	water	⅓ cup
1	egg*	1
2 tablespoons	margarine or butter, cut up	3 tablespoons
3 cups	bread flour	4 cups
2 tablespoons	sugar	3 tablespoons
¾ teaspoon	salt	1 teaspoon
¼ teaspoon	ground nutmeg	½ teaspoon
1 teaspoon	active dry yeast or bread machine yeast	1¼ teaspoons
½ cup	strawberries	⅔ cup
½ cup	raspberries	⅔ cup
½ cup	blackberries	⅔ cup
¼ cup	sugar	⅓ cup
2 teaspoons	cornstarch	1 tablespoon
½ teaspoon	finely shredded lemon peel	¾ teaspoon
	Sifted powdered sugar	

204

DIRECTIONS

☞ Select the recipe size. Add the first 9 ingredients to the machine according to the manufacturer's directions. Select the dough cycle. When cycle is complete, remove dough from machine. Punch down. Cover and let rest for 10 minutes.

☞ Meanwhile, for filling, in a food processor bowl or blender container combine berries; cover and process or blend until nearly smooth. Press the berries through a sieve and discard seeds. In a medium saucepan stir together the ¼ or ⅓ cup sugar and cornstarch. Stir in sieved berries. Cook and stir until thickened and bubbly. Stir in lemon peel.

☞ *For the 1½-pound recipe:* Divide the dough in half. Press half of the dough into a greased 11-inch tart pan, letting dough rest a few minutes occasionally. Spread with the filling to within ½ inch of the edges. On a lightly floured surface, roll the remaining dough into an 11-inch circle; cut into ¾-inch-wide strips. Weave the strips over filling in a lattice pattern. Trim ends as necessary; press against bottom dough to seal.

☞ Cover and let rise in a warm place about 30 minutes or until nearly double. Bake in a 375° oven for 25 minutes. If necessary, loosely cover with foil last 10 minutes to prevent overbrowning. Cool slightly in pan on a wire rack. Dust with powdered sugar.

☞ *For the 2-pound recipe:* Prepare as above, except press half of the dough into a greased 12-inch pizza pan. Roll the remaining dough into a 12-inch circle; cut into ¾-inch-wide strips. Continue as above.

☞ **NOTE:** Our Test Kitchen recommends 1 egg for either size recipe.

RASPBERRY RIBBON COFFEE BREAD

The red ribbon running through this coffee cake is conveniently made from raspberry preserves. The streusel topping is a buttery, cinnamon mixture that will melt in your mouth.

Prep time: 20 minutes   **Rise time:** 1 hour   **Bake time:** 50 minutes

Nutrition facts per serving: 208 calories, 7 g total fat (4 g saturated fat), 37 mg cholesterol, 182 mg sodium, 32 g carbohydrate, 1 g fiber, 4 g protein.

1½-POUND (16 servings)	INGREDIENTS	2-POUND (20 servings)
⅔ cup	milk	¾ cup
⅓ cup	butter or margarine, cut up	½ cup
1	egg(s)	2
2 tablespoons	water*	2 tablespoons
3 cups	bread flour	4 cups
⅓ cup	granulated sugar	½ cup
¾ teaspoon	salt	1 teaspoon
1¼ teaspoons	active dry yeast or bread machine yeast	1½ teaspoons
⅓ cup	seedless red raspberry preserves or apple butter	½ cup
¼ cup	all-purpose flour or bread flour	⅓ cup
¼ cup	packed brown sugar	⅓ cup
½ teaspoon	ground cinnamon	1 teaspoon
3 tablespoons	butter	¼ cup
	Milk	

DIRECTIONS

☞ Select recipe size. Add first 8 ingredients to the machine according to manufacturer's directions. Select the dough cycle. When cycle is complete, remove dough from machine. Punch down. Cover and let rest 10 minutes.

☞ On a lightly floured surface, roll the 1½-pound dough into a 16×8-inch rectangle (roll the 2-pound dough into a 16×10-inch rectangle). Spread with the preserves or apple butter. Starting from a long side, roll up into a spiral. Bring ends together to form a ring. Moisten ends; pinch together to seal ring. Place in a greased 10-inch tube pan. Cover and let rise in a warm place for 1 to 1¼ hours or until nearly double.

☞ Meanwhile, for streusel topping, in a medium bowl stir together the all-purpose flour, brown sugar, and cinnamon. Cut in the 3 tablespoons or ¼ cup butter until crumbly.

☞ Brush the top of dough with a little milk; sprinkle with streusel topping. Bake in a 350° oven for 50 minutes. If necessary, loosely cover with foil last 10 minutes to prevent overbrowning. Cool in pan for 15 minutes; remove from pan and transfer to a wire rack. Serve warm or cool.

☞ **NOTE:** Our Test Kitchen recommends 2 tablespoons water for either size recipe.

LEMON TWISTS

DIRECTIONS

☞ Select the recipe size. Add the first 8 ingredients to the machine according to the manufacturer's directions. Select the dough cycle. When the cycle is complete, remove dough from machine. Punch down. Cover and let rest for 10 minutes.

☞ Meanwhile, for filling, in a small bowl combine walnuts, the ⅓ or ½ cup sugar, melted margarine or butter, and lemon peel.

☞ For the 1½-pound recipe: On a lightly floured surface, roll dough into a 16×12-inch rectangle. Spread with filling. Cut in half lengthwise to make two 12×8-inch rectangles. Brush long edges with water. Fold each rectangle in half lengthwise; seal long edges. Cut each crosswise into twelve 4×1-inch strips. Twist strips. Place strips on parchment-lined or greased foil-lined baking sheets. Cover and let rise in a warm place 20 to 30 minutes or until nearly double.

☞ Bake in a 375° oven for 12 to 15 minutes or until golden. Remove from baking sheets; cool on racks. Drizzle with Lemon Glaze.

☞ For the 2-pound recipe: Prepare as above, except roll dough into a 16-inch square. Fill and cut into two 16×8-inch rectangles. Fold each rectangle in half lengthwise; cut each crosswise into sixteen 4×1-inch strips. Continue as above.

☞ Lemon Glaze: In a small bowl stir together 1 cup sifted powdered sugar and 1 teaspoon lemon juice. Stir in enough milk (2 to 4 teaspoons) to make a glaze of drizzling consistency.

Prep time: 40 minutes **Rise time:** 20 minutes **Bake time:** 12 minutes
Nutrition facts per twist: 141 calories, 5 g total fat (1 g saturated fat), 10 mg cholesterol, 103 mg sodium, 21 g carbohydrate, 1 g fiber, 3 g protein.

1½-POUND (24 twists)	INGREDIENTS	2-POUND (32 twists)
⅔ cup	milk	¾ cup
¼ cup	dairy sour cream	½ cup
1	egg*	1
2 tablespoons	margarine or butter, cut up	3 tablespoons
3 cups	bread flour	4 cups
1 tablespoon	sugar	4 teaspoons
¾ teaspoon	salt	1 teaspoon
1¼ teaspoons	active dry yeast or bread machine yeast	1½ teaspoons
½ cup	finely chopped walnuts	⅔ cup
⅓ cup	sugar	½ cup
3 tablespoons	margarine or butter, melted	¼ cup
2 teaspoons	finely shredded lemon peel	1 tablespoon
	Lemon Glaze	

207

CINNAMON ORANGE PRETZELS

Prep time: 40 minutes **Bake time:** 24 minutes **Cook time:** 2 minutes per batch
Nutrition facts per pretzel: 111 calories, 3 g total fat (1 g saturated fat), 12 mg cholesterol, 113 mg sodium, 18 g carbohydrate, 1 g fiber, 3 g protein.

1½-POUND (20 pretzels)	INGREDIENTS	2-POUND (28 pretzels)
1 cup	milk	1⅓ cups
1	egg*	1
3 tablespoons	margarine or butter, cut up	¼ cup
3 cups	bread flour	4 cups
3 tablespoons	granulated sugar	¼ cup
2 teaspoons	finely shredded orange peel	2½ teaspoons
¾ teaspoon	salt	1 teaspoon
¾ teaspoon	ground cinnamon	1 teaspoon
1 teaspoon	active dry yeast or bread machine yeast	1½ teaspoons
1	slightly beaten egg white	1
1 tablespoon	water	1 tablespoon
	Coarse sugar	

DIRECTIONS

☞ Select the recipe size. Add the first 9 ingredients to the machine according to the manufacturer's directions. Select the dough cycle. When cycle is complete, remove dough from machine. Punch down. Cover and let rest for 10 minutes.

☞ On a lightly floured surface, roll the 1½-pound dough into a 12×10-inch rectangle. Cut into twenty 12×½-inch strips. (Roll the 2-pound dough into a 16×14-inch rectangle; cut into twenty-eight 16×½-inch strips.) Gently pull the strips into 16-inch-long ropes. Shape each pretzel by crossing one end over the other to form a circle, overlapping about 4 inches from each end. Take one end of dough in each hand and twist once at the point where the dough overlaps. Carefully lift each end across to the edge of the circle opposite it. Tuck ends under edges to make a pretzel shape; moisten ends and press to seal. Place on 2 or 3 greased large baking sheets.

☞ Bake in a 475° oven for 4 minutes. Remove from the oven. Reduce the oven temperature to 350°. Meanwhile, in a large pot bring 12 cups of water to boiling. Add pretzels, 3 or 4 at a time, and boil gently for 2 minutes, turning once. Using a slotted spoon, remove pretzels from water and drain on paper towels. Let stand a few seconds. Place pretzels about ½ inch apart on 2 or 3 well-greased large baking sheets.

☞ In a small bowl combine egg white and water; brush over pretzels. Sprinkle with the coarse sugar. Bake in the 350° oven about 20 minutes or until golden brown. Remove from baking sheets; cool on wire racks.

☞ **NOTE:** Our Test Kitchen recommends 1 egg for either size recipe.

208

BUTTERY SUGAR ROLLS

DIRECTIONS

☞ Select the recipe size. Add the first 8 ingredients to the machine according to the manufacturer's directions. Select the dough cycle. When cycle is complete, remove dough from machine. Punch down. Cover and let rest for 10 minutes.

☞ *For the 1½-pound recipe:* On a lightly floured surface, roll dough into a 12×8-inch rectangle. Spread with the softened butter or margarine. Starting from a long side, fold a third of the dough over the center third. Fold remaining third of dough over center third, forming 3 equal layers. Moisten and seal edges. Cut crosswise into twelve 1-inch-wide strips.

☞ Place, cut sides down, in a greased 15×10×1-inch baking pan. Cover and let rise in a warm place about 30 minutes or until nearly double. Combine 1 beaten egg and water; brush over rolls. Sprinkle with coarse sugar. Bake in a 375° oven for 15 to 18 minutes or until golden brown. Remove from pan; transfer to wire racks. Serve warm.

☞ *For the 2-pound recipe:* Prepare as above, except divide dough in half. Roll each half into a 10×8-inch rectangle. Spread each rectangle with half of the softened butter or margarine. Fold each rectangle as directed above; cut each into ten 1-inch-wide strips. Continue as above.

☞ ***NOTE:** Our Test Kitchen recommends 1 egg and ¼ teaspoon salt for either size recipe.

Good Advice!

When a recipe calls for sugar, use white granulated sugar, sold in fine granulation. Coarse sugar, also called pearl and decorator's sugar, is a coarse granulation that adds glitter and sweetness to the tops of cookies, cakes, and breads. Superfine (also labeled ultrafine or caster sugar) is a finer grind that dissolves readily—the choice for frostings, meringues, and beverages.

Prep time: 30 minutes   **Rise time:** 30 minutes   **Bake time:** 15 minutes
Nutrition facts per roll: 225 calories, 8 g total fat (5 g saturated fat), 54 mg cholesterol, 137 mg sodium, 31 g carbohydrate, 1 g fiber, 6 g protein.

1½-POUND (12 rolls)	INGREDIENTS	2-POUND (20 rolls)
¾ cup	milk	1 cup
¼ cup	butter or margarine, cut up	⅓ cup
1	egg*	1
3 cups	bread flour	4 cups
¼ cup	granulated sugar	⅓ cup
1 teaspoon	finely shredded lemon peel	1¼ teaspoons
¼ teaspoon	salt*	¼ teaspoon
1½ teaspoons	active dry yeast or bread machine yeast	2 teaspoons
3 tablespoons	butter or margarine, softened	¼ cup
1	beaten egg	1
1 tablespoon	water	1 tablespoon
1 tablespoon	coarse sugar	4 teaspoons

209

GRAPE CLUSTER BREAD

Prep time: 25 minutes   **Rise time:** 30 minutes   **Bake time:** 20 minutes
Nutrition facts per serving: 149 calories, 5 g total fat (1 g saturated fat), 33 mg cholesterol, 145 mg sodium, 22 g carbohydrate, 1 g fiber, 4 g protein.

1½-POUND (15 servings)	INGREDIENTS	2-POUND (20 servings)
⅔ cup	milk	¾ cup
1	egg(s)	2
¼ cup	butter or margarine, cut up	⅓ cup
2 tablespoons	water	3 tablespoons
3 cups	bread flour	4 cups
2 tablespoons	sugar	3 tablespoons
¾ teaspoon	salt	1 teaspoon
1 teaspoon	active dry yeast or bread machine yeast	1¼ teaspoons
1	egg yolk	1
1 teaspoon	water	1 teaspoon
½ teaspoon	poppy seed	1 teaspoon

210

DIRECTIONS

☞ Select the recipe size. Add the first 8 ingredients to the machine according to the manufacturer's directions. Select the dough cycle. When cycle is complete, remove dough from the machine. Punch down. Cover and let rest for 10 minutes.

☞ *For the 1½-pound recipe:* Remove one-fourth of the dough; cover and set aside. Divide the remaining dough into 30 portions. Using lightly floured hands, shape each portion into a smooth ball. Arrange on a greased baking sheet in the shape of a bunch of grapes. In a small bowl combine the egg yolk and 1 teaspoon water; brush some over dough. Sprinkle with poppy seed.

☞ On a lightly floured surface, roll the reserved dough into an 8×4-inch rectangle; cut in half crosswise. Cut each square in half diagonally to form grape leaves. If desired, score leaves to resemble leaf veins. Place leaves on top of the widest end of bunch of grapes. Brush the leaves with remaining egg yolk mixture. Cover and let rise in a warm place for 30 to 40 minutes or until nearly double.

☞ Bake in a 375° oven for 20 to 25 minutes or until bread sounds hollow when lightly tapped. If necessary, loosely cover with foil last 5 to 10 minutes to prevent overbrowning. Remove; cool on a wire rack.

☞ *For the 2-pound recipe:* Prepare as above, except divide the dough in half. Set aside one-fourth of each half of dough. Shape each remaining half into 20 balls. Form 2 bunches of grapes on 2 greased baking sheets. Continue as above, baking in a 375° oven for 15 to 20 minutes.

CINNAMON SUGAR BRAID

Prep time: 30 minutes   **Rise time:** 45 minutes   **Bake time:** 20 minutes
Nutrition facts per slice: 150 calories, 4 g total fat (1 g saturated fat), 27 mg cholesterol, 148 mg sodium, 23 g carbohydrate, 1 g fiber, 4 g protein.

1½-POUND (16 slices)	INGREDIENTS	2-POUND (22 slices)
¾ cup	milk	1 cup
¼ cup	margarine or butter, cut up	⅓ cup
1	egg*	1
3 cups	bread flour	4 cups
¼ cup	sugar	⅓ cup
1 teaspoon	ground cinnamon	1¼ teaspoons
¾ teaspoon	salt	1 teaspoon
⅛ teaspoon	ground nutmeg	¼ teaspoon
1¼ teaspoons	active dry yeast or bread machine yeast	1½ teaspoons
1	beaten egg	1
1 tablespoon	sugar	4 teaspoons
¼ teaspoon	ground cinnamon	½ teaspoon

DIRECTIONS

☞ Select the loaf size. Add first 9 ingredients to the machine according to manufacturer's directions. Select dough cycle. When cycle is complete, remove dough from machine. Punch down. Cover; let rest 10 minutes.

☞ *For the 1½-pound recipe:* Divide dough into thirds. On a lightly floured surface, roll each portion into an 18-inch-long rope. To shape, line up the ropes, 1 inch apart, on a greased large baking sheet. Starting in the middle, loosely braid by bringing the left rope under the center rope. Bring the right rope under the new center rope. Repeat to end. On the other end, braid by bringing the outside ropes alternately over the center rope to center. Press ends together; tuck under.

☞ Cover and let rise in a warm place about 45 minutes or until nearly double. Brush with the beaten egg. In a small bowl combine the 1 tablespoon or 4 teaspoons sugar and ¼ or ½ teaspoon cinnamon; sprinkle over loaf. Bake in a 350° oven for 20 to 30 minutes or until golden brown. Remove from baking sheet; cool on a wire rack.

☞ *For the 2-pound recipe:* Divide the dough into fourths. Roll each portion into a 14-inch-long rope. Line up 2 ropes, 1 inch apart, on a greased baking sheet. Loosely twist the ropes together; tuck ends under. Repeat with remaining 2 ropes. Continue as above.

212

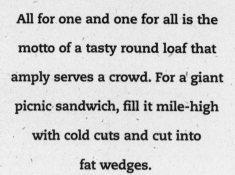

All for one and one for all is the motto of a tasty round loaf that amply serves a crowd. For a giant picnic sandwich, fill it mile-high with cold cuts and cut into fat wedges.

CRACKED WHEAT BREAD

Prep time: 20 minutes **Rise time:** 45 minutes **Bake time:** 35 minutes

Nutrition facts per slice: 121 calories, 3 g total fat (1 g saturated fat), 14 mg cholesterol, 113 mg sodium, 20 g carbohydrate, 2 g fiber, 5 g protein.

DIRECTIONS

☞ Select the loaf size. Bring 1 cup water to boiling; remove from heat. Stir in the cracked wheat. Let stand for 3 minutes; drain well. Add milk. Add the cracked wheat mixture and the next 8 ingredients to machine according to the manufacturer's directions. Select the dough cycle. When cycle is complete, remove dough from machine. Punch down. Cover and let rest for 10 minutes.

☞ On a lightly floured surface, shape the 1½-pound or 2-pound dough into a ball. Place on a lightly greased baking sheet; flatten slightly to a 6-inch round loaf. Cover and let rise in a warm place about 45 minutes or until nearly double.

☞ In a bowl combine the beaten egg and 1 tablespoon water; brush over loaf. If desired, sprinkle with fresh rosemary leaves. Bake in a 350° oven for 35 to 40 minutes or until bread sounds hollow when lightly tapped. If necessary, loosely cover with foil last 5 to 10 minutes to prevent overbrowning. Remove from baking sheet; cool on a wire rack.

☞ ***NOTE:** Our Test Kitchen recommends 2 tablespoons oil for either size recipe.

1½-POUND (16 slices)	INGREDIENTS	2-POUND (22 slices)
⅓ cup	cracked wheat	½ cup
1 cup	milk	1¼ cups
2 tablespoons	cooking oil*	2 tablespoons
2 cups	whole wheat flour	2½ cups
1 cup	bread flour	1½ cups
1 tablespoon	brown sugar	2 tablespoons
1 tablespoon	gluten flour	4 teaspoons
¾ teaspoon	salt	1 teaspoon
½ teaspoon	dried rosemary, crushed, or	¾ teaspoon
1½ teaspoons	snipped fresh rosemary	1 tablespoon
1¼ teaspoons	active dry yeast or bread machine yeast	1½ teaspoons
1	beaten egg	1
1 tablespoon	water	1 tablespoon
1 tablespoon	fresh rosemary leaves (optional)	1 tablespoon

213

PEPPER CHEESE BREAD

Prep time: 20 minutes   **Rise time:** 30 minutes   **Bake time:** 35 minutes
Nutrition facts per slice: 124 calories, 4 g total fat (1 g saturated fat), 4 mg cholesterol, 165 mg sodium, 18 g carbohydrate, 1 g fiber, 5 g protein.

1½-POUND (16 slices)	INGREDIENTS	2-POUND (22 slices)
1 cup	water	1⅓ cups
2 tablespoons	olive oil or cooking oil	3 tablespoons
2 cups	bread flour	2⅔ cups
1 cup	whole wheat flour	1⅓ cups
1 teaspoon	cracked black pepper	1½ teaspoons
¾ teaspoon	salt	1 teaspoon
1 teaspoon	active dry yeast or bread machine yeast	1¼ teaspoons
½ cup	shredded provolone cheese	⅔ cup
¼ cup	grated Parmesan cheese	⅓ cup
1	slightly beaten egg white	1
1 tablespoon	water	1 tablespoon

DIRECTIONS

☞ Select the loaf size. Add first 7 ingredients to the machine according to manufacturer's directions. Select the dough cycle. When cycle is complete, remove dough from machine. Punch down. Cover and let rest 10 minutes.

☞ *For the 1½-pound recipe:* On a lightly floured surface, roll dough into a 12×10-inch rectangle. Sprinkle with the provolone and Parmesan cheeses. Starting from a long side, roll up into a spiral. Moisten edge; pinch firmly to seal. Pinch and pull ends to taper. Place, seam down, on a greased baking sheet. Cover and let rise in a warm place for 30 to 45 minutes or until nearly double.

☞ With a very sharp knife, make 3 or 4 diagonal cuts about ¼ inch deep across the top of loaf. In a small bowl combine the egg white and 1 tablespoon water; brush over loaf. Bake in a 375° oven for 15 minutes. Brush with remaining egg white mixture. Bake for 20 to 25 minutes more or until bread sounds hollow when lightly tapped. Remove from baking sheet; cool on a wire rack.

☞ *For the 2-pound recipe:* Prepare as above, except divide the dough in half. Roll each half into a 10×8-inch rectangle. Sprinkle each rectangle with half of the provolone and Parmesan cheeses. Continue as above.

214

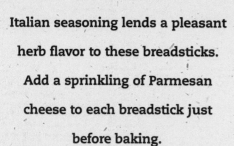

Italian seasoning lends a pleasant herb flavor to these breadsticks. Add a sprinkling of Parmesan cheese to each breadstick just before baking.

DIRECTIONS

☞ Select the recipe size. Add the first 8 ingredients to the machine according to the manufacturer's directions. Select the dough cycle. When cycle is complete, remove dough from machine. Punch down. Cover and let rest for 10 minutes.

☞ Divide 1½-pound dough into 24 portions (divide the 2-pound dough into 32 portions). On a lightly floured surface, roll each portion into an 8-inch-long rope. Place the ropes, 2 inches apart, on greased baking sheets. Cover and let rise in a warm place about 30 minutes or until nearly double.

☞ In a small bowl combine the egg white and 1 tablespoon water; brush over breadsticks. Sprinkle with the 1 or 2 tablespoons Parmesan cheese. Bake in a 350° oven for 15 to 20 minutes or until golden brown. Remove from baking sheets; cool on wire racks.

PARMESAN HERB BREADSTICKS

Prep time: 30 minutes **Rise time:** 30 minutes **Bake time:** 15 minutes
Nutrition facts per breadstick: 78 calories, 2 g total fat (1 g saturated fat), 1 mg cholesterol, 100 mg sodium, 12 g carbohydrate, 1 g fiber, 3 g protein.

1½-POUND (24 breadsticks)	INGREDIENTS	2-POUND (32 breadsticks)
1 cup	water	1¼ cups
2 tablespoons	cooking oil or olive oil	3 tablespoons
2⅓ cups	bread flour	3 cups
⅔ cup	whole wheat flour	1 cup
⅓ cup	grated Parmesan cheese	½ cup
1 teaspoon	dried Italian seasoning, crushed	1¼ teaspoons
¾ teaspoon	salt	1 teaspoon
1 teaspoon	active dry yeast or bread machine yeast	1¼ teaspoons
1	slightly beaten egg white	1
1 tablespoon	water	1 tablespoon
1 tablespoon	grated Parmesan cheese	2 tablespoons

215

ONION MUSTARD FLATBREAD

Delightfully different, this crisp and savory flatbread is wonderful for your appetizer tray. Serve with thin slices of prosciutto, a selection of cheeses, and cut-up fresh fruit.

Prep time: 20 minutes   **Bake time:** 11 minutes

Nutrition facts per serving: 155 calories, 5 g total fat (1 g saturated fat), 1 mg cholesterol, 140 mg sodium, 23 g carbohydrate, 1 g fiber, 4 g protein.

1½-POUND (16 servings)	INGREDIENTS	2-POUND (24 servings)
2 cups	finely chopped onion	2⅔ cups
1 tablespoon	bottled minced garlic	4 teaspoons
2 tablespoons	olive oil or cooking oil*	2 tablespoons
4 teaspoons	mustard seed	2 tablespoons
4 teaspoons	Dijon-style mustard	2 tablespoons
1 teaspoon	dried thyme, crushed	1½ teaspoons
1 cup	milk	1⅓ cups
3 tablespoons	olive oil or cooking oil	¼ cup
3 cups	bread flour	4 cups
1 tablespoon	sugar	4 teaspoons
¾ teaspoon	salt	1 teaspoon
1 teaspoon	active dry yeast or bread machine yeast	1¼ teaspoons

DIRECTIONS

☞ Select loaf size. In a large skillet cook onion and garlic in the 2 tablespoons hot oil until tender. Stir in mustard seed, Dijon mustard, and thyme. Cook and stir for 1 minute. Cool slightly.

☞ Add ⅓ cup (1½-pound) or ½ cup (2-pound) of the onion mixture and remaining ingredients to machine according to manufacturer's directions. Select dough cycle. When cycle is complete, remove dough from machine. Punch down. Cover; let rest 10 minutes.

☞ Divide the 1½-pound dough in half (divide the 2-pound dough into thirds). On a lightly floured surface, roll each portion into a 12-inch circle. Transfer each circle to a greased large baking sheet or 12-inch pizza pan. Using a fork, prick the entire surface of each circle several times. Spread the circles with the remaining onion mixture. *Do not let rise.*

☞ Bake in a 400° oven for 11 to 13 minutes or until crisp and browned. (If baking more than one pan at a time, rotate halfway through baking.) Remove from pans; transfer to wire racks. Serve warm or cool. Store in an airtight container to maintain crispness.

☞ ***NOTE:** Our Test Kitchen recommends 2 tablespoons oil for either size recipe when cooking onion and garlic.

FOUGASSES

This rustic flat country loaf with its distinctive ladder shape makes a pretty table presentation. The sage and whole wheat combination will guarantee its popularity.

DIRECTIONS

☞ Select the loaf size. Add all ingredients, except the milk, to the machine according to manufacturer's directions. Select the dough cycle. When cycle is complete, remove dough from machine. Punch down. Cover and let rest 10 minutes.

☞ Divide the 1½-pound dough in half (divide the 2-pound dough into thirds). On a lightly floured surface, roll each portion into an 8×4-inch rectangle. Make three or four 3-inch-long diagonal cuts through each rectangle to within 1 inch of the edges. Stretch dough slightly to widen the slits.

☞ Place each loaf on a greased large baking sheet. Cover; let rise in a warm place about 30 minutes or until nearly double. If desired, brush with a little milk. Bake in a 375° oven for 20 to 25 minutes or until lightly browned and bread sounds hollow when tapped. Remove from baking sheets; cool on wire racks.

Prep time: 25 minutes   **Rise time:** 30 minutes   **Bake time:** 20 minutes
Nutrition facts per slice: 97 calories, 1 g total fat (0 g saturated fat), 0 mg cholesterol, 101 mg sodium, 18 g carbohydrate, 1 g fiber, 3 g protein.

1½-POUND (16 slices)	INGREDIENTS	2-POUND (24 slices)
1 cup	water	1⅓ cups
1 tablespoon	olive oil or cooking oil	4 teaspoons
2 cups	bread flour	2⅔ cups
1 cup	whole wheat flour	1⅓ cups
1 teaspoon	sugar	1½ teaspoons
1 teaspoon	dried sage, crushed, or	1½ teaspoons
1 tablespoon	snipped fresh sage	4 teaspoons
¾ teaspoon	salt	1 teaspoon
1 teaspoon	active dry yeast or bread machine yeast	1¼ teaspoons
	Milk (optional)	

DIRECTIONS

☞ Select the recipe size. Add the first 5 ingredients to the machine according to the manufacturer's directions. Select the dough cycle. When cycle is complete, remove dough from machine. Punch down. Cover and let rest for 10 minutes.

☞ Meanwhile, for filling, in a large skillet cook the sausage over medium heat until brown. Drain off fat, reserving about 1 tablespoon drippings in skillet. Add the mushrooms and onion. Cook and stir over medium heat until vegetables are tender. Drain off any liquid. Stir in the pizza sauce and roasted peppers. Set aside.

☞ *For the 1½-pound recipe:* Grease bottom and side of a 9×3-inch springform pan. Shape one-fourth of the dough into a small ball. Shape the remaining portion of dough into a large ball. On a lightly floured surface, roll the large ball into a 16-inch circle. Fit dough into the bottom of the prepared pan; press dough up the side of the pan, allowing dough to extend slightly over edge for easier filling. Sprinkle with half of the cheese; top with meat mixture. Sprinkle with the remaining cheese; press lightly into meat mixture.

☞ Roll the small ball into a 9-inch circle; place on top of meat mixture. In a small bowl combine the egg and 1 tablespoon water; brush over dough. Fold edge of bottom dough over top dough; press lightly to seal. Brush again with egg mixture; cut slits in dough. Sprinkle with sesame seed.

☞ Bake in a 350° oven for 45 to 50 minutes or until golden brown. Cool in pan on a wire rack for 20 minutes. To serve, use a metal spatula to loosen the pie from edge of pan; remove side of pan. Cut into wedges.

☞ *For the 2-pound recipe:* Prepare as above, except use a greased 10×3-inch springform pan. Roll the large ball into a 17-inch circle and roll the small ball into a 10-inch circle.

PIZZA RUSTICA

Prep time: 35 minutes　**Bake time:** 45 minutes　**Cool time:** 20 minutes
Nutrition facts per serving: 420 calories, 18 g total fat (6 g saturated fat), 67 mg cholesterol, 824 mg sodium, 44 g carbohydrate, 2 g fiber, 20 g protein.

1½-POUND (8 servings)	INGREDIENTS	2-POUND (10 servings)
1 cup	water	1⅓ cups
4 teaspoons	olive oil or cooking oil	2 tablespoons
3 cups	bread flour	4 cups
¾ teaspoon	salt	1 teaspoon
1½ teaspoons	active dry yeast or bread machine yeast	2 teaspoons
1 pound	bulk hot or sweet Italian sausage	1¼ pounds
2 cups	sliced fresh mushrooms	2½ cups
1 cup	chopped onion	1¼ cups
1 cup	pizza sauce	1¼ cups
½ of a 7-ounce jar	roasted red sweet peppers, drained and chopped	one 7-ounce jar
1 cup	shredded mozzarella cheese	1¼ cups
1	beaten egg	1
1 tablespoon	water	1 tablespoon
2 teaspoons	sesame seed	2 teaspoons

219

HONEY MUSTARD SPIRALS

A small amount of honey mustard is added to the dough of these attractive spirals. Their flavor makes them ideal for serving with a baked ham dinner.

Prep time: 25 minutes **Rise time:** 30 minutes **Bake time:** 10 minutes
Nutrition facts per spiral: 83 calories, 1 g total fat (0 g saturated fat), 1 mg cholesterol, 65 mg sodium, 15 g carbohydrate, 0 g fiber, 3 g protein.

1½-POUND (24 spirals)	INGREDIENTS	2-POUND (32 spirals)
¾ cup	milk	1 cup
¼ cup	honey mustard	⅓ cup
2 tablespoons	margarine or butter, cut up	3 tablespoons
1 tablespoon	water	2 tablespoons
3 cups	bread flour	4 cups
1 tablespoon	brown sugar	4 teaspoons
½ teaspoon	salt	¾ teaspoon
⅛ teaspoon	pepper	¼ teaspoon
1 teaspoon	active dry yeast or bread machine yeast	1¼ teaspoons
1	slightly beaten egg white	1
1 tablespoon	honey mustard	1 tablespoon

DIRECTIONS

☞ Select the recipe size. Add the first 9 ingredients to the machine according to the manufacturer's directions. Select the dough cycle. When cycle is complete, remove dough from machine. Punch down. Cover and let rest for 10 minutes.

☞ Divide the 1½-pound dough in half. On a lightly floured surface, roll each half into a 12×6-inch rectangle. Cut each rectangle into twelve 12×½-inch strips. (Divide the 2-pound dough in half. Roll each half into a 12×8-inch rectangle; cut each into sixteen 12×½-inch strips.) Coil each strip into a spiral.

☞ Place spirals, 2 inches apart, on greased baking sheets. Cover and let rise in a warm place about 30 minutes or until nearly double. In a small bowl combine the egg white and 1 tablespoon honey mustard; brush over spirals. Bake in a 375° oven for 10 to 12 minutes or until golden brown. Remove from baking sheets; cool on wire racks.

220

BASIL SHALLOT BRAID

DIRECTIONS

☞ Select recipe size. Add first 9 ingredients to the machine according to manufacturer's directions. Select the dough cycle. When cycle is complete, remove dough from machine. Punch down. Cover and let rest 10 minutes.

☞ Meanwhile, for filling, in a small saucepan cook the shallots in hot oil until tender. Remove from heat. In a small bowl combine the basil, Parmesan cheese, and pine nuts; stir in shallot mixture.

☞ On a lightly floured surface, roll the 1½-pound dough into a 15×12-inch rectangle. Cut into three 15×4-inch strips. (Roll the 2-pound dough into a 17×12-inch rectangle; cut into three 17×4-inch strips.) Spread one-third of the filling down center of each strip; moisten edges. Bring long edges together over filling and pinch to seal.

☞ To shape, line up the ropes, 1 inch apart, on a greased baking sheet. Starting in the middle, loosely braid by bringing the left rope under the center rope. Bring the right rope under the new center rope. Repeat to end. On the other end, braid by bringing the outside ropes alternately over the center rope to center. Press ends together; tuck under. Cover and let rise in a warm place about 40 minutes or until nearly double.

☞ Bake in a 350° oven about 25 minutes or until bread sounds hollow when lightly tapped. If necessary, loosely cover with foil the last 5 minutes to prevent overbrowning. Remove; cool on a wire rack.

☞ **NOTE:** Our Test Kitchen recommends 1 tablespoon water for either size recipe.

Prep time: 25 minutes   **Rise time:** 40 minutes   **Bake time:** 25 minutes
Nutrition facts per slice: 146 calories, 5 g total fat (1 g saturated fat), 15 mg cholesterol, 157 mg sodium, 21 g carbohydrate, 2 g fiber, 5 g protein.

1½-POUND (16 slices)	INGREDIENTS	2-POUND (24 slices)
¾ cup	milk	1 cup
1	egg(s)	2
2 tablespoons	margarine or butter, cut up	3 tablespoons
1 tablespoon	water*	1 tablespoon
1½ cups	bread flour	2¼ cups
1½ cups	whole wheat flour	2 cups
2 tablespoons	sugar	3 tablespoons
¾ teaspoon	salt	1 teaspoon
1 teaspoon	active dry yeast or bread machine yeast	1¼ teaspoons
½ cup	finely chopped shallots	⅔ cup
1 tablespoon	olive oil or cooking oil	3 tablespoons
½ cup	snipped fresh basil	⅔ cup
¼ cup	grated Parmesan cheese	⅓ cup
¼ cup	pine nuts, toasted	⅓ cup

221

BREAD SOUP BOWLS

Wow your family with their favorite soup served in a bowl that looks (and is) good enough to eat. The bread machine does almost all the work—but you don't have to tell anyone.

Prep time: 30 minutes   **Bake time:** 20 minutes
Nutrition facts per bowl: 559 calories, 17 g total fat (6 g saturated fat), 71 mg cholesterol, 626 mg sodium, 80 g carbohydrate, 3 g fiber, 19 g protein.

1½-POUND (4 bowls)	INGREDIENTS	2-POUND (6 bowls)
⅔ cup	milk	¾ cup
1	egg(s)	2
3 tablespoons	margarine or butter, cut up	¼ cup
3 cups	bread flour	4 cups
1 tablespoon	sugar	4 teaspoons
¾ teaspoon	salt	1 teaspoon
1 teaspoon	active dry yeast or bread machine yeast	1¼ teaspoons
½ cup	shredded cheese, such as cheddar, Swiss, or Monterey Jack	¾ cup

DIRECTIONS

☞ Select the recipe size. Add the first 7 ingredients to the machine according to the manufacturer's directions. Select the dough cycle. When cycle is complete, remove dough from machine. Punch down. Cover and let rest for 10 minutes.

☞ Meanwhile, generously grease the outside of four (or six for 2-pound) 10-ounce custard cups or individual casseroles. Place, upside-down, on a greased large baking sheet(s), leaving 3 to 4 inches between cups.

☞ Divide 1½-pound dough into 4 portions (divide the 2-pound dough into 6 portions). On a lightly floured surface, roll each portion into a 12×6-inch rectangle. Sprinkle about 2 tablespoons cheese onto half of each rectangle to within ½ inch of the edges. Moisten edges; fold each rectangle in half to form a 6-inch square. Seal edges.

☞ Drape the dough squares over the greased cups, pressing lightly. *Do not let rise.* Bake in a 350° oven for 20 to 25 minutes or until golden brown. If necessary, loosely cover with foil last 10 minutes to prevent overbrowning. Remove the bread bowls from cups; cool on wire racks.

222

GARLIC HERB BREAD

The garlic has already been roasted for you to use in this recipe. Look for jars of convenient roasted garlic in the produce section with regular minced garlic.

Prep time: 40 minutes **Rise time:** 35 minutes **Bake time:** 25 minutes
Nutrition facts per slice: 100 calories, 2 g total fat (1 g saturated fat), 1 mg cholesterol, 126 mg sodium, 16 g carbohydrate, 1 g fiber, 3 g protein.

1½-POUND (20 slices)	INGREDIENTS	2-POUND (24 slices)
1 cup	water	1⅓ cups
2 teaspoons	olive oil or cooking oil	1 tablespoon
3 cups	bread flour	4 cups
⅓ cup	grated Parmesan cheese	½ cup
2 teaspoons	sugar	1 tablespoon
¾ teaspoon	salt	1 teaspoon
1 teaspoon	active dry yeast or bread machine yeast	1¼ teaspoons
1½ teaspoons	bottled minced roasted garlic	2 teaspoons
2 tablespoons	margarine or butter	3 tablespoons
⅔ cup	snipped parsley	1 cup
½ cup	snipped fresh chives	¾ cup

224

DIRECTIONS

☞ Select recipe size. Add first 7 ingredients to the machine according to manufacturer's directions. Select the dough cycle. When cycle is complete, remove dough from machine. Punch down. Cover and let rest 10 minutes.

☞ Meanwhile, for filling, in a small saucepan cook the roasted garlic in hot margarine or butter for 30 seconds. Remove from heat. Stir in the parsley and chives.

☞ *For the 1½-pound recipe:* Divide the dough in half. On a lightly floured surface, roll each half into a 16×10-inch rectangle. Spread each rectangle with half of the filling almost to the edges. Starting from a long side, loosely roll up into a spiral. Moisten edge; pinch firmly to seal. Place, seams down, on a greased large baking sheet, tucking ends under.

☞ Cover and let rise in a warm place for 35 to 45 minutes or until nearly double. Bake in a 350° oven for 25 to 30 minutes or until bread sounds hollow when lightly tapped. Remove; cool on a wire rack.

☞ *For the 2-pound recipe:* Prepare as above, except divide the dough and filling into thirds. Roll each portion into a 12×10-inch rectangle. Continue as above, using 2 greased large baking sheets.

Experience a lively taste of Italian "street" life. You create this herb-seasoned flatbread by snipping off pieces of dough and letting them fall randomly into the pan. The result? Cobblestone bread.

QUICK COBBLESTONE BREAD

Prep time: 15 minutes **Rise time:** 25 minutes **Bake time:** 30 minutes
Nutrition facts per serving: 176 calories, 5 g total fat (1 g saturated fat), 2 mg cholesterol, 229 mg sodium, 26 g carbohydrate, 1 g fiber, 5 g protein.

DIRECTIONS

☞ Select the recipe size. Add the first 8 ingredients to the machine according to the manufacturer's directions. Select the dough cycle. When cycle is complete, remove dough from machine. Punch down. Cover and let rest for 10 minutes.

☞ *For the 1½-pound recipe:* Using kitchen scissors sprayed with nonstick coating, snip the dough directly into a well-greased 11×7×1½-inch baking pan. Cut into ¾- to 1-inch irregular pieces, covering pan evenly in 1 or 2 layers. Cover and let rise in a warm place about 25 minutes or until nearly double.

☞ Meanwhile, in a small mixing bowl stir together the melted margarine or butter, the ½ or ¾ teaspoon Italian seasoning, and garlic salt. Drizzle over dough. Bake in a 350° oven about 30 minutes or until golden brown. Cool slightly in pan on a wire rack. Serve warm.

☞ *For the 2-pound recipe:* Prepare as above, except use a well-greased 13×9×2-inch baking pan.

☞ **★NOTE:** Our Test Kitchen recommends ¼ teaspoon garlic salt for either size recipe.

1½-POUND (12 servings)	INGREDIENTS	2-POUND (16 servings)
1 cup	water	1⅓ cups
2 tablespoons	margarine or butter, cut up	3 tablespoons
3 cups	bread flour	4 cups
⅓ cup	grated Parmesan cheese	½ cup
1 tablespoon	sugar	4 teaspoons
½ teaspoon	salt	¾ teaspoon
½ teaspoon	dried Italian seasoning, crushed	¾ teaspoon
1¼ teaspoons	active dry yeast or bread machine yeast	1½ teaspoons
	Nonstick spray coating	
2 tablespoons	margarine or butter, melted	3 tablespoons
½ teaspoon	dried Italian seasoning, crushed	¾ teaspoon
¼ teaspoon	garlic salt*	¼ teaspoon

225

PINWHEEL BREAD

Prep time: 30 minutes   **Rise time:** 30 minutes   **Bake time:** 20 minutes
Nutrition facts per serving: 281 calories, 8 g total fat (2 g saturated fat), 56 mg cholesterol, 308 mg sodium, 41 g carbohydrate, 2 g fiber, 10 g protein.

1½-POUND (8 servings)	INGREDIENTS	2-POUND (16 servings)
¾ cup	milk	1 cup
1	egg*	1
3 tablespoons	margarine or butter, cut up	¼ cup
2 tablespoons	water	3 tablespoons
3 cups	bread flour	4 cups
1 tablespoon	sugar	4 teaspoons
¾ teaspoon	salt	1 teaspoon
1 teaspoon	active dry yeast or bread machine yeast	1¼ teaspoons
2 tablespoons	grated Parmesan cheese	3 tablespoons
½ teaspoon	dried Italian seasoning, crushed	¾ teaspoon
2 tablespoons	sesame seed	3 tablespoons
1	beaten egg	1
1 tablespoon	water	1 tablespoon

DIRECTIONS

☞ Select the recipe size. Add the first 8 ingredients to the machine according to the manufacturer's directions. Select the dough cycle. When cycle is complete, remove dough from machine. Punch down. Cover and let rest for 10 minutes.

☞ Meanwhile, on a sheet of waxed paper, combine the Parmesan cheese and Italian seasoning. Place the sesame seed on another sheet of waxed paper. Set aside.

☞ Divide 1½-pound dough into 8 portions. On a lightly floured surface, roll each portion into a 10-inch-long rope. In a small bowl combine the beaten egg and 1 tablespoon water; brush over the ropes. Roll half of the ropes in the cheese mixture and half in the sesame seed.

☞ Arrange the ropes on a well-greased large baking sheet to form a spoke shape, alternating the cheese- and sesame-coated ropes. Press the ends in the center together to seal. Curve each of the ropes into a half-circle to form a pinwheel shape, allowing each rope to touch the next one. Cover and let rise in a warm place about 30 minutes or until nearly double. Bake in a 350° oven about 20 minutes or until golden brown. Remove from baking sheet; cool on a wire rack.

☞ *For the 2-pound recipe:* Prepare as above, except divide the dough into 16 portions; roll each portion into an 8-inch-long rope. Form 2 pinwheels on 2 well-greased large baking sheets. Continue as above.

These impressive little bundles, tied with a jaunty chive ribbon, look very black tie but toss together as easily as a T-shirt and jeans. They suit every occasion from brunch to cocktails.

BEGGAR'S PACKAGES

Prep time: 45 minutes   **Rise time:** 30 minutes   **Bake time:** 20 minutes
Nutrition facts per package: 132 calories, 4 g total fat (2 g saturated fat), 19 mg cholesterol, 114 mg sodium, 20 g carbohydrate, 1 g fiber, 4 g protein.

DIRECTIONS

☞ Select the recipe size. Add the first 7 ingredients to the machine according to the manufacturer's directions. Select the dough cycle. When cycle is complete, remove dough from machine. Punch down. Cover and let rest for 10 minutes.

☞ Meanwhile, for filling, stir together the cream cheese, walnuts, the 1 tablespoon or 4 teaspoons flour, and snipped chives.

☞ For the 1½-pound recipe: Divide the dough in half. On a lightly floured surface, roll each half into a 10-inch square. Cut each square into sixteen 2½-inch squares. Place about 1½ teaspoons filling in the center of half of the squares. Moisten edges; place remaining squares on top. Seal edges by pressing with tines of a fork. Place on greased baking sheets. Cover and let rise in a warm place about 30 minutes or until nearly double. In a small bowl combine egg yolk and 1 teaspoon water; brush over dough.

☞ Bake in a 350° oven about 20 minutes or until golden. Remove from baking sheets; cool slightly on wire racks. If desired, use a chive to tie a "string" around each package.

☞ For the 2-pound recipe: Prepare as above, except divide the dough into thirds.

1½-POUND (16 packages)	INGREDIENTS	2-POUND (24 packages)
1 cup	water	1¼ cups
1 tablespoon	olive oil or cooking oil	4 teaspoons
3 cups	bread flour	4 cups
1 teaspoon	sugar	1½ teaspoons
¾ teaspoon	garlic salt	1 teaspoon
½ teaspoon	dried Italian seasoning, crushed	¾ teaspoon
1 teaspoon	active dry yeast or bread machine yeast	1¼ teaspoons
one 3-ounce package	cream cheese	½ of an 8-ounce package
2 tablespoons	chopped walnuts, toasted	¼ cup
1 tablespoon	bread flour	4 teaspoons
1 tablespoon	snipped fresh chives	4 teaspoons
1	egg yolk	1
1 teaspoon	water	1 teaspoon
	Fresh chives (optional)	

227

LAMB & FETA STUFFED BUNDLES

Sharp feta cheese and lamb combine for the filling of these hearty sandwiches. Add a Greek salad and you'll have the perfect casual dinner.

Prep time: 25 minutes **Bake time:** 20 minutes

Nutrition facts per bundle: 389 calories, 16 g total fat (5 g saturated fat), 64 mg cholesterol, 476 mg sodium, 43 g carbohydrate, 3 g fiber, 18 g protein.

1½-POUND (8 bundles)	INGREDIENTS	2-POUND (10 bundles)
¾ cup	buttermilk	1 cup
¼ cup	margarine or butter, cut up	⅓ cup
1	egg*	1
1 tablespoon	water	4 teaspoons
2 cups	bread flour	2⅔ cups
1 cup	whole wheat flour	1⅓ cups
2 tablespoons	sugar	3 tablespoons
¾ teaspoon	salt	1 teaspoon
1¼ teaspoons	active dry yeast or bread machine yeast	1½ teaspoons
12 ounces	ground lamb	1 pound
½ cup	crumbled feta cheese	¾ cup
¼ cup	sliced green onions	⅓ cup
2 tablespoons	chopped pitted ripe olives	¼ cup
⅛ teaspoon	garlic salt	¼ teaspoon
2 teaspoons	margarine or butter, melted	1 tablespoon
one 8-ounce carton	plain yogurt	1½ cups
1 teaspoon	snipped fresh mint	1½ teaspoons

228

DIRECTIONS

☞ Select the recipe size. Add the first 9 ingredients to the machine according to the manufacturer's directions. Select the dough cycle. When cycle is complete, remove dough from machine. Punch down. Cover and let rest for 10 minutes.

☞ Meanwhile, for filling, in a large skillet cook the lamb until brown. Remove from heat; drain off fat. Stir in the feta cheese, green onions, olives, and garlic salt. Cool slightly.

☞ Divide 1½-pound dough into 8 portions (divide the 2-pound dough into 10 portions). On a lightly floured surface, roll each portion into a 6-inch circle. Place about ¼ cup filling in the center of each circle. Bring the dough up around filling, pleating and pinching dough firmly to seal. Place the bundles, sealed sides down, about 2 inches apart on a greased large baking sheet. *Do not let rise.*

☞ Bake in a 350° oven for 20 to 25 minutes or until golden brown. Remove from baking sheet; cool slightly on wire racks. Brush with the melted margarine or butter. For sauce, in a small bowl stir together the yogurt and mint. Serve with the bundles.

☞ ***NOTE:** Our Test Kitchen recommends 1 egg for either size recipe.

SAUSAGE MUSHROOM STROMBOLI

Discover the joys of these spicy, savory pies. Filled with a zesty mushroom and sausage mixture, they're hearty enough to satisfy a crowd of hungry football fans gathered 'round the TV.

Prep time: 25 minutes **Bake time:** 30 minutes

Nutrition facts per serving: 463 calories, 17 g total fat (5 g saturated fat), 32 mg cholesterol, 873 mg sodium, 58 g carbohydrate, 3 g fiber, 18 g protein.

DIRECTIONS

☞ Select the recipe size. Add the first 7 ingredients to the machine according to the manufacturer's directions. Select the dough cycle. When cycle is complete, remove dough from machine. Punch down. Cover and let rest for 10 minutes.

☞ Meanwhile, for filling, in a large skillet cook sausage, mushrooms, and onion until sausage is brown and onion is tender. Remove from heat; drain off fat. Pat with paper towels. Return to pan. Stir in pizza sauce.

☞ Divide the 1½-pound dough in half. On a lightly floured surface, roll each half into an 11-inch circle. (Divide the 2-pound dough in half; roll each half into a 13-inch circle.) Transfer each circle to a greased large baking sheet. Spread half of each circle with half of the filling to within 1 inch of the edge. If desired, sprinkle with cheese. Moisten edge; fold the dough in half over filling. Seal edges by pressing with tines of a fork. Cut slits in top; brush with a little milk. *Do not let rise.*

☞ Bake in a 425° oven for 30 to 35 minutes or until lightly browned. Remove from baking sheets; cool slightly on wire racks.

1½-POUND (6 servings)	INGREDIENTS	2-POUND (8 servings)
1 cup	water	1⅓ cups
2 tablespoons	olive oil or cooking oil	3 tablespoons
3 cups	bread flour	4 cups
2 teaspoons	dried Italian seasoning, crushed	1 tablespoon
2 cloves	garlic, minced	3 cloves
¾ teaspoon	salt	1 teaspoon
1 teaspoon	active dry yeast or bread machine yeast	1¼ teaspoons
12 ounces	bulk Italian sausage	1 pound
2 cups	sliced fresh mushrooms	3 cups
1 cup	chopped onion	1⅓ cups
1 8-ounce can	pizza sauce	1 15-ounce can
1 cup	shredded mozzarella cheese (optional)	1½ cups
	Milk	

229

CALZONES

Ground beef, vegetables, and pizza sauce fill these turnoverlike Italian favorites. If you have fresh basil on hand, substitute 2 or 3 tablespoons for the 2 teaspoons or 1 tablespoon dried basil.

Prep time: 35 minutes   **Bake time:** 12 minutes

Nutrition facts per calzone: 329 calories, 10 g total fat (3 g saturated fat), 33 mg cholesterol, 392 mg sodium, 41 g carbohydrate, 2 g fiber, 17 g protein.

1½-POUND (8 calzones)	INGREDIENTS	2-POUND (12 calzones)
1 cup	water	1⅓ cups
2 tablespoons	olive oil or cooking oil	3 tablespoons
3 cups	bread flour	4 cups
2 teaspoons	dried basil, crushed	1 tablespoon
1 teaspoon	bottled minced garlic	1½ teaspoons
¾ teaspoon	salt	1 teaspoon
1¼ teaspoons	active dry yeast or bread machine yeast	1½ teaspoons
12 ounces	lean ground beef	1 pound
¾ cup	sliced fresh mushrooms	1 cup
⅓ cup	chopped green pepper	½ cup
¾ cup	shredded mozzarella cheese	1 cup
¾ cup	pizza sauce	1 cup
1 tablespoon	milk	4 teaspoons

230

DIRECTIONS

☞ Select the recipe size. Add the first 7 ingredients to the machine according to the manufacturer's directions. Select the dough cycle. When cycle is complete, remove dough from machine. Punch down. Cover and let rest for 10 minutes.

☞ Meanwhile, for filling, in a large skillet cook the ground beef, mushrooms, and green pepper until meat is brown. Remove from heat; drain off fat. Stir in the cheese and the pizza sauce.

☞ Divide the 1½-pound dough in half. On a lightly floured surface, roll each half into a 10-inch square. Cut each square into four 5-inch squares. (Divide the 2-pound dough in half. Roll each half into a 15×10-inch rectangle; cut each rectangle into six 5-inch squares.) Divide the filling among the squares; moisten edges. Lift a corner of each square and stretch to opposite corner over filling. Seal edges by pressing with tines of a fork.

☞ Transfer calzones to greased baking sheets. Prick tops with a fork. Brush with the milk. *Do not let rise.* Bake in a 425° oven for 12 to 15 minutes or until golden brown. Remove from baking sheets; cool slightly on wire racks. If desired, serve calzones with additional warmed pizza sauce.

DRIED TOMATO FOCACCIA RINGS

Dried tomatoes are now a bumper crop in supermarkets year-round. So even on winter's darkest days, you can make this appealing ring of tomatoey rolls, created to sop up a thick spaghetti sauce.

Prep time: 30 minutes   **Rise time:** 30 minutes   **Bake time:** 20 minutes
Nutrition facts per serving: 174 calories, 5 g total fat (1 g saturated fat), 1 mg cholesterol, 159 mg sodium, 26 g carbohydrate, 1 g fiber, 5 g protein.

1½-POUND (12 servings)	INGREDIENTS	2-POUND (16 servings)
4	dried tomatoes (not oil-packed)	6
	Boiling water	
¾ cup	water	1 cup
¼ cup	olive oil or cooking oil	⅓ cup
3 cups	bread flour	4 cups
1 teaspoon	sugar	1½ teaspoons
¾ teaspoon	dried rosemary, crushed, or	1 teaspoon
2 teaspoons	snipped fresh rosemary	1 tablespoon
¾ teaspoon	salt	1 teaspoon
1 teaspoon	active dry yeast or bread machine yeast	1¼ teaspoons
1	slightly beaten egg white	1
2 tablespoons	grated Parmesan cheese	3 tablespoons
	Spaghetti sauce, warmed (optional)	

DIRECTIONS

☞ Select the recipe size. Place the dried tomatoes in a small bowl; add enough boiling water to cover. Let stand for 10 minutes. Drain well and pat dry. Snip tomatoes. Add the tomatoes and the next 7 ingredients to the machine according to the manufacturer's directions. Select the dough cycle. When cycle is complete, remove dough from machine. Punch down. Cover and let rest 10 minutes.

☞ Meanwhile, grease the outside of a 6-ounce custard cup. Place, upside-down, on a greased baking sheet.

☞ Divide 1½-pound dough into 24 portions (divide the 2-pound dough into 32 portions). Using lightly floured hands, shape each portion into a smooth ball. Place the balls of dough, about ½ inch apart, in rings around the custard cup. Brush dough with egg white; sprinkle with Parmesan cheese. Cover and let rise in a warm place for 30 to 45 minutes or until nearly double.

☞ Bake in a 375° oven for 20 to 25 minutes or until golden brown. Cool on baking sheet for 10 minutes; remove cup. Remove bread; cool slightly on a wire rack. If desired, serve with warmed spaghetti sauce.

GOAT CHEESE & ONION FOCACCIA

Slightly sweet cooked onion and tangy goat cheese strike a perfect flavor balance on this delectable focaccia. It's great served with soups or salads or as a bread for sandwiches.

Prep time: 35 minutes   **Rise time:** 30 minutes   **Bake time:** 18 minutes

Nutrition facts per serving: 191 calories, 7 g total fat (2 g saturated fat), 8 mg cholesterol, 190 mg sodium, 26 g carbohydrate, 1 g fiber, 6 g protein.

DIRECTIONS

☞ Select the recipe size. Add the first 7 ingredients to the machine according to the manufacturer's directions. Select the dough cycle. When cycle is complete, remove dough from machine. Punch down. Cover and let rest for 10 minutes.

☞ Meanwhile, for filling, in a large skillet cook the onions and rosemary in 1 tablespoon hot oil about 2 minutes or just until onions are tender. Cool slightly.

☞ Divide the 1½-pound dough in half. Place the dough on 2 greased 11- or 12-inch pizza pans. (Divide the 2-pound dough in half; place on 2 greased 13- or 14-inch pizza pans.) Using the palms of your hands, pat the dough into even rounds, just slightly smaller than the pans. Using your fingertips, poke each round all over to dimple the surface. Spread with the filling.

☞ Cover and let rise in a warm place about 30 minutes or until nearly double. Sprinkle with the goat cheese. Bake in a 400° oven for 18 to 20 minutes or until edges are golden brown. Remove from pans; cool slightly on wire racks.

☞ **★NOTE:** Our Test Kitchen recommends 1 tablespoon oil for either size filling.

1½-POUND (12 servings)	INGREDIENTS	2-POUND (16 servings)
1 cup	water	1¼ cups
2 tablespoons	olive oil or cooking oil	3 tablespoons
3 cups	bread flour	4 cups
1 tablespoon	snipped fresh basil or	4 teaspoons
½ teaspoon	dried basil, crushed	¾ teaspoon
1 teaspoon	sugar	1½ teaspoons
¾ teaspoon	salt	1 teaspoon
1 teaspoon	active dry yeast or bread machine yeast	1¼ teaspoons
2 medium	onions, sliced	2 large
1 tablespoon	snipped fresh rosemary or	2 tablespoons
½ teaspoon	dried rosemary, crushed	1 teaspoon
1 tablespoon	olive oil or cooking oil★	1 tablespoon
4 ounces	goat cheese (chévre), crumbled	6 ounces

233

Tips and Facts

metric cooking hints

By making a few conversions, cooks in Australia, Canada, and the United Kingdom can use these recipes with confidence. The charts on this page provide a guide for converting measurements from the U.S. customary system, which is used throughout this book, to the imperial and metric systems. There also is a conversion table for oven temperatures to accommodate the differences in oven calibrations.

Product Differences: Most of the ingredients called for in the recipes in this book are available in English-speaking countries. However, some are known by different names. Here are some common American ingredients and their possible counterparts:

- Sugar is granulated or castor sugar.
- Powdered sugar is icing sugar.
- All-purpose flour is plain household flour or white flour. When self-rising flour is used in place of all-purpose flour in a recipe that calls for leavening, omit the leavening agent (baking soda or baking powder) and salt.
- Light-colored corn syrup is golden syrup.
- Cornstarch is cornflour.
- Baking soda is bicarbonate of soda.
- Vanilla is vanilla essence.
- Green, red, or yellow sweet peppers are capsicums.
- Golden raisins are sultanas.

Volume and Weight: Americans traditionally use cup measures for liquid and solid ingredients. The chart, below, shows the approximate imperial and metric equivalents. If you are accustomed to weighing solid ingredients, the following approximate equivalents will be helpful.

- 1 cup butter, castor sugar, or rice = 8 ounces = about 250 grams
- 1 cup flour = 4 ounces = about 125 grams
- 1 cup icing sugar = 5 ounces = about 150 grams

Spoon measures are used for smaller amounts of ingredients. Although the size of the tablespoon varies slightly in different countries, for practical purposes and for recipes in this book, a straight substitution is all that is necessary.

Measurements made using cups or spoons always should be level unless stated otherwise.

equivalents: U.S.=Australia/U.K.

⅛ teaspoon = 0.5 ml
¼ teaspoon = 1 ml
½ teaspoon = 2 ml
1 teaspoon = 5 ml
1 tablespoon = 1 tablespoon
¼ cup = 4 tablespoons = 2 fluid ounces = 60 ml
⅓ cup = ¼ cup = 3 fluid ounces = 90 ml
½ cup = ⅓ cup = 4 fluid ounces = 120 ml
⅔ cup = ½ cup = 5 fluid ounces = 150 ml
¾ cup = ⅔ cup = 6 fluid ounces = 180 ml
1 cup = ¾ cup = 8 fluid ounces = 240 ml
1¼ cups = 1 cup
2 cups = 1 pint
1 quart = 1 liter
½ inch =1.27 cm
1 inch = 2.54 cm

baking pan sizes

American	Metric
8×1½-inch round baking pan	20×4-cm cake tin
9×1½-inch round baking pan	23×3.5-cm cake tin
11×7×1½-inch baking pan	28×18×4-cm baking tin
13×9×2-inch baking pan	30×20×3-cm baking tin
2-quart rectangular baking dish	30×20×3-cm baking tin
15×10×1-inch baking pan	30×25×2-cm baking tin (Swiss roll tin)
9-inch pie plate	22×4- or 23×4-cm pie plate
7- or 8-inch springform pan	18- or 20-cm springform or loose-bottom cake tin
9×5×3-inch loaf pan	23×13×7-cm or 2-pound narrow loaf tin or pâté tin
1½-quart casserole	1.5-liter casserole
2-quart casserole	2-liter casserole

oven temperature equivalents

Fahrenheit Setting	Celsius Setting*	Gas Setting
300°F	150°C	Gas Mark 2 (slow)
325°F	160°C	Gas Mark 3 (moderately slow)
350°F	180°C	Gas Mark 4 (moderate)
375°F	190°C	Gas Mark 5 (moderately hot)
400°F	200°C	Gas Mark 6 (hot)
425°F	220°C	Gas Mark 7
450°F	230°C	Gas Mark 8 (very hot)
Broil		Grill

*Electric and gas ovens may be calibrated using Celsius. However, for an electric oven, increase the Celsius setting 10 to 20 degrees when cooking above 160°C. For convection or forced-air ovens (gas or electric), lower the temperature setting 10°C when cooking at all heat levels.